CRITICAL A
FOR *TRAVELE*

"The *Travelers' Tales* series is altogether r
—Jan Morris, author of *Journeys, Locations,* ...
Trieste and the Meaning of Nowhere

"For the thoughtful traveler, these books are an invaluable resource.
There's nothing like them on the market."
—Pico Iyer, author of *The Global Soul*

"This is the stuff memories can be duplicated from."
—*Foreign Service Journal*

"I can't think of a better way to get comfortable with a destination
than by delving into *Travelers' Tales*...before reading a guidebook, before
seeing a travel agent.
—Paul Glassman, Society of American Travel Writers

"*Travelers' Tales* is a valuable addition to any predeparture reading list."
—Tony Wheeler, founder, Lonely Planet Publications

"*Travelers' Tales* delivers something most guidebooks only promise: a real
sense of what a country is all about...."
—*Hartford Courant*

"The *Travelers' Tales* series should become required reading for anyone
visiting a foreign country who wants to truly step off the tourist track
and experience another culture, another place, firsthand."
—*St. Petersburg Times*

"If there's one thing traditional guidebooks lack, it's the really juicy travel
information, the personal stories about back alleys and brief encounters.
The *Travelers' Tales* series fills this gap with an approach that's all anecdotes,
no directions."
—*Diversion*

TRAVELERS' TALES

ALASKA

TRUE STORIES

TRAVELERS' TALES

ALASKA

TRUE STORIES

Edited by

BILL SHERWONIT,

ANDROMEDA ROMANO-LAX

AND ELLEN BIELAWSKI

Series Editors
JAMES O'REILLY AND LARRY HABEGGER

TRAVELERS' TALES
SAN FRANCISCO

Art Direction: Michele Wetherbee
Interior design: Kathryn Heflin and Susan Bailey
Cover photograph: © *Steven Nourse/Getty Images. Aurora Borealis, Alaska Range.*
Page layout: Cynthia Lamb, using the fonts Bembo and Remedy

Distributed by: Publishers Group West, 1700 Fourth Street, Berkeley, California 94710.

Library of Congress Cataloguing-in-Publication Data

Travelers' Tales Alaska : true stories / edited by Bill Sherwonit, Andromeda Romano-Lax, and Ellen Bielawski.— 1st ed.
     p. cm.
  ISBN 1-885211-96-1 (pbk.)
  1. Alaska—Description and travel—Anecdotes. 2. Alaska—History, Local—Anecdotes. 3. Frontier and pioneer life—ALaska—Anecdotes. 4. Outdoor life—ALaska—Anecdotes. 5. Alaska—Biography—Anecdotes. 6. Travelers—Alaska—Biography—Anecdotes. 7. Adventure and adventurers—Alaska—Biography—Anecdotes. 8. Travelers' writings, American. I. Sherwonit, Bill, 1950- II. Romano-Lax, Andromeda, 1971- III. Bielawski, E.
  F910.5 .T73 2003
  917.9804'51'0922—dc22

                                   2003014901

                              First Edition
                      Printed in the United States
                         10 9 8 7 6 5 4 3

…Who comes here, to this whiteness, this far and frozen place, in search of something he cannot name? Not wealth, it may be, but a fortune of the spirit, a freshness denied him in the place he came from."

—JOHN HAINES, "Stories We Listened To"
The Stars, The Snow, The Fire

Table of Contents

Part Three
GOING YOUR OWN WAY

Part Four
IN THE SHADOWS

Part Five
THE LAST WORD

Alaska: An Introduction

by David Roberts

With six college friends, I first arrived in Alaska in June 1963, having driven a VW bus up the Alcan (not yet the Alaska Highway) in order to assault the then-unclimbed north face of Mt. McKinley (not yet Denali). As we started hiking at midnight across the tundra toward the Peters Glacier, I was one scared twenty-year-old. At the moment, there were many other places I would rather have been than Alaska. The gigantic, avalanche-swept mountain wall we had chosen to attack, I felt in my gut, would prove too much for the modest talents of our gang, trained as we were on the diminutive crags and gullies of New England.

Thirty-five days later, as we staggered out of the wilderness, having not only climbed the Wickersham Wall but traversed over both summits of McKinley, I was hooked. Hooked on Alaska—though to be honest, it was Alaska's mountains that had set the lure. For the next twelve years, I returned every summer, seeking out virgin faces and peaks all over the state. The sheer plenitude of untrodden glaciers and ridges in Alaska dazzled me; I felt like a classical scholar who had stumbled upon a cache of unknown scrolls. In 1967, we even got to name a whole range—the Revelation Mountains—that had never been explored.

During those thirteen years, Alaska was by far the most *real* place on earth for me. During the "off-season," as I trudged through college, grad school, and a teaching career, I longed for the Alaskan ranges as a troubadour poet pined for his unattainable mistress. Yet never for a moment did I consider moving to the 49th state, as several of my alpinist cronies did. On the way in and out of the mountains, what I saw of Alaskan culture dismayed rather than enthralled me. A get-rich-quick opportunism seemed to dominate the sprawling burgs of Anchorage and Fairbanks. The bush was steeped in a frontier ethic, the resourceful pluck of the homesteader leavened by his provincialism. There was no ignoring the xenophobia that ran deep through Alaska's boom-or-bust mentality, and the squalor and alcoholism that pervaded many an Inuit or Indian village that I visited seemed heartbreaking.

In my ex cathedra take on Alaska I was, of course, acting like the Eastern snob I was sometimes accused of being. There was, I had to admit, as much provincialism and squalor in Boston or New York as there was in Alaska.

Still, it was the Alaskan wilderness that spoke to me. Like most mountain climbers, the more passionate I was about new routes on unnamed peaks, the less curious I was about the cultural matrix that embraced that wilderness. It was only as my career as a climber started to taper off that I began to probe deeper into Alaska's unique and puzzling history and culture.

As the twenty-six narratives assembled in this beguiling collection testify, I was hardly alone in my response to Alaska. Again and again in these tales, it is the power and peril of the wilderness that the authors celebrate. The rare exceptions— Ellen Bielawski's "Camping at Wal★Mart" or Mike Grudowski's mordant portrait of Whittier—only reinforce the centrality of wilderness in Alaskan life, by evoking parodic inversions of the myth of the limitless outback. This emphasis is not surprising. Alaska does indeed teem with some of the most magnificent and daunting back country on earth, on the edges of which a mere 627,000 inhabitants (55 percent of them nestled in Anchorage and Fairbanks) cling to their livelihoods. As a result, the literature of Alaska, unlike that of, say, Tuscany or Virginia, focuses almost obsessively on man's (and woman's) encounter with nature.

Thirty years ago, Margaret Atwood, in a polemic called *Survival*, argued that Canadian literature would never come of age until it got over its preoccupation with adventurers battling the wilderness. As a feminist, Atwood saw this fixation as a predominantly male hang-up. At its core, "survival" was reduced for Canadian writers to a morally simplistic, anti-intellectual machismo.

Does the same stricture hold for Alaska? I think this anthology of some of the freshest writing in recent years makes a strong case to the contrary. The classic Alaskan narratives of the first half of the twentieth century—works such as Belmore Browne's *The Conquest of Mount McKinley,* Charles Brower's *Fifty Years Below Zero*, and Robert Marshall's *Arctic Wilderness*—wove lyrical and heroic fantasias around the monotonic theme of an explorer or pioneer confronting the wilderness. In the present collection, in contrast, there are twenty-six different voices ranging, with a thoroughly postmodern sense of irony, across a dozen themes more ambiguous than survival or wilderness.

And yet, in *Traveler's Tales Alaska* there lingers (as I would guess is true for very few other places in the world) a fundamental choose-up-sides distinction between writers who live in the state and those who hail from Outside (the metaphoric tag could not be more apt). At its most tendentious, the attitude of Alaskans toward writers (and travelers) from the Lower 48 is that they can't possibly get it right. The countervailing prejudice (exemplified in Joe McGinnis's brilliantly unfair *Going to Extremes*) is that Alaskans, being country bumpkins, are best explicated by a visitor from the heartland of American sophistication (read the East Coast)—just as three generations of Victorian colonialists thought they had better takes on Borneo or Sudan or India than anybody who had the misfortune to be born and raised in those benighted purlieus.

Nowhere is this us-them dichotomy more vivid than in the reception of the bestseller *Into the Wild*. The Alaskan response to Jon Krakauer's evocation of Chris McCandless's demise, as he tried to live solo off the land north of Denali, was more negative than the book garnered anywhere else in the world. The knee-jerk Alaskan fix on McCandless/Krakauer could be paraphrased as, "One more clueless, screwed-up hippie buys the farm 'cause he doesn't know what he's doing up here. Why romanticize and glorify the poor sucker?"

Yet McCandless's saga proved to have a universal resonance. In this volume, Sherry Simpson's complex meditation, "I Want to Ride on the Bus Chris Died In," captures the full spectrum of reactions to McCandless's unwittingly symbolic quest and fate, and thus punctures the ultimately foolish us-versus-them split between writers and witnesses who live in Alaska and those who visit from Outside.

In this context, the editors have performed a salutary service by saving for last Nancy Lord's wonderfully wistful essay, "In the Giant's Hand." Lord, who moved to Alaska in the wake of a profound wilderness experience in the Brooks Range at the age of nineteen, and who has lived there ever since, manages to look back on the naive idealist she once was from the vantage point of three decades of living in and writing about the 49th state. In a mere eight pages, Lord dismantles the us-them dichotomy (for she is both in one person), finding her own truths in the universal human dramas of desire and aging and coming to terms with one's own mortality. Here is the kind of writing that, we can only hope, Alaska will provoke from her celebrants as the twenty-first century unveils new ways of comprehending the Great Land.

David Roberts is a mountaineer and adventurer who has climbed the 20,000-foot Quenehar in Argentina to discover the remains of Inca sacrificial victims, made the first descent of the Tekeze in Ethiopia, and been stranded in China during the Tiananmen Square massacre. He has journeyed from academia where he was an associate professor of literature, to Alaska and the Yukon where he led thirteen climbing expeditions (including more than six first ascents), to the literary world where he has written or edited sixteen books and won numerous awards, including the Prix Méditerrané, the Prix du Salon de Livre de Passy, the Prix d'Autrans, and the American Alpine Club Literary Award. He has also written for National Geographic, Outside, Smithsonian, The Atlantic Monthly, The New York Times Magazine, Travel and Leisure, Conde Nast Traveler, *and more.*

PART ONE

ESSENCE OF ALASKA

JEFF FAIR

✳

Sixty-Five

*A transplanted Easterner gets a cold reception
in the far, frigid north.*

A FEW YEARS AGO I LEFT BEHIND MY JOB, THE OLD
family cookstove, several loved ones, and Magalloway, Maine,
to make my way to Alaska once and for all. My plan was to
travel overland in the American tradition, staying in touch
with the landscape and its climates and thus better understand
the meaning of my journey. I chose January because it was
earlier than June or even April. Couldn't wait to get going.

Shortly after the holidays, I packed the Trooper (outfitted
with a new engine-block heater, cord slithering out through
the grille like the tongue of a snake) with all the worldly pos-
sessions that fit, inverted the canoe on top, summoned my travel
companions (a pair of Brittany spaniels), and motored off.

We made good time to the Missouri River, with one ominous sign: The venison I'd stowed in the bow of the canoe
began to thaw. At fifty-four degrees in Mitchell, South
Dakota, not a patch of snow in sight, I had to buy ice. In
January. I felt spiritually deprived, but things improved by way
of a cold front near Shelby, Montana. In a motel lot in

Whitecourt, Alberta, I plugged in the block heater for the first time, barely able to suppress my glee. Twenty below.

The following night in Fort Nelson, British Columbia (forty below), not a room was available. "Oilman's convention," the clerk explained. "Your best bet is Fort St. John." But that was the wrong direction. I phoned ahead and secured a room at Toad River Lodge, 122 miles up the road according to my map. I asked what time they closed.

"What time you coming through?" asked the proprietress.

"I'm leaving Fort Nelson now," I said.

"If you're not here by ten we'll come up the road looking for you."

"You're kidding," I said.

She was not, and scribbled down a description of my rig. By ten P.M. I had parked by the lodge and was feeling around the grille for my electrical cord. A woman appeared at the door.

"I have a block heater," I explained.

"Congratulations," she said. "Everyone else just lets their motor run." Something about the modern plastic belts that turn brittle at forty below and shatter to pieces at morning ignition.

I let the dogs out and locked the doors with the engine idling. My companions marched in place as they relieved themselves, unable to tolerate the touch of the subfrozen ice for more than a second at a time. Dance of the deep freeze.

Next morning at breakfast I inquired about the temperature. "Forty-eight centigrade," the cook said. Meaning *minus* forty-eight. Below-zero temperatures out here this time of year are referred to by numerics alone.

We rolled out into a world of bold, naked, granitic peaks, blanketed in snow and the orange glow of dawn. Warm at first, the truck began to exhibit a noticeable sluggishness, particularly on the uphill grades. Cold bearings, I figured, and a colder engine (forgot the cardboard for the radiator again). Another problem arose: panting like marathoners in the dry air, the dogs were frosting the inside of the windshield. When I diverted heat from the heater to the defroster, my feet began to freeze. Couldn't keep up with both. This, along with a coarse whine in the gearbox, stole from the peaceful joy of my morning. I couldn't shake the nagging thought of some malignancy in the transfer case which had denied me access to low range for several months. Should've had that looked at back in Maine.

At Muncho Lake we hit a surprise curve (I was steering with my knee at the time, scraping a rime of dog breath off the inside of the windshield with a credit card), requiring emergency maneuvers to avoid sliding down the bank. However, what had been a loose clutch first thing this morning had tightened up in the cold wind, requiring great pressure to disengage, and then a toe-pry off the floor to re-engage. The brake behaved similarly. We made it, barely, and then paused to allow the pedal linkages to warm up.

A few miles later, on the downward side of a long hill, I eased off the gas, but we continued to accelerate, speeding nearly out of control. In a panic I shut off the key, forfeiting power assistance to brakes and steering, and barely got us stopped upright and on the road. Gas pedal frozen down. I pried it up, restarted the engine, and drove on, careful to slip the edge of my boot under the accelerator and lift it any time I wished to decelerate.

Our road was wider now, but a bit rougher. We struck an unexpected mogul, took a small leap, and lurched about on frozen shocks, shaking loose the tail of a snowshoe lashed to the canoe, which rotated rather slowly down to touch the windshield, brittle at fifty below, decorating it with a scrim of cracks. One more badge of travel, another rite of passage.

We limped across the border into the Yukon (the Yukon!), and pulled up at the Contact Creek roadhouse for the ceremonial dog dance, fuel, and advice.

"Get a belly tarp," the owner suggested.

I inquired about the current temperature.

"Sixty-five."

"Centigrade or Fahrenheit?" I asked.

He smiled. "Don't matter," he said.

At Watson Lake I purchased a belly tarp, a swath of brown canvas that covered the front of the radiator and lapped halfway back beneath the engine, maintaining a bubble of engine heat under the hood, warming the heater and pedal linkages.

The next day, after 4,800 miles of hard and happy driving, I crawled out of the cab into the gelid air of Alaska, to celebrate my passage. I stared at the high peaks of the Wrangells a hundred miles off to the south, and westward along the Tanana flowage, out over the infinite frozen silent timeless beatific landscape. But what I drank to was the surest confirmation of my latitude: the wild, beautiful, penetrating cold.

Author and independent field biologist Jeff Fair follows loons and other wild spirits, including his own, across the North to study and write about them. A wildlife biologist by formal training, he had, prior to his emancipation, trapped and radio-collared grizzly bears in Yellowstone, worn the badge and uniform of a Utah game warden (one career arrest), and introduced snakes to tourists as a USFS naturalist in Oklahoma. He now lives in Alaska and spends a considerable amount of time hitchhiking by bush plane around the hinterlands with his notebook, bedroll, and the stub of a No. 2 pencil. The pay is lean, but it's a good living.

ED READICKER-HENDERSON

* * *

Surrounded by Bears

*Why bother with humans, when there are
so many salmon to eat?*

THIS IS MY JOB: I REASSURE PEOPLE. I TELL THEM, "HEY, don't worry. Bears don't like the taste of GORE-TEX."

Nobody looks reassured. Maybe it's the t-shirt I'm wearing, the one that says, "Tourists: The Other Red Meat."

We're on a path, a mile or so long, full of blind corners. This walk into Anan Bear Observatory, near Wrangell in Southeast Alaska, is every Tarzan jungle walk you ever watched on a Saturday matinee, the blue screen of the TV opening up the impossible world beyond. Each time the boardwalk gives way to mud, there are fresh bear tracks on the trail. Some of the tracks are the size of your head. Beside the path, there are tree trunks that bears have clawed just for the fun of it. Some of the claw marks are ten feet up.

Something has been eating the bridge.

"Shouldn't we have brought pepper spray?" Jean, the woman behind me, asks. She's here bravely trying to overcome a lifelong fear of bears, but her husband stayed back in town, and behind her, the other three clients look like they might turn and run any minute.

But I'm here to reassure. It's part of my summer job. I'm here to keep the tourists happy, keep them safe. These people are paying my bills, so reassuringly, I say, "Pepper spray doesn't work on wet bears. The capsaicin molecules don't bond well with water. In rain like today, we'd just be spraying air freshener in the bear's face. Besides, every single person I know who has ever gone out with bear spray has ended up on the ground after blasting themselves in panic while the bear wandered off into the woods. The screaming is never pretty."

At each blind corner—I'm not afraid of bears, right? That's why I'm the guide—I call out, "Hey, bear," just in case the bears are listening. Rule one: Never surprise animals with mouths bigger than your face. A startled bear is an unhappy bear.

The bears are here because each July and August Anan Creek is so jammed with returning pink and chum salmon that the eddies look like one solid fin. For those two months, over a half-million fish beat themselves again and again against a waterfall eight feet high and twenty feet wide. In the turbulence of the falls, the leaping fish are dark slashes that disappear, tossed back by the force of the water, faster than you can blink. The falls themselves almost glow because the treetops lace together so closely that directly over the stream is the only place you can see sky.

The place smells like somebody opened a thousand cans of tuna and then forgot all about them. There are fish carcasses—partial and whole—lining the stream's banks, where the bears wait. The fish start dying the instant they hit fresh water; their bodies are able to process it only long enough to get upstream, spawn, and die gasping. But the bears get an awful lot of them first.

Jean reaches the viewing platform with a sigh of relief, as if she's safe now. Proving that the man who hired me to help him schlep tourists out here should have thought about it longer, I tell her that a week or two ago, a bear came up onto the platform, chasing a photographer around. Nobody seriously thought the bear wanted to eat the guy. It was a game, a break between meals. Really, for all our atavistic fears of being eaten alive, from the bears' point of view, with this many fish in the river, it's just too much work to try and eat a person. Hiking boots don't digest well, and no self-respecting bear wants to spend a week spitting up Nike logos.

We're on the platform only five minutes before a black bear wades into the stream, grabs a fish on the first stab—there are so many it's hard to miss—and walks back up, perching on a log to eat. He's less than ten yards away.

After the first few days of

——————✹——————

Bears annually congregate along hundreds of Alaska's creeks and rivers to fish for salmon; a handful of those streams have become especially well-known for their bear-viewing programs. Anan Creek is one. Pack Creek on Admiralty Island, Fish Creek near the Alaska-British Columbia border, and the Brooks River in Katmai National Park are others. The best known—and the standard by which all other bear-viewing areas are measured—is the McNeil River State Game Sanctuary, on the Alaska Peninsula. The focal point of the gathering is McNeil Falls, where dozens of brown bears congregate each July and August to feed on chum salmon. As many as 144 bears (adults and cubs) have been identified along McNeil River in a single season. And in July 1997, biologists counted 70 bears at the falls at one time.

—Bill Sherwonit

the salmon run, once they've had their post-hibernation fill, the bears only eat the fattiest parts of the fish—the skin and the roe, the brains and stomach—letting the rest fall for the scavengers that move in as soon as the bear shuffles off to get another fish. There are gulls, terns, kingfishers. River otters move like oil slicks, and thirty bald eagles perch on the banks and in the trees. Far above us, ravens call, sounding like drippy faucets. There's so much life here. There were a dozen seals at the river's mouth, and we'd passed harbor porpoise on the boat ride in, their black fins cutting the gray water, chasing leaping fish ahead of them. Everybody is eating somebody else. Even the plant life within a half-mile of the stream banks depends on the nutrients of fish bits the animals drop.

So the odds are, if the bears think of us at all, they just think we are incredibly stupid. We're the only ones not fishing, not eating. Each and every other animal in sight—except, of course, for the dying fish themselves—is acting like it's the final night's buffet on a cruise ship. We humans are just standing around like morons, staring, eyes and mouths wide open.

Six or seven more bears come and go. Meanwhile, the fish keep hurling themselves against the waterfall. Not a single one seems to make it. Some must—I can see fish in eddies above the falls, waiting while they gather strength to move into the calm water upstream—but below the falls, all I see is failure after failure, thousands of fish not making the cut. It's Nature throwing an infinity of solutions at a small problem. In order to get one fish, you need ten thousand fish.

A black bear comes down the opposite side of the stream. She sits, sniffing the air for a moment, and her caution is rewarded: a brown bear comes out of the brush. The black bear turns into a blur, running away, picking a course that takes her through the thickest brush and up a nearly vertical rock face. She has completely disappeared in seconds.

Anan is one of the very few places in the world where black and brown bears share a river, but it's obvious the brown bears, the grizzlies, are at the top of the pecking order here. This brown is a full-grown female. She's close enough for us to see that she's lactating, but there are no cubs. They must have died recently, taken by a wolf or by disease, or even by another bear. Like the fish hurling themselves at the waterfall, this bear hurled herself, her progeny, into the world. And like the fish she's chewing on, her progeny fell short.

As many as a hundred bears—eighty black, twenty brown—come to Anan during any given year. Today, I lose count. There's a bear in the pilings of the platform, chasing fish into a dead-end cave. There's another on the hill opposite, twenty yards or so off. A third is hiding by crouching next to the platform stairway. Jean, a huge smile on her face, lifelong fear gone in sheer wonder, points out one in a cave on the other side of the stream. There are two more in the upper river. There's a brown bear, a yearling, in the stream below, pouncing on fish with legs splayed, butt in the air, body not yet sure what to do with the knees, while the fish get away.

There is no way to keep all the bears in sight at the same time. The forest is so thick there could be a dozen more out there, patiently waiting their turn at the river.

And this is a good thing. It's good to find out that nature still has you hopelessly outnumbered.

On our way back to the boat, a brown comes out of the bush and sits on the trail in front of us. In the movies, bears crash through the bushes, making as much noise as a freight train, but they'd be lousy predators if they did that. This one appears as silently as a ghost. She's three, maybe four years old, 600 pounds or so. She has a huge scar on her hind leg from a fight with another bear. She's about ten feet away. She looks at me. I look at her. A few minutes ago I'd watched her dissect a fish, her claws as agile as a surgeon's scalpel, as dexterous as chopsticks, but the size of butcher knives.

I bow to her, in respect. She scratches her ear and walks into the bush, utterly indifferent.

She smells like a very large, very wet dog.

Here's the lesson from the bears, what I think Jean's taking home with her: Tarzan was never lord of the jungle. It's just that the jungle was so full, the animals didn't get around to eating him. What Tarzan was yelling about was not danger, but sheer joy. There's so much of it. More than we ever imagine.

Ed Readicker-Henderson has been traveling in Alaska since 1978, and is the co-author of eight guidebooks on the state. Over the years, he's been chased by wolves, charged by moose, attacked by eagles, ravens, and snow geese, and once had to deal with an enraged pika. Bears, though, are never a problem.

JON KRAKAUER

* * *

The Flyboys of Talkeetna

*Glacier landings and flying blind without
instruments are routine for the off-strip set.*

IT'S AN ORDINARY JUNE MORNING IN DOWNTOWN
Talkeetna, cultural hub of Alaska's upper Susitna Valley, population maybe 250 on a good day. The dawn breeze carries the
scent of spruce and wet earth; a moose wanders across the
hamlet's deserted main drag and pauses to rub her head against
the fence of the local ballpark. Abruptly, out on the airfield at
the edge of town, the peace of the young day is shattered as
the engine of a small red airplane coughs two or three times
and then catches with a roar.

The fellow in the pilot's seat is a big shaggy bear of a man
named Doug Geeting. As he taxis his craft to the end of the
runway, Geeting gets on the radio and files a flight plan in the
terse, cryptic argot that's the *lingua franca* of aviators everywhere. "Talkeetna, four-seven-fox. We've got four souls to the
Southeast Fork of the Kahiltna. Three hours fuel. Hour and
thirty on the route."

"Four-seven-fox, roger. Wind three-five-zero at six, favor-
ing three-six. Altimeter two-niner-eight-niner."

※

Alaskans have long debated the proper name for North America's highest mountain. Though it's officially been called Mt. McKinley since 1897, many residents believe the peak should be given the name that Athabascans living north of the Alaska range used for centuries: Denali, "The High One." Among those to prefer Denali was Hudson Stuck, leader of the first expedition to reach the great peak's 20,320-foot summit in 1913 and author of *The Ascent of Denali.* In Stuck's view, the use of McKinley was an affront to both the mountain and the region's Native peoples: "There is, to the author's mind, a certain ruthless arrogance that grows more offensive to him as the years pass by, in the temper that comes to a 'new' land and contemptuously ignores the Native names of conspicuous natural objects, almost always appropriate and significant, and overlays them with names that are, commonly, neither the one nor the other."

—Bill Sherwonit

"Two-niner-eight-niner, roger. Away we go." With that, the thirty-five-year-old pilot pulls back on the throttle, the din of the engine rises to an unholy wail, and the little airplane leaps off the tarmac in the huge Alaskan sky.

Beyond Talkeetna's two airstrips, half-dozen dirt streets, and ramshackle assemblage of log cabins, trailers, Quonset huts, and souvenir shops lies a vast plain of black spruce, impenetrable alder, and water-logged muskeg—a mosquito's idea of paradise that's flat as a griddle and barely 350 feet above sea level. Just fifty miles away, however, the immense ramparts of Mt. McKinley— the highest point in North America—erupt out of these lowlands without preamble. No sooner is Geeting in the air than he banks sharply to the left, buzzes west over the broad, silty braids of the Susitna

River, and points the airplane squarely toward that hulking silhouette.

Geeting's craft is a Cessna 185, a six-seater with about as much room inside as a small Japanese station wagon. On this particular flight he is carrying three passengers, who are jammed into the cabin like sardines beneath a heap of back-packs, sleeping bags, skis, and mountaineering paraphernalia that fills the airplane from floor to ceiling. The three men are climbers, and they have each paid Geeting two hundred dol-lars to be flown to a glacier at the 8,500-foot elevation on Mt. McKinley, where they will spend the better part of a month trying to reach the 20,320-foot summit.

Approximately one thousand climbers venture onto the slopes of McKinley and its satellite peaks each year, and land-ing them on the high glaciers of the Alaska Range is Doug Geeting's bread and butter. "Glacier flying"—as this demand-ing, dangerous, little-known facet of commercial aviation is generally termed—is practiced by only a handful of pilots the world over, eight or nine of whom are based in Talkeetna. As jobs go, the pay isn't great and the hours are horrible, but the view from the office is tough to beat.

Twenty-five minutes out of Talkeetna, the first snaggle-toothed defenses of the McKinley massif rise sharply from the Susitna Valley, filling the windshield of Geeting's Cessna. Ever since take-off the airplane has been laboring steadily upward. It has now reached an altitude of 8,000 feet, but the pickets of snow-plastered rock looming dead ahead stand a good 1,500 feet higher still. Geeting—who has logged some fifteen thou-sand hours in light planes, and has been flying this particular route for more than fifteen years now—appears supremely unconcerned as the plane bears down on the fast-approaching mountain wall.

A few moments before collision seems imminent—by

which time the climbers' mouths have gone dry and their knuckles turned white—Geeting dips a wing hard, throws the plane into a dizzying right turn, and swoops through a narrow gap that appears behind the shoulder of one of the loftier spires. The walls of the mountainside flash by at such close range that individual snow crystals can be distinguished glinting in the sunlight. "Yeah," Geeting casually remarks on the other side, "that notch there was what we call 'One-Shot Pass.'"

"The first rule of mountain flying," the pilot goes on to explain in the laid-back tones of his native California, "is that you never want to approach a pass straight on, because if you get into some unexpected downdraft and aren't able to clear the thing, you're going to find yourself buying the farm in a big hurry. Instead of attacking a high pass directly, I'll approach it by flying parallel to the ridge line until I'm almost alongside the pass, and then turn sharply into it so that I move through the notch at a forty-five-degree angle. That way, if I lose my lift and see that I'm not going to be high enough to make it over, I'm in position to turn away at the last instant and escape. If you want to stick around very long in this business, the idea is to leave your back door open and your stairway down and clear at all times."

On the far side of the pass is a scene straight from the Pleistocene, an alien world of black rock, blue ice, and blinding-white snow stretching from horizon to horizon. Beneath the Cessna's wings lies the Kahiltna Glacier, a tongue of ice two miles across and forty miles long, corrugated by a nubbly rash of seracs and crevasses. The scale of the setting outside the plane's windows beggars the imagination: The peaks lining the Kahiltna rise a vertical mile and more in a single sweep from glacier to summit; the avalanches that periodically rumble down these faces at a hundred-plus miles per hour have so far to travel that they appear to be falling in slow motion. Against this immense landscape, Geeting's airplane is but a miniscule red mote, an all-but-invisible mechanical gnat droning its way through the firmament toward McKinley.

Ten minutes later the gnat makes a ninety-degree turn onto a tributary of the main Kahiltna called the Southeast Fork and settles into its descent. A crude snow-landing strip, delineated by a series of plastic garbage bags tied to bamboo tomato stakes, materializes in the middle of the glacier ahead amid a maze of gargantuan crevasses. As the plane gets closer, it becomes apparent that the glacier here is far from flat, as it had appeared from a distance; the strip, in fact, lies on a slope steep enough to give a novice skier pause.

The thin air at this altitude has severely cut into the Cessna's power, and the plane will be landing uphill into a cul de sac of mile-high granite walls. Hence, Geeting cheerfully allows, "When you land here, there's no such thing as a go-around. You've got to nail your approach perfectly the first time." To avoid any unpleasant surprises, he scans the surrounding ridges for wisps of blowing snow that might tip off the existence of hazardous wind conditions. Several miles away, up at the head of the main arm of the glacier, he spies a blanket of wispy cotton-like clouds creeping over a 10,300-foot saddle called Kahiltna Pass. "Those are foehn clouds," he says. "They indicate extremely turbulent downslope winds—rotors we call 'em. You can't see it, but the air is churning down those slopes like breaking surf. You take an airplane anywhere near those clouds and I guarantee you'll get the crap kicked out of you."

As if on cue, the Cessna is buffeted by a blast of severe turbulence, and the stall-warning shrieks as the airplane bucks wildly up, down, and sideways. Geeting, however, has anticipated the buffeting, and has already increased his airspeed to counter it. Serenely riding out the bumps, he guides the plane on down until the glacier rises to meet the craft's stubby aluminum skis with an easy kiss. Geeting taxis the Cessna to the uppermost end of the strip, spins the plane around with a burst of power so that it will be pointed downhill for takeoff, then shuts off the engine. "Well, here we are," he offers, "Kahiltna International Airport."

Geeting's passengers crawl hastily out into the glacial chill, and three other alpinists, their faces purple and peeling from a month on the hill, eagerly climb on board for a lift back to the land of beer, flush toilets, and green growing things. After five minutes at Kahiltna International, Geeting snaps off a crisp Junior Birdman salute to the dazed-looking crew he's just unloaded, fires up his Cessna one more time, and roars down the strip in a blizzard of prop-driven snow to pick up the next load of climbers, who are already impatiently awaiting his arrival back in Talkeetna.

From May through late June, the busiest climbing season on McKinley, it is not unusual for the skies over Talkeetna to reverberate with the infernal whine of ski-equipped Cessnas, Helio Couriers, and cloth-winged Super Cubs from five in the morning to well after midnight. If the racket ever cuts short anybody's beauty rest, however, no complaints are registered, for Alaska without airplanes would be as unthinkable as Iowa without corn.

"Alaskans," writes Jean Potter in *The Flying North*, a history of bush pilots, "are the flyingest people under the American flag and probably the flyingest people in the world.... By 1939 the small airlines of the Territory were hauling twenty-three times as many passengers and a thousand times as much freight, per capita, as the airlines of the United States. The federal government and large corporations had little to do with this." The driving force behind the development of Alaska aviation, Potter points out, was a ragtag assortment of self-reliant, seat-of-the-pants bush pilots—larger-than-life figures like Carl Ben Eielson, Joe Crosson, Noel Wien, and Bob Reeve, who cheated death on a daily basis to deliver groceries and medicine and mail to outposts at the edge of the earth—of whom Doug Geeting and his glacier-baiting rivals in Talkeetna are very much the spiritual heirs.

A 12,800-foot peak overlooking Kahiltna International's makeshift glacial airstrip now bears the name of Joe Crosson, which is fitting, because it was Crosson, in April, 1932, who pulled off the first Alaskan glacier landing, on McKinley's Muldrow Glacier, where he delivered a scientific expedition to measure cosmic rays. According to one of the expedition members, Crosson took the momentous initial landing "much as a matter of course, and lit a cigar before leaving the plane," though Jean Potter reports that the job resulted in "such risk and such damage" to the aircraft that Crosson's employer, Alaskan Airways, subsequently forbade him to engage in any further glacier sorties.

It was left to Bob Reeve—a high-strung Wisconsin-born barnstormer and bon vivant—to perfect the art of glacier flying. Beginning in 1929, the twenty-seven-year-old Reeve had been introduced to mountain aviation while pioneering extremely hazardous long-distance air-mail routes over the Andes of South America between Lima, Santiago, and Buenos Aires, where he occasionally shared a bottle between flights with a dapper, romantic French airman named Antoine de Saint-Exupéry, who would soon thereafter write both *The Little Prince* and an intensely lyrical, hugely popular record of the early flying life, *Wind, Sand, and Stars*.

Reeve left South America in 1932 after incurring the wrath of his superiors by smashing up an expensive Lockheed Vega. Back in the States, he promptly lost all his money in the stock market and contracted polio. Finding himself flat broke and seriously ill at the height of the Depression, he stowed away on a freighter to Alaska seeking a change of luck, and wound up in the seedy port city of Valdez.

Unfortunately, Alaska had already attracted a host of hungry pilots in those Depression years, and there weren't enough paying customers to go around. Desperate for work, Reeve decided to specialize in a corner of the aviation market that not even the territory's boldest aviators had dared to go after: landing gold miners and their heavy supplies on the glaciers that flowed down from the jumble of high peaks surrounding Valdez. By trial and error, Reeve quickly developed a sense for steering clear of hidden crevasses, discovered that the incline of a glacier could be an aid, rather than an impediment, to making short-field landings and take-offs, and learned that by dropping a line of spruce boughs or gunny sacks onto the snow before setting down, he could establish a horizon and judge the lay of a slope on cloudy days when it was otherwise impossible to tell exactly where the ground was....

By the 1950s, though, Reeve had moved on from Valdez and was unavailable for glacier work, so mountaineer and mapmaker Bradford Washburn was forced to turn elsewhere when he needed a full-time pilot for an ongoing nine-year cartographic survey of Mt. McKinley. A fearless young Talkeetna-based flyer named Don Sheldon was recommended. Washburn says that when he asked Reeve what he knew about Sheldon, Reeve replied, "He's either crazy and he's going to kill himself, or he'll turn out to be one hell of a good pilot." The latter proved to be the case.

Taking advantage of the newly invented "wheel-ski" landing gear—which permitted a pilot to take off with wheels on a dry runway, and then, while airborne, lower a set of skis into position for landing on snow—Sheldon flew commercially out of Talkeetna for twenty-seven years, routinely logging more than eight hundred hours each summer in the malevolent skies over the Alaska Range. Along the way he went through forty-five airplanes—four of them totaled in violent crashes—but he never injured either himself or a single passenger. His nervy high-altitude landings and life-saving rescue missions were legendary not only throughout Alaska, but in much of the world at large. At the time of his death from colon cancer in 1975, the name Don Sheldon had become synonymous with heroic glacier flying.

Sheldon's career coincided with the mushrooming popularity of mountaineering on McKinley; over the last decade of his life Sheldon was so busy flying climbers that in the spring and summer months he averaged just four or five

Alaska is hailed as the "flyingest" state, with more private pilots per capita than anywhere else in the nation. It's also one of the most dangerous places to fly. Alaska's crash rate is five times above the national average and forty-five people, on average, are killed in plane crashes annually. Bad weather, inadequate or non-existent navigation systems, and pilot error are to blame. Only a handful of the state's 435 runways have control towers and many are unpaved and unlit—and those are the easier places to land. Where airports don't exist, small planes equipped with skis, floats, and fat tires touch down on glaciers, lakes, and gravel bars.

—Andromeda Romano-Lax

hours sleep a night. Even with the onerous workload, though, most years Sheldon barely made enough money to pay the bills. "Nobody gets rich owning an air-taxi business," explains Roberta Reeve Sheldon—Don's widow and Bob Reeve's daughter—who still lives in Talkeetna in a modest wood-frame house at the end of the village airstrip. "All the money you make goes back into the airplanes. I remember once we went to the bank and borrowed forty thousand dollars to buy a new Cessna 180. Three months later Don totaled it on Mt. Hayes. I'll tell you, it hurts to be making payments on an airplane you don't even have anymore."

Sheldon's financial woes were exacerbated by the existence of a second, equally talented glacier pilot in town, one Cliff Hudson, who started working out of Talkeetna a few years after Sheldon did. It was not a friendly rivalry: Sheldon and Hudson were forever stealing each other's customers, and longtime Talkeetnans still vividly recall a fistfight between the two pilots that splintered the candy counter in the B & K Trading Post and left both men with black eyes and split lips. Things got so bad between them that Sheldon once allegedly buzzed Hudson at extremely close range in midair, an incident that wound up in the courts and nearly cost Sheldon his license.

Sheldon—a cocky, ruggedly handsome ex-cowboy from Wyoming—looked every inch the dashing bush pilot. In marked contrast, Hudson—who is still alive and flying— might easily be mistaken for a stray panhandler from the Bowery, thanks to the soiled wool shirt, shiny polyester slacks, and cheesy black loafers that make up his standard flight uniform. Hudson's sartorial shortcomings, however, haven't diminished his reputation as a masterful glacier pilot.

The primary windsock for the village airstrip sits atop the roof of an infamous local watering hole called the Fairview Inn. It is not uncommon, within the Fairview's dimly lit chambers, to overhear barstool aviators bickering over the relative abilities of Hudson and Sheldon in the manner of baseball fans comparing Maris and Ruth, or Bonds and McGuire. There are denizens of the Fairview who argue that Hudson is at least as good a pilot as Sheldon was, pointing out that

Hudson—incredibly—has yet to wreck a single airplane despite having logged more hours of glacier flying than any other man alive.

After Sheldon's death, Hudson enjoyed a few relatively flush years without serious competition, but only a few: by 1984 there were no fewer than four air-taxi companies operating full-time out of Talkeetna—Hudson Air Service, Doug Geeting Aviation, K2 Aviation, and Talkeetna Air Taxi—all specializing in glacier flying, and all headed by brilliant pilots hell-bent on being top dog. Jim Okonek, the owner of K2 Aviation, candidly allows that "each of us considers himself the best pilot in town, and can't imagine why a person would ever want to fly with anybody else."

Not surprisingly, the confluence of so many robust egos in such a small place throws off sparks from time to time. Insults are traded, clients are rustled. The pilots are constantly reporting each other to the authorities for real or imagined breaches of regulations....

All of the pilots now regularly take planeloads of tourists, ordinary vacationers from Philadelphia and Des Moines, on sightseeing flights to the glaciers. These trips have become so routine, in fact, that cynics suggest that the risk and romance has all but disappeared from the job—that glacier flying today isn't much different from

---

Jim Okonek and Lowell Thomas Jr. have retired from commercial flying and Cliff Hudson has turned over his company's flying chores to son Jay, but Talkeetna's contemporary "flyboys"—which still include Doug Geeting—remain a competitive and adventurous bunch who transport climbers and an ever-increasing number of flightseers to and from the Alaska Range.

—Bill Sherwonit

driving a cab. Okonek, a retired Air Force colonel who flew helicopters in Viet Nam, disagrees, insisting that "this has got to be the best flying job anywhere. Jacques Cousteau's pilot recently called to ask me for a job; top commercial pilots from all over the world have expressed interest in working here.

"I take quite a few airline pilots up to the glacier on their layover days," Okonek continues, "guys who fly 747s for Swissair and Quantas, and it bowls them over to see the places we land, the terrain we fly over. Glacier flying still holds plenty of challenge. Pilots lacking mountain experience will fly up the Kahiltna for a look around and get disoriented by the incredible scale of the peaks. All of a sudden their little airplane is out of breath, they're out of ideas about what to do, and they ' crash onto the glacier. We see it year after year."

And green, amateur flyers are not the only ones who smash airplanes into the Alaska Range. In 1981, an experienced Talkeetna pilot named Ed Homer took two friends on an afternoon joyride around McKinley, got caught in a downdraft while crossing Kahiltna Pass, and slammed his Cessna into the mountainside. By the time rescuers reached the wreckage four days later, one passenger was dead, the other had lost both his hands to frostbite and Homer had lost both his feet. "We're often up against a fine line in this business," Lowell Thomas emphasizes. "It's just a question of whether you can recognize when you're stepping too far over that line. And there are definitely times—usually when we're called upon to rescue climbers who've gotten themselves into trouble—when we step over the line quite a ways, and do things that are extremely marginal."

Geeting handles more than his share of those marginal flights. Several years ago, a climber plunged 70 feet into a hidden crevasse on Mt. Foraker—a 17,400-foot peak next to McKinley—and suffered massive head injuries. After two days of stormy weather stymied several rescue attempts, a doctor on the scene radioed in desperation that the victim would die if he didn't get to a hospital soon. "It was completely socked-in," Geeting recalls. "Visibility was zero-zero from the surface of the glacier all the way up to eleven thousand feet. But I'd landed beneath Foraker before, and I'd memorized the layout of the surrounding peaks and ridges, so I decided to take a shot at evacuating the guy."

Geeting's plan was to approach Foraker above the clouds, get his bearings, and then establish a precise descent pattern into the soup. "I'd fly straight for exactly one minute," he explains, "then turn for one minute, fly straight for another minute, turn again for a minute. It was a total whiteout—I couldn't see a freaking thing—but I trusted the course I'd worked out ahead of time and stuck to it. For a reference point, I asked the people on the glacier to give me a shout on the radio every time they heard me pass overhead."

From the time he dropped into the cloud bank, Geeting was irrevocably committed. The peaks looming unseen in the mists beyond his wingtips left absolutely no room for error: If the pilot were to complete a turn a few seconds late, or steer a few degrees too far to the left or right, with each subsequent maneuver he would unwittingly compound the mistake, and the airplane would eventually plow blindly into one of a dozen icy mountainsides at 110 miles per hour.

"I made my way down through the cloud between the mountain walls," Geeting says, "watching the compass, the clock, and the altimeter real close, listening for the climbers to yell, 'Now' when I buzzed over them. I figured touchdown would be right at seven thousand feet, so when the altimeter showed seventy-five hundred I lined up for final, slowed to landing speed and went on in. It was a real odd feeling, because in a whiteout like that you can't tell where the sky stops and the glacier begins. All of a sudden my airspeed went down to nothing, and I thought, 'Son of a bitch!' Then I looked out the window and saw these climbers running out of the cloud toward the airplane. Damned if I wasn't on the ground."

Jon Krakauer is an outdoor and adventure writer and the author of Into the Wild, Into Thin Air: A Personal Account of the Mt. Everest Disaster, *and* Eiger Dreams: Ventures Among Men and Mountains, *from which this story is excerpted. A contributing editor to* Outside, *he writes for many national magazines and newspapers. He lives in Seattle.*

BARBARA BROWN

Kayaking through a Timeless Realm of Rain, Bugs, and B.O.

A paddler finds soggy serenity.

THE PADDLE ENTERS THE WATER WITH A SCATTERING of splashes and a *plonk*. It glides backward, rises from the water, and the *plonk* moves to the other side of the kayak, to the other paddle. *Plonk, plonk. Plonk, plonk.* One thousand-one, one thousand-two. This is the only rhythm of my week. This and the tides. High tide in the afternoon, high tide late at night.

My husband, Tim, and I have thoughtfully arranged this trip in Prince William Sound to coincide with the one week of rainy weather all summer. We are out in weather that would lead Californians to say, "Let's just reschedule; the weather will be great another day." But as my friend Ann says, "There is no bad weather, only bad gear." And as my friend Rob says, "If the weather were great, this place would be as crowded as California."

So we get rain and privacy, rain and emptiness. It's a good trade. If it weren't raining, I wouldn't know that tiny silver bubbles are released when raindrops hit the water. I wouldn't know that when my rain hood is up and I can't see to the sides or even turn my head around, I am in a silent, solitary world. The mist hangs over the landscape. There are no mountains, no faraway distances. Just the immediacy of this cove, this gravel bar, and nothing moving faster than a kayak, nothing moving faster than the *plonk, plonk* of my paddle metronome.

And then the sky clears and there are mountains and glaciers. I take off my hood, rediscover Tim, our friends Rob and Mark. We peel off rain jackets and long underwear; I'm down to my life jacket and sunglasses. Oh, rain is so good because it feels so good when it stops. A day is good when we get the tents set up before the rain. A day is bad when the rain picks up and beats down on us just as we find a campsite. A day is good when the rain starts just as we slip into our fully loaded kayaks for another paddle.

A day is really good when we manage to escape the bugs. The gnats are clouds around us, bites on our bodies, bumps everywhere. Sometimes we race for the tents at night, right on the brink of psychosis, but then I get to fill the tent walls with gnat corpses and I feel better. Mark is new to Alaska; he lives in his head net. I take the route of personal poison: I pump bug dope all over. Tim says I will smell of bug dope when I perspire, but at least I can look at the scenery without a seam down my face.

I already look like the Elephant Man when I'm bit on the lip. It swells up huge. I have Barbara Hershey collagen-stuffed lips. Suddenly I want to make big smooshy kisses with Tim. I feel like there's a berry in my lip and that if I kiss him, berry juice will run through us. If all my DEET doesn't poison us first.

So I line up at the tent, ready to race inside before the bugs follow me in. I dive in...and reel backwards from the stench inside. "Zip the door," Tim shouts.

"It stinks in here," I gasp. Old wool, he says, polypro long underwear, bug dope. Personal hygiene, I say, bodily functions. GAS. With the rain and the bugs, our tents are factories of scent, cesspools of odors. Our hygiene is so bad I am eating meals prepared by fingernails dirtier than an auto mechanic's. We fish bugs out of our hot chocolates and then give up. We would never eat bug corpses from our tent walls, but we are eating them in our food.

We sleep eleven hours. The rhythm of our days is clockless, timeless. We watch for high tide, are relieved when it passes our tents by, and then sleep till whenever. We eat our meals and beg each other to eat more. Should we eat to reduce volume or weight? Why did we bring so much food?

We boil water for cooking. It's good when it rains; we just put pots under the corners of the tarp. On sunny days, we have to filter. On rainy days, it's easy, but our drinking water tastes like tarp. We eat a lot of things like cheese and crackers, chocolate chips, salami, gorp. I go out in the wilderness to be healthy and I eat things I'd never eat at home.

We see otters and seals, bears and porcupines, eagles everywhere. I collect stones, each one smoother than the last, stones that have been smoothed for eons. I am traveling with three men, and they are collecting stones for a skipping tournament, best three out of five. They gang up, say I use more than my fair share of toilet paper.

I'm paddling to the rhythm of the kayak. *Plonk, plonk.* I am neither fast nor slow. I am the only time of the Sound, the only time of the water. My mind is so clear, the water clear. I look at my bare arms. I have strong biceps, I think. I am the earth, the water, the rain, the air. I turn back to Tim.

"Man," he says, "your armpits stink."

Barbara Brown and her ten-year-old daughter, Sophie, spent the summer of 2002 crossing America by waterpark. They began at home in Anchorage, Alaska and ended back there after 10,000 miles, 24 waterparks, 10 stitches to the head, and 3 demolished bathing suits. Husband Tim kept the home fires burning and Barbara is now at work on the book. Barbara was a weekly columnist at the Anchorage Daily News *for the past eight years and is now the Director of Leadership Anchorage for the Alaska Humanities Forum, and a regular commentator on public radio. She is also the "Storytime Lady" for the Alaska Botanical Garden.*

DANIEL HENRY

Eating Edward Curtis at the Ugruk Café

A tribe's wealth includes knowing
where its food comes from.

BROWN FACES ARE THE ONLY SKIN SHOWING ON PEOPLE with dip nets by the side of the highway. Early May breeze leaves a winterish afterbite, so everyone is bundled up. A pickup bed sags with eulachon, the local smelt treasured for its sweet grease. You swerve onto the gravel shoulder and lean against your rental car, a black techno-shaman soul-stealer dangling from your neck. As a reformed representative of the conquering nation, you are titillated by your presumed guilt, so saunter over. Conscious of a photo op with aboriginal flame-keepers, you wait for acknowledgement. A man with long raven hair chews on a strip of red fish jerky. He offers it to the man next to him, who hands it to his brother or uncle. Emboldened by ancient ritual, you ask for a bite. Time passes.

They are amicable, quiet. Syllables gurgle and splash within the river's rushing discourse. David, you think you hear the oldest man say by way of introduction. He meets your gaze, ducks a greeting with the bill of his ball cap, returns his sentinel stare to blue-black streaks in frothwater. Feebly: How's the fishing? Spring flood swallows your words. You stare, too, unwilling to intrude further into the eyes of men in prayerful duty.

The river answers your question with each netload bent to strobe-balls wrangled from glacial milk in the flat, slobbering light. Like these men, you are transfixed by thousands of fish muscling through current the color of wet cement. You focus your shaman's eye at the rain-slickered row of backs bowing to this river called Chilkat, or "salmon storehouse," by people whose surroundings speak to them constantly in dialects of water. Flash. Flashes of fish in silvery death dance, flashes in faces looking away. Somewhere before your thoughts circle around the pictures' monetary value, the ancient images tip-toe past the closed door of your ethics. Maybe the door is ajar enough for you to wonder if this story is really yours to tell. You seek comfort in knowing that six or seven generations of photographers have already opened the door, captured their prizes, and slammed it shut.

Did frontier photographer Edward Curtis feel this way when he appropriated hundreds of Native American faces a century ago? The question threatens to kick open your shadowy door as you return to the safety of your white coupe. You see them everywhere: sepia-tone images staring back proudly from posters, book jackets, the flickering campfires of cyberspace. Surely Curtis yearned to span the same unbridgeable separateness from his subjects, and you want to know how he did it. How did he know when it was time to squeeze the bulb on his hulking Kodak?

Something primal and awkward pulls a grin across your face as you drive on. Like Curtis, you've crossed through time and have the pictures to prove it. You may even convince yourself in stories told back home that these men were, in a way, your friends, or at least companions along the river. But you know better. Friends invite friends to the table. Only intimates or intruders barge in. Strangers are fed by grace.

It's likely that you are not the type to stop and bother Native fishers, but it happens. In my twenty years of knocking around a North known by its disconnection with all things Southerly, I've often driven my rusting Subaru hatchback past curious non-Natives along the sides of roads as they earnestly invested their ten minutes to bridge the gap between Burger King and subsistence people. Those tableaus may be frozen in your memory as well. Voyeurs with high-optic cameras distance themselves from the threat of an actual encounter. Drive-by shootings flash from braking SUVs. Without the shield of cultural ambiguity, Edward Curtis was compelled to listen at length to the stories of his subjects. He may have grasped the forearms of men in welcome, or lifted a small child to his shoulders. Names were exchanged. Meals were dished up. Through his images, Curtis transformed the magical events of photographic portraiture into commerce, sold to the conquerors' spawn so we may at any moment meet the eyes of the vanquished.

But this is not about blame or guilt. It is about sharing. The gap that some contend exists between ancient and contemporary peoples is an interface, really. As Tlingit poet-linguist Nora Dauenhauer suggests in her poem, "How to Cook Fresh Salmon from the River," perceived cultural chasms may be bridged by the contents of a paper plate: "Serve to all relatives and friends/You have invited to the bar-b-q/And those who love it./And think how good it is/That we have good spirits/That still bring salmon and oil." Like wolves and hounds, teachers and students, parents and offspring, the blood that courses under our deceptive skins defines our commonalities. And long before prejudice or love, the pulse within our bodies burns with the heat of food.

The smooth faces of a young Inupiaq family gazed up at me from a glass bowl a few winters back at a neighborhood potluck near my home of Haines, Alaska. Dark, shining eyes found mine as I daubed away sauce-drenched morsels of Thai stir-fry while the rich steaming clatter of feeding friends swirled around the hewn-log room. Wolverine ruff flared from self-assured faces etched into smoky glass, faces so beatific and rare that I stared long enough for a friend to reveal the bowl's garage-sale lineage. Part of a Curtis set traded locally, over and over. She showed me her Chief Joseph, his powerful jaw set in pride and sorrow, and another bowl containing the haunting visage of "Papago Woman," whose deep eyes peered from behind yellowish globs of tapioca.

From each set of burnished eyes peering eternally into Curtis' lens, I sense a profound love of place; the oneness beaming from Inupiaq faces, or the yearning in Joseph's. Each possesses tribal knowledge of sunken halibut ledges and meadows of wild asparagus, bear trails, and sea lion haul-outs. Like others who came from someplace else to set roots in the glacially scoured soils of Haines, I moved here for the same reasons that local Tlingits used to justify their aggressive defense of territory: fish, birds, wild game, berries and plants for the gathering. Access from tidewater to trade routes penetrating a dry Interior in Alaska and Yukon. Most important, it was where they belonged. Home.

The Chilkat and Chilkoot watersheds proved an ample homeland for up to a thousand residents in four villages. That they were fierce proprietors of an extraordinarily rich territory was widely understood, earning ethnographer Aurel Krause's nomination for "the mightiest of all the Tlingit tribes." Their wealth was measured by the sweep of legendary terrain as well as the fabulous artwork used to prove their ownership, carved in totemic design or woven into Chilkat blankets. But among trading partners they were known best for eulachon oil, a treasured food that supplied the namesake for their closely guarded route to the Interior, the so-called Grease Trail.

In 1879 the tribe's sense of ownership shifted when a preacher-explorer named John Muir delivered his "brotherhood of man" oration to hundreds in Yendestucke, at the mouth of the Chilkat. The shaman followed Muir's speech with an acknowledgement that, "for the first time, the Indian and the white man are on the same side of the river." Crossing the spiritual gap was a piece of cake for Muir compared to the epicurean gulf to come.

At the invitation of Chief Don-na-wuk, Muir partook in a celebratory meal, a "feast of fat things" prepared for the "Ice Chief" and his missionary friend Samuel Young. In a memoir published a year after Muir's death, Young described the meal served to the two white men in "huge washbowls of blue Hudson Bay ware." The first course consisted of dried salmon stacked in each guest's trencher like

---

Isu'iq piturnertuq means "the seal tastes good." Seals, sea lions, porpoises, and whales produced meat for food, oil for light, hides for boat coverings, and bone and sinew for tools.... It was important to strike a seal after it took a breath of air, so the injured animal would not sink.

—Amy Steffian and Florence Pestrikoff, *Alutiiq Word of the Week: Lessons in Alutiiq Language and Culture*

---

kindling, drenched in seal oil. Then the tubs were washed out and returned with a second course, "great long hunks" of deer back fat drowned in seal gravy. Following this, bowls were again washed and set before the visitors, this time heaped with walnut-sized Russian potatoes ascending from a puddle of oil. For dessert, fleshy rosehips as big as plums overflowed from their bowls, again dripping with grease. After a period of exquisite moans and lip-smacking by his gracious hosts, Muir leaned toward Young and exclaimed, "Mon, mon! I'm fashed we'll be floppin' about i' the sea, whiles, wi' flippers an' forked tails."

Traditional foods were discouraged at the Presbyterian mission that followed two years later. Beef, poultry, and flour became staples in the boarding school through which each Tlingit child passed. The same language used expertly by Reverend Young to translate his and Muir's speeches was banned among Native speakers. However, despite non-Native efforts to squelch an identity centuries in the making, Tlingit ways persist today. Even the gradual settlement of a couple thousand non-Natives in this venation of green valleys walled by glacier-draped crags has not deterred the rule of citizens waxing Tlingit by blood or association. They never signed a treaty, never relinquished the power that they now share with the strangers who came to their table. And I have felt the grace of their generosity.

Consider the contents of these pages a tribute to the generous spirit of subsistence people. Their blood flows with blueberry shine, sockeye wiggle, rain, wind, and impetuous sunlight. Described herein are two pathways, both of which I have trod. Each leads to a scene made familiar in the history of the world when people share food: one, like Muir's banquet, is by auspicious invitation. The other, like the roadside scene, is a bungling intrusion. I carry the lessons from these occasions as reassurance and warning, reminders of my place as a guest at the table.

✳

Green-bottle tones glint from the clear water that tumbles a rocky mile from Chilkoot Lake to the sea at Lutak Inlet. Filling the narrow wooded valley is the same liquid conversation that once spoke to a village of about one hundred twenty L'koot Tlingits, people of the Sockeye clan. On this day in late May, 1991, perhaps two dozen descendents scurry between work stations, their spirited palaver punctuating the river's drone with ancient grammar and laughter rarely displayed on Main Street in Haines, ten miles distant. Their chief, Austin Hammond, is called Donawak, after the leader who invited John Muir to his banquet. Austin has asked me to come out, take pictures, pose "good questions," and watch with white man's eyes as clan members attend to the business of cultural survival.

Diaphanous boundaries of kin and culture keep Tlingit folk distinct from non-Native residents, but their presence in Haines insinuates itself on nearly every level: politics, religion, education, business, food. Subsistence sets Alaska Natives apart from most other shoppers on the continent. Their traditional ways define an ancient culture with each recipe for salmon or seal gut, with each prayer for bountiful harvest. Beyond consumerism, though, Natives operate with a set of principles based on stewardship of the places that supply their groceries. Overharvest threatens their identity, disrespect can insult the spirits of plants and animals on which people depend. Food usually arrives when it is supposed to arrive, although fish stocks and other species have declined dramatically in parts of the state. Even the legendary tribes of eulachon, whose runs still contribute to local Tlingit status, have become sporadic.

"Now you get to see how Tlingits really act," Hammond says as he steps out of a thick coil of steam vapor to shake my hand. "Like our eulachon brothers, we are the last who know the ways." A purplish flush creeps up the eighty-one-year-old man's wizened neck, tinting his already dark face with burning radiance; his eyes twinkle with lipid-induced euphoria. He grins, a kid eating birthday cake. Guffaws burst from the other elders sitting in lawn chairs just up the riverbank. They dip celery and Ritz crackers into a salad bowl brimmed with honey-colored solution while calling out advice and jokes to the younger tribal members who work below. Austin nudges me, revealing ravaged dental work, and spreads both arms broadly toward the workers and the river gushing past them. "I am a wealthy man," he says. "To be here cooking eulachon with my children and grandchildren. This is my wealth." He runs a gnarled hand across his close-cropped salt-and-pepper hair, widens his eyes. "It gets so your ears tingle. Then you know the eulachon's working for you."

Young men shoveled a truckload of the oily fish into a pit ten days earlier, then covered it with a sheet of plywood until today. Sammy carefully lowers himself into the hole until he is out of sight. His hand reappears grasping the bale of a steel bucket overfilled with fermented eulachon. Fumes emanate from the putrefying mass. Insect clouds hover over the eight-by-ten-foot excavation. A potent bouquet punches me when I peer into the pit. Tears well in my eyes and a fist of nausea clenches my stomach. Austin lightly touches my elbow to bring me back from the edge.

The bucket goes to Ozzie, a young man I usually see in town swimming through a bottomless pool of alcohol, who now sloshes the bucket's contents into a washtub. Ozzie and his friend Pete waltz gingerly to the fire with their precious haul, then pour it gradually into the forty-gallon cast iron cauldron. Thick white steam erupts from the bubbling stew which envelopes Austin's middle-aged granddaughter, Lena, as she stirs with both hands pushing a sawed-off canoe paddle. She recognizes my wife, Jeannie, and waves her toward another paddle on the ground near the woodstove. Jeannie and Lena fall into a rhythm of slow, steady stirring, meant to thoroughly break apart the fish bodies to release every molecule of the precious oil.

The chief steps into the white steam and inhales sharply. Clouds billow and thicken each time fish is added. Austin wraps himself completely in the hot vapor blanket. When a slight breeze unravels his ethereal cloak, the man's eyes meet mine, smiling. The steam has restorative powers, Austin says. "It can cure a bad sunburn; does the same thing to your insides." Lena hands me her paddle and walks up the bank to take a photo of Jeannie and me stirring, swaddled in steam. "Say cheese," she says, giggling. Flash. One at a time the old men and women in lawn chairs stand with effort and hobble down to the cauldron for their turn in the steam. I lean into it and suck long draughts. Instead of the heat blast I expect, steam slides down my throat and coats my innards completely with warm velvet. Instantly, my body relaxes. I step back from the vat as others move in to skim the creamy froth for oil. A grin stretches across my face.

The elders nod and laugh and point at the white guy wearing an eulachon smirk. One of the grandfathers, George Lewis, waves a long stalk of wild celery and points with it to an empty lawn chair. Like passing a baton, he slaps the peeled stalk into my palm, points with his open hands to the salad bowl on a firewood round. "Try our elixir of life," he urges. I dip into the bowl and withdraw the stalk drenched in what could pass as olive oil. Tastebuds prepared for rancid shock are disoriented by a mild, cloying flavor that only hints of fish. When the celery is gone, my hosts offer crackers and bread sticks. George says that during the 1898 gold rush the trading value of eulachon oil was many times that of the precious mineral that lured at least 20,000 adventurers past these waters to Skagway, just fifteen miles up the fjord. Another man adds that his grandfather was paid in gold to be a packer escorting crowds over Chilkoot Pass, but traded his wages for oil when he came off the mountain.

Someone passes around a Mason jar of darker oil, prompting a lively discourse on the varying grades, tastes, potency. Braids of steam drift and unravel through our semi-circle facing the sonorous river. More jars are tested. My ears begin to tingle.

> I longed to lift the lid on a Dutch oven filled with tender ribs and onions, the unctuous steam rising up to slick my cheeks and my forehead. My father, after twelve years of successful hunts, once failed to get his moose. That was the year that mountain goat, black bear, and caribou filled our freezer. I was born to game meat, and I craved its smell, taste, and energy.
>
> —Steve Kahn, "The Hard Way Home"

Two eulachon seasons later and more than a thousand air miles across Alaska, Jeannie and I are exploring the tundra north of Kotzebue. On the eighth day of a cross-country walk through the Igichuk Hills we climb to the wind-blasted summit of Mt. Noak for a view across the Bering Strait. We imagine a brooding Russian horizon, although our actual view is obscured by low fog far out to sea. Crouched behind lichen-gold boulders for hours of squinting and imagining, we commit to film and memory the rare summer scenes of a green Arctic land slumping into ice-free seawater.

To the south, across the two-mile mouth of Hotham Inlet,

Kotzebue crowds the exposed point of Baldwin Peninsula, a long, low finger extending into the shallow basin of Kotzebue Sound. Beyond rises the Seward Peninsula, a rumpled black shoulder jutting to a westward plunge into the Strait. To the east and north spread the Kobuk and Noatak rivers over dendritic deltas which narrow back to the mountains of their origins. When our landscape sweep returns to Kotzebue we spy a charcoal smudge slanting back through town from the prevailing sea breeze. In minutes, the slender column thickens into a dreary funeral plume, smothering signs of humanity's tentacle sprawl. Town, airport, roads—swallowed completely.

Somebody lit the dump again, people tell us when we return to civilization two days later. Happens a few times a year. The choking fog burns our eyes and throats whenever we step outside, but few seem concerned. The fire is a tradition on Fourth of July, attracting young people who stand at the brink of the Mephistophelean pit to laugh, gossip, and cough. This time, the fire department rushed out to douse the blaze, producing pallid cloud mountains until the next afternoon when the fire's noxious rebirth brings back the black.

Three thousand subsistence-dependent Inupiaq people comprise most of Kotzebue, sometimes called the "largest village" in Alaska. As in other northern cultures, no one seems to sleep during summer months, preparing or recovering from fish camp. Outboards and four-wheelers gutter and whine at all hours. Dogs roam the unpaved streets in shifts. Incessant light spills from the Arctic sun.

Our national park friend, Andy, is eager to show us around. When I show interest in local subsistence food, he applies a park interpreter's zeal to call several households. Phones ring unanswered. Finally he talks with Robert, the grown son of Jonas, an Inupiaq elder employed by the national parks as a "subsistence specialist." Andy says that they still have bearded seal left over from the winter, maybe muktuk, too. Both are considered delicacies, especially muktuk, the chewy strips of whale blubber prized by northern people for fat content. We order a pizza to be picked up in an hour and pedal single-speed bicycles across town for a taste of local fare.

Five-year-old Martha meets us at the Arctic entrance of a mobile home held together by odd-sized strips of plywood nailed to tar paper over metal sheathing. She pirouettes in the dust, her traditional *kuspuk* skirts flaring around her velveteen middle. Names and intentions exchanged, she pulls aside the Army surplus blanket hanging in the doorway like a magician revealing an astonishing climax. We are assured by her happy chatter, and duck into the small, dark space.

Two opposite windows in the dim interior let in enough light to illuminate curls of trash-fire smoke still clinging to us. Martha points to a man slumped achingly low on a couch in a corner of the L-shaped living room/kitchen and introduces him as her father, Robert. We dutifully identify ourselves. In a voice that booms with nervous authority, Andy explains that Jeannie and I are guests from Haines; he describes at length the location of our home in relation to Kotzebue. Robert rises from his sprawl to shake hands, then settles back to the couch where he refocuses on an ancient blaring television. Farrah Fawcett tugs a man's leather-jacketed elbow behind his back. "Do you watch *Charlie's Angels?*" Martha asks.

Undaunted, Andy explains the purpose of our visit. "Bearded seal or muktuk. I think I told you on the phone. You said you had some."

"*Ugruk.* Kitchen table," Robert says to Farrah.

Martha seizes both of Jeannie's hands and demands to be swung around by the arms. Difficult to maneuver in the clutter, but anything to distract from our growing sense of trespass. Andy and I step back to the table where we see a blackened

shoulder roast on a platter. Next to it is a stack of small, col-
orful paper plates, the kind kids use at birthday parties. Unsure
of our next move, we stare at the meat until a man emerges
from a back room. He introduces himself as Jonas's uncle Ivan,
visiting for a Friends convention in town. A spare, neat
Inupiaq man in his sixties, Ivan brought his family five hours
in an open boat down the Kobuk from Noorvik. He sits at the
table, facing us. He is careful not to look at the ugruk.

For the lack of anything better to fill the long, stifling si-
lences, Andy embarks on a rapid-fire series of questions.
Whenever he pauses, I follow with further questions. Ivan's
slow, careful answers turn terse, jerky, automatic. He often
pauses and chuckles into his fist. The behavior prompts flights
of fidgety interrogation until Ivan expels a long, pent-up
breath and holds up both hands. "You white people," he says,
shaking his head, smiling at the floor. He lifts his eyes to find
ours. "You think you can know everything by asking all these
questions. Sometimes. You. Have. To. Listen." He motions to
the *ugruk*. "Here. Have some."

Silence. Farrah grunts as she heaves another flack to the
floor. Martha has led Jeannie outside to play. No one moves.
My ears burn like candles, hot wax dripping on cheeks and
neck. Then Andy: "How do you eat *ugruk*?"

Ivan bursts into loud laughter that forces him to tightly
cross his arms over his chest. He wipes tears away with a
folded white handkerchief as he gradually catches his breath.
"How do you eat bacon or steak?" he returns. More laughter,
this time shared by the three of us.

Smoke wisps trail Jonas as he pushes through the blanket
doorway. Andy brightens at his friend's entrance, but the elder
hardly notices us. Waiting outside is a vanload of Friends who
need housing for the night. We shake hands and Jonas apolo-
gizes for being so busy, but the church conference demands his

full attention. Three elderly women duck through the entrance and cluster around the telephone. They make several calls, all in Inupiaq. Whoever is on the phone often breaks into giggles, then relays messages to the other women who titter excitedly.

Andy raises his voice above the commotion: "My friends from Haines are only here for the night. They are wondering if they can try some muktuk."

A sudden hush amplifies the *oofs* and smacks of three beautiful TV crime-fighters taking out the last thugs of the show. The whale blubber strips about which Andy inquires are food for celebration and family. Like it is with fine wines, if you have to ask, you're probably not in the loop. Ivan smiles into his hand. Jonas flashes a quizzical look at us. "Wrong season. Besides, it's in the freezer and I'm in a hurry." He shrugs at the women. "We've got a convention going on."

Tendrils of toxic fog creep under the hanging blanket and settle just above the floor. More chuckles around the phone. No one mentions the *ugruk* rising like a promontory from its puddle of congealed grease. Robert turns down the TV volume, walks to the table. Looks at the *ugruk*, then at us. Patiently, curiously, the men watch their white interlopers.

Shame and hunger rings in my ears. "Pizza must be ready now," I say to Andy. The men nod their heads, chuckle agreeably. We excuse ourselves in a round of hasty handshakes, then exit into the roiling haze.

As I write from this remote, roadless shore of home, thousands of birds scream from the tideflat that stretches into mirroring fjordwater. Last week silver-blue balls of herring rolled into our little bay for their annual spawning frenzy. The bursting females laid a two-inch rime of roe on swaths of bladderwrack, bull kelp, dulse. Milky surface froth represented the final, best work of males driven by moonlight and destiny. On this bright May morning, surf scoter, gull, eagle, plover, sandpiper, duck, crow, and heron gorge themselves on the pale pudding exposed by one of the lowest tides of the year. I watch seal, sea lion, and otter patrol the glassy water for stray herring or their gilled pursuers. Cutting wakes among them are skiffs and diesels with nets outstretched on a bet that enough fish might persist for bait or pickling. With Jeannie close behind, our three-year-old Charlie lurches along the high tide mark seeking egg-studded fronds to festoon a "wombat stew" over-flowing with pebbles, clamshells, dandelions, beach-hay. I sit at this keyboard thinking about the power of instinct, how life attracts life. And the yawning gulf between computers and wild food.

This week, subsistence burns in the hearts of many more than those gathered outside my window. In Anchorage, an eight hun-dred-mile road trip from here, nearly two thousand advocates marched yesterday for a "We the People" rally declaring the right of Native and rural Alaskans to a sub-sistence "preference." Signs tell the story: "Subsistence Feeds Our Families," "First Come, Last Served," "Great Nations Keep Their Word."

⁂

Talk about real food: According to the *Alaska Almanac*, rural Alaskans eat on average about one pound of wild food per person daily. Forty-four million pounds are harvested annually, along with another 10 million that urban residents procure and take home. The harvest is primar-ily fish (60 percent by weight), followed by land mammals (20 percent), ma-rine mammals (14 percent) and birds, shellfish, and plants (2 percent each).

—Ellen Bielawski

In a state once blessed with abundant resources, a battle rages between subsistence users and commercial interests. As human population grows and wild stocks diminish, competition heightens over the remaining fish, berries, caribou, whale. Should food leave Alaska to be mounted on walls or gussied up for gourmet markets? Who most "deserves" the animals that each season fulfill their genetic contracts to return to the creek mouths and mountain passes dedicated by human elders to their grandchildren? Many more questions persist, none of which may be answered simply. After generations of inviting guests to the table, traditional peoples are forced to inventory their larder, perhaps to turn some of us away.

It is a somber stewardship, this new way of looking at food. It means confrontation with non-Native bureaucrats and corporations. It means leaving one's village and wearing a white man's suit to Washington, D.C. or Anchorage. It means uncertainty about future supplies. Sharing a meal with outsiders, once a source of great pride for our original hosts, has been reduced to an exercise in scarcity.

In the early 1980s, Canadian justice Thomas Berger held a sweeping series of hearings throughout Alaska to record villagers' views about the success of the Alaska Native Claims Settlement Act, especially as it pertained to subsistence. The results of his study for the Alaska Native Review Commission were published in the keystone book, *Village Journey*. Like Edward Curtis seventy-five years before him, Berger came to listen, watch, and record, keenly aware of his role in preserving essential aspects of a culture in transition.

I observed Justice Berger's procedure during hearings in Klukwan, a Tlingit village twenty miles up the Chilkat River from Haines. Other than a plain explanation of purpose and an open invitation to speak, Berger said little to the crowd that spilled from the old tribal house to the muddy street beyond.

Oratory is a highly regarded skill among the Chilkats and

Chilkoots. Even so, the speeches that followed were remarkable. Words spoken in English and Tlingit supplied concise, poetic descriptions of a vibrant people whose identity hinges on the food of their place. But more than eloquent proclamations, pressing questions comprised the backbone of most presentations.

From her wheelchair, eighty-four-year-old Annie Hotch spoke in Tlingit about the pain of "losing our total lifestyle." Fewer fish, she lamented, would starve them: "Do you suppose that a non-Native would allow it if she were told to use only four or five dozen eggs a season? How can we live with four or five dozen salmon?" Young mother Lani Strong Hotch asked a similar question pinned to their tenuous future: "What's going to happen if they decide, 'The Natives don't need that fish, they can buy hamburger from the store?'" Chilkoot chief Austin Hammond wondered how whites could, in good conscience, supplant Tlingit stewardship traditions. Natives, he declared, should manage subsistence fish and game because "if we don't take care of it right the bears are going to get mad at us." As Berger noted near the end of the evening, the villagers' testimony reflected concerns that were much deeper than allocation of resources, "it is, rather, an issue of a different order of magnitude—the survival of village Alaska."

Tribal members gave their views over several hours, often dressed in their finest regalia passed down through generations. Shoulders draped with priceless Chilkat blankets, headdresses rimmed with brown bear claws and porcupine quills, smocks and shawls covered completely with impeccable beadwork. These are the images, too, that caught the eyes of Edward Curtis and a handful of other early photographers whose work reflects the grandeur of a richly artistic culture. It may even be that some of the finery displayed at the hearings appeared in those first portraits.

Few cameras flashed that drizzly October evening. As I work now through the details of my notes and memory, the singular image is that of a man in nondescript clothing—a sweater, jeans, vest. Justice Berger sits in a folding chair, bent deeply toward each speaker. Hands support his chin in an attitude of prayer. His eyes are nearly closed by the weight of his brow's furrowed concentration. Mouth. Shut. Tight.

Daniel Henry is a Pushcart-winning debate coach who began carving his niche in the Alaska wilderness culture more than twenty years ago. He has been treed by grizzlies, chased by fry-pan-wielding women, and weathered in at some of the most obscure communities in America. He is an assistant professor of communication at the University of Alaska Anchorage.

KATHLEEN DEAN MOORE

* * *

The Only Place Like This

*In an unnamed Southeast fishing town,
residents ponder hard choices and wonder
what the next tide will bring.*

AS A BALD EAGLE COASTS OVER HIS HEAD, A LITTLE BOY
walks along the boardwalk toward school, wearing a life
jacket, clutching a handful of daffodils. He passes an old man
on a four-wheeler.

"Hiya," the boy says. "How are you today?"

"Home, sick in bed," the old man announces. Then without waiting for the boy to figure out the joke, he laughs,
downshifts, and trundles off, rattling the planks of the boardwalk past the Cold Storage Plant and a boarded-up house. By
the post office, a little dog is sitting square in the middle of the
walkway, not moving. The old man stops, turns off his engine,
and devotes ten minutes to the project of scratching the dog.
Close by, two men in yellow rain-pants lean over the railing,
talking in low voices, watching a school of herring. Frank and
I sit on a wooden bench in front of the restaurant, looking
across the boardwalk to the inlet and the mountains beyond.
Our backs are erasing "borscht" from the chalkboard menu.

Wildland shoulders in on the little town from all directions,

49

jagged snow-covered peaks and fjords as deep as the mountains are high. Because the mountains plunge so steeply into the sea, the town is built on stilts over the water. Buildings line up on both sides of the boardwalk that runs along the bluffs, graying wooden cottages connected by narrow planks with railings. Even the school sits at the end of a pier, on posts above the tidal flats. Twice each day, tides move in under the town, and twice each day they move out again, stranding starfish.

The nearest road is seventy miles away. When the weather is good—which it rarely is—a floatplane might land at the dock and off-load a fisherman, or a dog, or some groceries. We flew in on yesterday's floatplane, imported from outside to teach in the school for a few days. Low clouds forced us to fly below the cliffs along arms of the sea, skimming close to the waves like a pelican. The ferry comes only once a month. When the schoolteacher's piano arrived by barge, the town turned out to haul the piano up the gangway and along the boardwalk on the back of the only suitable vehicle in town, the garbage ATV. Now the teacher trades piano lessons for halibut and jam and considers herself ahead in the bargain.

This little town is home to 160 people, more or less, people who take the word "home" seriously. When I ask my writing students what marks this place as home, the seven children in the high school put their heads together and make me a list:

The Boardwalk
Boringness
Dogs barking
My boat
TOO MUCH RAIN.
Bears
The restaurant
The river.

I press them for the names of the inlet, the restaurant, the river, the bears, and they debate for some time, but really, the question makes no sense. What's the use of proper names, when there's only one of each? But the children consult among themselves and tell me that the bears are brown bears. They wander into town in April looking for something to eat, but head back to the mountains when the snows melt. "They have their space and we have ours and it works out pretty good," says a student. All the same, she spent the night with a friend, having been warned not to walk home past the place a bear had been seen. When townspeople visit each other at night, they carry cowbells and pepper spray. And when word comes round that a bear is on the boardwalk just past the church, the teacher leaves her meeting and walks home to bring her dog inside.

There are more docks than boardwalks in this town, and more boats than houses. Amidst the working boats, a couple of sailboats hunker down under blue tarps. "Tourists," the sheriff explains. He laughs, holding his cigarette between his forefinger and

---

I'd read two things about this place. One: that the people were friendly to tourists. And two: that they were not. Timing, temperament, season, and weather made the difference, I guessed.

It didn't bother me too much, though. There was something about this village: the drawn shades, the rare walker striding past with collar up and face hidden, the casual service in the town's only open eatery, that made me feel the very opposite of pandered to, and somehow better able to rest, turn inward, and feel hidden away myself. Here, on a gray day, overly chipper smiles would have been out of place.

—Andromeda Romano-Lax,
Walking Southeast Alaska

thumb. Lacking much business in the crime department, he has joined us on the bench. We look out together at the boats in the moorage and give the sun time to work its way into our shoulders. "Had one woman stand here on her boat and ask how many feet above sea level we were. Had another lady fly in over the glacier and ask what we did with all that Styrofoam. 'We mine it,' I told her, 'and ship it south for picnic coolers.'" He laughs again and then it's quiet on the dock except for the sound of waterfalls streaming down the mountains across the inlet.

"I don't know why they call it tourist season, if we're not allowed to shoot 'em." But he's only joking, just running through his repertoire of dumb-tourist jokes, and here comes the next one: "Some guy asked me how much rain we forecast, and I said I expected it to fill the inlet about eight more feet by suppertime." Then the law looks over at us, so obviously strangers, and remembers his manners. "Aw, a few tourists aren't so bad. As long as they go home."

A boy runs past, carrying a fishing pole. A few others bunch on the boardwalk, jostling and wrestling without ever dismounting from their bikes. Their parents are out on the boardwalk too, gathered in small groups to talk and tease, enjoying the first clear evening in a long, long time. "I don't think I'd like to live anywhere else but here," a sixteen-year-old tells me. "Doesn't seem all that nice in other places. Except maybe I'll go to college, if there's a college in a place like this."

What she doesn't know is that she may live in the only place like this.

This was a company town, built for packing salmon in 1930. For decades the people got by, prosperity ebbing and flowing with the schools of herring that brought in the Chinook. But last year, the long-line fisherman who doubles as town manager received a letter over his fax machine: *The fish plant will close on Friday*. Word spread quickly the length of the boardwalk, past the wet-goods store, past the store-front "steambaths and showers," past the bar-and-grill and the restaurant, past the fire station and the boatyard where crab traps pile up off-season, to the row of little company houses along the boardwalk, the school, the river, and the end of town.

Some families moved away. Some fathers left to get jobs outside, leaving their families behind. Other parents divided their children among the neighbors and went off to find work. Somebody cobbled together financing to run the fish plant for a few months a year, other people set up their boats for halibut, off-loading their catch on fish-buying boats. The people who remain in this little town get by whatever way they can and wonder what will happen next. On the docks, we overhear the worried conversations, the patched-together plans. In the school, I listen to the children. They want to know about the Seattle Sonics, but I can't help them. Their parents are holding on to a way of life as tightly as the town clings to the mountainside, but they know it's going to take more than a life jacket to keep their children from drifting away.

So it's complicated when a corporation from outside announces plans to build a floating lodge near the town and fly in paying guests. The site the corporation has chosen is close enough to town that the people will see floatplanes coming and going, day after day, bringing in people, taking out trophy fish. The corporation plans to moor its lodge in a place rare and wonderful, anchoring its cables to pilings in front of the only beach in the fjord, a beach where townspeople have always come to dig for clams, and where long-line fishermen—grandfathers and fathers and sons—angle for salmon and halibut. The place where mothers bring their children for picnics, running out to the beach in skiffs.

"The people don't want the lodge," says a songwriter whose family has lived in the town from the beginning, when the first corporation came in three generations ago. "None of us want it. It won't bring *us* any jobs. And even if it did, they wouldn't be worth it. But what can we do?" And sure enough, when a representative of the corporation comes to town, the people are polite, the way they are polite to the bears and the occasional tourist. People don't argue here, said a fourteen-year-old girl. "In a town as small as this, you can't just say whatever you're thinking."

But the people know the value of what they would be giving up. Scarcity raises the value of anything. As peace and solitude and wildlands disappear under bulldozers in the south, their price increases proportionately. Peace becomes a commodity, like board feet of cedar or kilos of frozen fish. Solitude is precious. Unspoiled beauty sells for a premium. Anyone who figures out how to extract these resources will make a fortune.

The townspeople call a meeting, gathering in the town hall just down from the dry goods store. "What the corporation plans to do," a bearded man says, "is take the peace and solitude that belong to this community, the same peace and solitude the people have been saving for their children." They will take it without asking, without giving anything in return, as if it belonged to them. Then they will package it and sell it to strangers for something around $2,500, a five-day package deal. "There's a word for this," a woman says, holding her son on her hip. "But I can't put my finger on it. Isn't it 'theft'?"

The schoolteacher pushes back her chair and stands up. "This isn't about just one fishing lodge," she says. "It's about this one and the next one and the next. Is this the kind of life we want? Is this what we want for the children?"

"I wouldn't know," says the corporate representative. "That's a philosophical question."

But the people know. What they want for their children are salmon and yellow cedar, the river, the inlet, and a little town where wooden houses stand on stilts above great schools of fish. A place you know is home because, as a teenager explained it to me, when you open the door "there's a row of boots and raincoats and some firewood, and your little brother is waiting to beat you up." A place where bears roll boulders on the beach, sucking up crabs and sculpin. Where gardens grow in milk crates stacked above the tide—daffodils and garlic, and rhubarb for pies. A place where women's voices call to children across the docks, and salt wind carries the laughter of men. A place where people can make a living, but not a fortune. A place where enough is great riches.

Kathleen Dean Moore is the chair of the Philosophy Department at Oregon State University, where she is a prize-winning teacher and director of the Spring Creek Project for Ideas, Nature and the Written Word. Riverwalking, *her first book, won the 1996 Pacific Northwest Booksellers Association Award. Her second,* Holdfast: At Home in the Natural World, *from which is story was excerpted, won the Sigurd Olson Nature Writing Award. Her essays have appeared in a wide variety of magazines and journals.*

S U S A N   B E E M A N

✦ ✦ ✦

From Scratch

The trek to her parents' old homestead
is a ritual return to the bush.

EVERY AUGUST, I LOAD UP THE CAR WITH SLEEPING BAG, cook stove, food, and tubs for picking blueberries. As I pack, I remember the sound, the *tink, tink, tink* the first fat berries make when they hit the bottom of the tub and how that sound becomes muffled the fuller it gets, until all the city chatter inside my mind is muffled too, and I'm just there on the mountainside picking quietly.

Headed north from Anchorage on the Parks Highway, I tune the radio to NPR for Saturday morning's "Savvy Traveler" and pretend I'm a savvy traveler. Where will I stop? Will I meet locals when I take a break from the wheel, and talk to them about the weather or the fishing or this year's berry crop? Or will I keep silent and eavesdrop on the old men who wear baseball caps with hunting lodge logos and drink coffee from thick white mugs? What new stories will I bring home? I relax into the road. No need to hurry. The blueberries are getting sweeter every hour, since nights are almost freezing.

I sing along to Mary Black and Natalie Merchant and Deep Forest through the long stretch of dull road between Willow and the Talkeetna junction, then settle into the silence of the road, the rhythm of driving. Birch trees, still hanging on to green leaves, line the roadside and wave me gently north toward an old family treasure at Byers Lake.

My parents' decaying cabin hunkers on one of the hidden knolls above the lake. It's been falling into itself for years now. At the trailhead, I study the piece of weathered paper taped to the Alaska State Parks sign to find out about the most recent bear sightings. Every year, the paper is taped here, with comments scrawled in pencil or pen. The most recent ones are these:

8/15, grizzly sow with two cubs by inlet;
8/17, small blackie in campground;
8/18, black bear hanging around outhouse, Alder Loop;
8/20, fresh tracks by old cabin.

But nothing for the last two days.

I follow the muddy trail over tree roots into the cool forest of birch and spruce, where mushrooms and mosses grow underfoot and high bush cranberries reach up to glint red in the dappled light, and I think of my parents living here forty-odd years ago, before the highway was punched through. I picture them snowshoeing these woods, Dad wearing wool pants that Mom hemmed to fit him; she setting a failed loaf of brick-heavy bread outside the cabin window for the gray jays and black-capped chickadees to peck. My parents launched their married life here in 1959, snuggled together in a bed frame made of sturdy spruce poles hammered together with spikes and a mattress of pungent boughs laid beneath sleeping bags.

Trumpeter swans chortle and loons lament on the lake to my right as I walk deeper into the forest. Voices echo across

A three-hour drive north of Anchorage, Denali State Park is among the most accessible of all Alaskan parklands, bisected by the Parks Highway (which connects Anchorage and Fairbanks) and bordered on its eastern edge by the Alaska Railroad. Yet many travelers headed north to bigger and better-known Denali National Park speed through "Little Denali" without even realizing the gems it holds. Just off the highway at Mile 147 is Byers Lake, rimmed with spruce-birch forest. Visitors may boat, fish, hike, picnic, or stay in one of two public-use cabins. Loons, beavers, swans, bears, and moose inhabit the lake or its edges and salmon spawn here in fall.

Not far from Byers Lake is Kesugi Ridge, one of Southcentral Alaska's premier backpacking routes. One reason is the view: several of the Alaska Range's grandest peaks dominate the western horizon, culminating in the snow- and ice-capped throne of 20,320-foot Mt. McKinley.

—Bill Sherwonit

the water from a couple paddling a canoe or someone fishing from the walk-in campground on the far side of the lake, but I can't hear what they say. Were those high-pitched noises really people, or just gulls crying? I glance behind me. Maybe it was a bear cub.

At the kinked birch my family used as a marker I turn off the main path onto the wide new trail to the cabin. We used to bushwhack to get here, back when we'd come on the weekend or school holidays, before we sold the cabin to the government as it swallowed more land for Denali State Park.

As I approach the cabin, I come to what once was a small clearing. It is overgrown now with devil's club, willows, grass, and young trees, but a tall cache used to stand in the clearing, its four thick spruce legs covered with cut-open tin cans, flattened and nailed around the legs to keep bears and squirrels from climbing up. Fox, lynx, and wolverine furs were stored in the cache. Moose meat, too, and big sacks of flour for bread and pies.

The jagged metal corner of the cabin's porch sticks out from behind brush and I notice how tall the spruce and birch trees growing from the top of the grassy roof have become and how moss thicker than a down quilt hangs from the top of the sinking cabin.

I pad slowly around to the front, careful not to lean too close to the sharp-edged porch overhang, the rusty corrugated tin roofing bent down by many wet winter snows. I peek in the side window, the glass long shattered, to see the living room where my parents cooked and ate and sang and skinned pelts and read aloud to each other by Coleman lantern light. Where they built wood fires each frigid morning in December when the day would not brighten until the sun glowed at its zenith behind Curry Ridge at noon. Only remnants of those days remain now. Over the years the cabin has been vandalized, cleaned out. Even the spruce-pole couch frame Dad built is now gone, ashes in a campfire somewhere nearby. The little table he made still sits in the corner, though, and candle wax is still pooled where it dripped so long ago, next to flies twenty years dead.

I pull my head carefully back from the empty window frame. Out front, I trace with the tip of my index finger the official wood-burned state parks sign that reads in neat loopy letters, *Beeman's Cabin 1959.*

Another sign outside reads *Unsafe—Keep Out.* Visitors aren't supposed to crawl inside the cabin, where they might break an ankle jumping over the root cellar built into the middle of the living room floor, collapsed onto itself with rotten planks jutting up from below. Or a person might whack his forehead on the low log over the doorway between the

living room and the bedroom, the doorway where my parents
stapled a cutout magazine photo of a mallard so they wouldn't
forget to duck. Visitors might squeeze into the bedroom and
sit down on the edge of a bunk bed to see more clearly the
drawings my brother and I sketched on the ceiling and the
frame could crack, injuring them.

But I'm not a visitor. I crouch through the front entrance
and step carefully over the root cellar in the dim light and
duck into the bedroom to see the old artwork. Yes, those were
my horses. I did lie there thirty years ago, drawing long-
backed stallions with squarish legs and foals with perky,
pointed ears, laughing and telling stories with my brother as
he uttered boy noises in the other bunk, drawing pistols and
bullets on his side of the room.

Now it is time to go, time to pick berries. I've seen all I can
see at the cabin. I've remembered all I can, the memories only
hints of what had gone before, more bird track than bird.

I drive on, through Cantwell, and park just past the Nenana
River. Carrying my empty tub, I walk the highway shoulder a
few hundred feet. Two huge boulders hug the edge of a tundra field on the left. I drop down the steep side of the roadbed
and push through tall grass, careful not to trip on hidden
deadwood underfoot, and crest the lip of the field. My hiking
boots sink into spongy mosses and lichens and I scan the
ground for blues.

It's a good year and the bushes hang thick with fruit, like
grape clusters, the blueberries fat and juicy and waiting to be
plucked before they freeze and shrivel. Late afternoon sun
shines up the valley, and across the river against the steep
mountainside, the train's rumble and whistle sounds. I'm not
far from the road, but once over the field's edge, kneeling on
my folded rain pants, and pulling fruit from the twigs, all is
quiet. The blueberry patch is my own private place. I pop a

few berries in my mouth and roll them around on my tongue before mashing them and tasting their sweet sourness.

When my knees and lower back get tired from leaning down to pick, I sit on my backside and spread my legs in a V and keep picking. The berries are so thick I can pull off five or six at once, with one hand, using a light touch, an open pluck, to separate berry from bush.

After a while, I take a break and wander across the field toward the bank overlooking the braided river. I've seen small bands of caribou down on the riverbar before, camouflaged by silvery willows and gray driftwood. But this time only the bushes are there, thick and yellow-green. I return to the patch and finish filling the tub with blueberries, plenty for a pie.

> When the tundra changed color, we went to the hills to pick berries. Wild cranberries slid off their bushes easily in solid handfuls, round and firm, into the warm palms of our hands. I thought of how good they'd taste with turkey come Thanksgiving. The air was crisp and fresh, the tundra smelled like fruit and spices, and we browsed like bears taking in the crisp air and the last warmth of summer, which left as the afternoon waned.
>
> —Dana Greci,
> "Plowing the Driveway"

As I head back through Broad Pass, fall colors dot the mountains on either side of the road. Muted reds of bearberry leaves cover the ground just above treeline, orangey-red dwarf birch whisk back and forth in the breeze, spruce point up darkly green to lead my eye to rocky patches of grass above long, slaty scree slopes. A magpie swoops at the windshield and lands on a bough unscathed, tipping back and forth for a moment to get its balance before it flies away, iridescent in the setting sun.

Rain begins to spit as I pull back into the Byers Lake campground, this time to sleep surrounded by other travelers: motorhome retirees relaxing beside a crackling fire, young twenty-somethings with bicycles atop their Subaru station wagon and a husky tied to a tree nearby, a lone man setting up his tent, radio perched on the picnic table spewing country music into the air. I camp far away from him, in a spot on Cranberry Loop, a quiet space where I build a fire and huddle under my waterproof hood and listen to raindrops patter softly on top of my head while eating dinner. I wonder if any of the other campers have discovered the cabin.

When I return home Sunday at midday, I prepare the kitchen for baking. I open my tub of blueberries and dump them gently into a mixing bowl. Lightly, so I don't squash them, I rake my fingertips through the purply fruit and pluck a couple of worms that have crawled out from hiding, and leaves and twigs still attached or stuck with moisture to the berries.

For the pie filling, I measure six cups of berries into another mixing bowl and bag the rest in Ziplocs to freeze for muffins or pancakes in December. The berries are the only ingredient I measure. From scratch means having a feel for something you love, making it up as you go along, building on the knowledge of the past and incorporating your own pinch of flavor into the creation, whether it is a pie or a new marriage in a small cabin.

Sugar hisses from the bag. Then a few squeezed drops of lemon juice, dashes of cinnamon and nutmeg shaken in, a small handful of flour for thickener, and a few gentle stirs to mix it all up. I make the crust next, rolling to the left, to the right, toward the wall, toward my belly, rolling this way and that until the dough is a circle bigger than the pan. On the top crust, I make slits for steam to escape as the berries plump in the heat.

With the dish in the oven and the timer set, I sink into a chair and call my parents. I invite them over for dessert while slowly the room, the house, even the air outside the kitchen fills with the sweet, hot tartness of blueberry pie.

A world traveler whose favorite countries visited so far are India, Nepal, and New Zealand, Susan Beeman always returns home to Anchorage, where she is an editor for Alaska Geographic. *When on the road she loves to sample local cuisine and has tried everything from "tomato nuddle soup" and "scrumble egg" in New Delhi to ice cream for breakfast in Rotorua, but never again will she eat steak in Kathmandu. She would, though, travel all the way back to Diu, on the tip of Gujarat, for more of Jay Shankar's fresh fish curry.*

PART TWO

SOME THINGS TO DO

TIM CAHILL

* * *

The Great White Philharmonic

Crushed ice, hold the suds; even a beer-ad guy
can appreciate Alaska's glacial symphony.

YOU KNOW HOW GUYS IN BEER ADS ARE ALWAYS PICTURED
doing stuff you wouldn't do—or shouldn't do—when you've
been drinking beer? In the Beer-Ad Universe guys continu-
ally engage in potentially dangerous activities like bungee
jumping, or roofing their houses, or talking to women.

Recently I discovered that I am a beer-ad guy.

It was a print campaign, and apparently there were posters,
along with a lot of those little cardboard tents they put on tables to encourage people to buy beer. The picture on the
posters and on the cardboard tents was of me. I was a small
speck of a guy in a kayak, surrounded by floating icebergs and
dwarfed by an enormous tidewater glacier looming 200 feet
above me.

I suspect the ad campaign was designed to suggest that this
beer is as cool and refreshing as a couple million pounds of ice
grinding down a mountainside.

The picture was taken in Glacier Bay National Park, about
sixty miles northwest of Juneau, Alaska. A guidebook I read

before my visit encouraged folks to book mid-summer trips, but it was late September and snowing maniacally when I arrived at park headquarters, at Bartlett Cove, near the mouth of the bay. Here I would hop a boat for the glaciers at Muir Inlet, starting point for a sixty-mile kayak trip back to Bartlett Cove—a journey that serves as a painless course on botany-in-action and is about as close as any of us will ever get to time travel. Throw in calving tidewater glaciers, the northern lights, mile-wide beds of mussels, friendly harbor seals, killer whales, wolves, bears, and bald eagles perched on icebergs, all roaming a seascape ringed by mountains that rise from sea level to 15,000 feet, and you've pretty much got the premier North American sea-kayaking trip. Even better: In late September you can have the place completely to yourself.

The next day I rented a kayak. The concessionaire said there was only one other rented out: Some crazy guy paddling around all alone in the snow. That was my partner, photographer Paul Dix, the future beer-photo entrepreneur.

I was a day late, but Paul had said he'd meet me in Muir Inlet, near the "snout" of McBride Glacier. Despite the delay, I suspected he'd still be there, waiting, because Paul takes his commitments seriously. Also I was bringing the food. I lugged my kayak through ankle-deep snow down to the tour boat, which would drop me at a gravel bar south of McBride Glacier, a place, I learned later, that Paul had renamed Hungry Point. It was a two-and-a-half-hour trip, and of course it snowed. You really couldn't see anything. Then the wind picked up.

The boat dropped me off at the gravel bar. Here, predictably, the snow was being driven horizontally by the wind. Worse, it was falling as corn snow, which consists entirely of exceedingly hard little pellets, so the situation was rather like being sandblasted with crushed ice.

The few tourists on the deck of the boat regarded me with that somber homage our society pays to the visibly deranged, which is to say they were pretty much doubled over laughing. So the boat pulled away, and I was left alone on a gravel bank, unable to see more than fifteen feet in any direction and feeling quite sorry for myself, when Paul Dix came paddling out of the ice storm and greeted me with a hearty "Where in hell's the food?"

We sat in the tent, and Paul filled me in on his ad-

> Tourism in Glacier Bay is nothing new, explains Karen Jettmar, author of *Alaska's Glacier Bay*. Inspired by John Muir's descriptions of ice-lined fjords, tourists began arriving by steamer in 1883. By the turn of the century, steamships had carried 25,000 visitors to Glacier Bay.
>
> —Andromeda Romano-Lax

ventures to date. There were Alaskan brown bears all over, which were like the grizzlies we were familiar with from Yellowstone, only bigger. Yesterday Paul had paddled into a sandy cove, looking for a place to camp. A bear had recently padded across the beach, and Paul was measuring his own foot (diminutive and pitiable) against one of the prints (colossal and appalling) when he noticed that the bear had left something else on the beach. What it had left wouldn't fit in a gallon pail and was still steaming. Paul decided to paddle on.

"Good thing you weren't carrying any food," I said.

"Yeah," Paul replied pointedly, "I sure was lucky."

In fact, we were lucky. The next day dawned clear. The sky was cobalt blue, there was not a breath of wind, and the sea was like glass, a mirror to the sky and the mountains on either end of the inlet, which was about a mile wide in that spot. We paddled over the reflections of snowcapped peaks on our way to Muir Glacier, as the sun shone and the temperature rose to a little over seventy degrees, which is about as warm as it ever gets in Glacier Bay.

And then, there in front of us, was the glacier, pouring off the mountain and into the sea. The enormous wall of ice, the terminus of the glacier is called the snout, and this one looked to be about 200 feet high and maybe a mile across.

The whole of Glacier Bay is shaped a little like a horseshoe, open end toward the ocean, with the inland section surrounded by mountains. Snow falls in the upper elevations, never melts, is compressed by the next year's snow, and the next decade's, until it turns into heavy, dense ice that flows downhill, as all water must. The ice makes pretty good time, too, sweeping down to the sea at the rate of two to five feet per day.

The snout is subject to tides that rise and fall as much as twenty feet, eating away at the base of the glacier so that great slabs of it "calve" off the main body and crash into the ocean in an explosion of spray. The sound of the glacier calving can be heard for miles, and the mountain across the inlet from Muir Glacier is called White Thunder Ridge.

Paul and I camped on a gravel slope below White Thunder Ridge, and we might have gotten some sleep except for the damn Northern Lights, which arced across an ebony star field like phosphorescent green smoke interspersed with dozens of red lightning bolts running in ultraslow motion. All the while the sound of calving ice rumbled off the ridge above. It was like having the whole New York Philharmonic come over to play Beethoven for you at midnight: The mindless and ungrateful go to sleep so they can rise fully rested and spiritually impoverished.

For the next few days, Paul and I played chicken with the glacier. Kayakers are cautioned to stay at least half a mile from the snout, but distances were impossible to calculate. I'd get in there, way too close, and hear what sounded like the amplified cracking of automatic gunfire. Then a great 200-foot-high block of ice would separate from the glacier and fall, slowly it seemed, into the sea with a roar that echoed against the mountains for a full minute. And afterward, maybe five minutes later, a small ripple of a wave would roll past my kayak. So I figured I could maybe move in a little closer.

I avoided the icebergs, big as mansions, and made my way through a watery field of bergy bits, smaller slabs of ice that pretty much covered the surface of the sea. There was a strange sound all around, a crackling, like static electricity, and it was getting louder as I paddled toward the foot of the glacier before me. It took a while to understand that the bergy bits themselves were doing the crackling, in the manner of an ice cube dropped into a glass of water.

There were harbor seals basking in the sun on the larger slabs of ice, and some of them dropped into the water, disappeared for a time, and then surfaced near my kayak. They had heads like wet Labrador retrievers—that same friendly curiosity—and one came close enough for me to touch with my paddle, had I wanted to. He tilted his head in a quizzical manner, dove, and then surfaced again, on the other side of the kayak. I thought he wanted to play tag and paddled toward him, at which point my kayak was rocked by a sound so loud it could actually be felt.

I looked up to see a block of ice the size of a twenty-story building falling in my direction. Time slowed, as it does in these situations, and I had the leisure to appreciate fully what an enormous horse's ass I was. Eventually, about a month later it seemed, the ice thundered into the sea far in front of my kayak. It threw up a wave that rolled toward me in a ten-foot-high crest, topped by pieces of ice ranging in size from fist to

Ford. I paddled forward to take the wave at a run so that it wouldn't crest over me. My kayak rolled easily over the top and slipped down the back side. The last rumble of the calving was echoing off White Thunder Ridge, and I could hear the bergy bits snapping all around. Some insane person was beating a drum hysterically inside my chest.

Which, I think, is when Paul—who was quite a ways behind me—snapped the picture that someone thought might sell beer.

The weather held for a week, and we paddled back down the inlet toward Bartlett Cove, a trip that is a time-lapse lesson in plant succession. Two hundred years ago, Captain George Vancouver mapped what was then Glacier Bay: a five-mile inlet capped by a 300-foot-high wall of ice. Over the past two centuries, since the end of the Little Ice Age, that immense glacier has retreated almost sixty-five miles, and the land it exposed is all barren rock and sterile gravel.

But the planet is modest, and she quickly clothes herself with life. Even under White Thunder Ridge, on land that had been exposed perhaps a few decades earlier, we found "black crust," an algal nap that retains water and stabilizes silt so that eventually mosses grow. They in turn support hardy pioneers like fireweed and dryas. These plants are plentiful a few miles from the retreating glaciers. Farther down the inlet, alders drop nitrogen-rich leaves, building a soil that enables spruce to take hold and eventually shade out the alders. At Bartlett Cove, which was under 200 feet of ice 200 years ago, there is a hemlock and spruce rainforest.

Down inlet from the alder breaks we thought we saw a kayaker, far out ahead of us, his paddle dipping from side to side. This was the first human being we'd seen in a couple of weeks, and we called out to him. The kayaker failed to respond, probably, we decided later, because he turned out to be a bull moose. It was his antlers swaying from side to side as he swam that had looked like a kayak paddle.

Paul, had he known he was going to sell a photo to a Canadian beer company, might have taken a picture of that moose's head. Instead, he got a horse's ass. I never did see the poster, but you'd think those Canadian beer execs would send me a few cases of their fine product so I could go bungee jumping and talk to women. At least get my roof fixed.

Tim Cahill is the author of many books, mostly travel-related, including Hold the Enlightenment, Jaguars Ripped My Flesh, Pecked to Death by Ducks, Pass the Butterworms, *and* Dolphins, *as well as the editor of* Not So Funny When it Happened: The Best of Travel Humor and Misadventure. *Cahill is also the co-author of the Academy Award-nominated IMAX film,* The Living Sea, *as well as the films* Everest *and* Dolphins. *He lives in Montana, and shares his life with Linnea Larson, two dogs, and two cats.*

IAN FRAZIER

* * *

Woe Is Me

There's no place like Nome...for embracing melancholy.

WHEN I WAS YOUNGER, I USED TO—NOT ENJOY, EXACTLY,
but take a certain satisfaction from being melancholy and depressed. As a single guy in an apartment in New York, I often
spent days at a time in an unbroken mood of gloom, regret,
self-recrimination, dislike for the world and for other human
beings, and general unearned despair. In later years, married
and with kids, I had to give up this indulgence. Walking
around depressed with no reason is disagreeable behavior for
which family and friends will rebuke you, rightly.

Plus I just didn't have the time for it anymore. Whenever
I'd get started on a good downslope of melancholy, family
concerns or pleasures would distract me, and I would abandon
my mood in irritation. Nowadays my only opportunity for an
old-fashioned, self-indulgent sulk comes when I'm traveling.

I had one opportunity recently in Nome, Alaska, a far-
northern town on the Bering Sea. I had gone there to do
some reporting, which bad weather made impossible. I sat in
my motel room for several days, getting gloomier and

gloomier. Rain fell constantly. The month was August, and the rainy twilight lasted from four in the morning until midnight. Outside my window Bering Sea waves the color of wet cement landed on the riprap shoreline with thuds. To say that Nome, Alaska, is mainly mud with pieces of rusted iron sticking out of it is to be unfair to that interesting place, but so it appeared to me at the time. On my motel-room bed I read obscure books to the sound of the rain and the waves, taking occasional breaks to stare at the ceiling. I saw almost no one, never cracked a smile, and was as sorry for myself as I could be. After three or four days, completely bummed out, I went to the airport and flew home. I arrived pale, monosyllabic, and wonderfully refreshed.

Ian Frazier is a frequent contributor to The New Yorker *and author of numerous books, including* Family, Great Plains, On the Rez, *and* The Fish's Eye. *He lives in Montclair, New Jersey.*

ELLEN BIELAWSKI

⋆ ⋆ ⋆

Camping at Wal★Mart

At the proverbial end of the road,
there's…a parking lot.

ANCHORAGE, AUGUST, FRIDAY AFTERNOON. CHOICES abound: the family cabin, backpacking in the Chugach, kayaking ocean or whitewater. Both new and familiar wild places are in easy reach of my home. I choose Wal★Mart.

All summer the question has gnawed at me: Why would anyone travel thousands of miles to Alaska, then camp at a big box store? We locals wonder aloud at the herd of RVs resting on the midtown pavement. Our fear and loathing of the wheeled vehicle set is such that we do not ask.

But I am a lapsed anthropologist. I have no excuse for avoiding the culturally insular. Indeed, dangerous as the expedition might be, I have a professional responsibility to explore the big box lot. After all, Wal★Mart is, well, *there.*

So I borrow a pickup truck with camper on the back, a cheap passport to the unnerving but intellectually enticing RV club. Friends are incredulous. "You're spending a *summer weekend* at Wal★Mart?" Some express pity. My mother, who came to Alaska alone in 1946, fears for me. "Will you be all right?" she quavers as she leaves for our cabin.

Despite the risk, I am as determined to conquer the pavement as I was to winter camp with Athabascan hunters last year. I climb up behind the high steering wheel, drive down the Seward Highway to Wal★Mart South (Anchorage is blessed with two Wal★Marts, one in midtown and this one, just off the highway to the Kenai Peninsula) and enter a strange new world.

Where to park? I cruise the lot a few times, finally picking a spot between a gargantuan RV and an SUV with a tiny trailer. It's a weak, compromise choice, but I have to get my feet on the blacktop somehow. I park with the back of the camper facing south towards Turnagain Arm (not that I can see it past Stephan's Tool Rentals). I set out the camper steps, then sit down with my door open, my notebook on my knees. Social scientists call this research method "participant-observation." I call it "hanging out." All I have to do is watch, then do—whatever the locals do.

Not very much, for a while. The owner of the rig next to mine fills a burrito with beans he's warmed over a propane stove on the tailgate of his SUV. He watched me make camp—along with my stairs, I put a bucket out below my camper drain spout—then leaned across the yellow line on the pavement. "I'm Rich." Now he gestures toward a truck and trailer with Michigan plates. "I know them from somewhere," he chews. Burrito in hand, he strolls over to speak with the disembarking couple. Calls to me, "It was Glennallen, a month ago, we camped at the same place."

Her name is Rose; his is Woody. His pate is as shiny as the buttons she's sewn all over her jean jacket. They move coolers from the truck to the trailer.

"Woody's a fisherman," Rose says, as if resuming a conversation we've been having throughout the nomadic season. "Fishing" explains the coolers, and the debate Rich and Woody are now engaged in, each jabbing at an Alaska road map. Picking spots to fish. Rose and Woody are spending the summer in Alaska, fishing; they'll winter on Texas's Gulf Coast, fishing. They travel year round, relying on Wal★Mart lots across the nation—campgrounds for retirees without a lot of income. "Where else can you afford to buy anything in Alaska?" she asks.

I head across the pavement to check out the perks of no-fee camping. A Wal★Mart greeter welcomes me pleasantly as I enter the store. The lights are very bright. The store is open from six in the morning to eleven P.M. The phones work. The bathroom is large and conveniently located. I can purchase innumerable Alaska souvenirs—mugs and caps bearing blurry salmon, eight stars of gold on everything from headbands to socks—at reasonable prices. Nearby fitness clubs offer showers. What's not to like?

Back outside, late afternoon sun filters through the remains of rain clouds. On the unshaded asphalt, it's t-shirt weather. The view of the Chugach Mountains is superb. I realize I've never seen it from Wal★Mart before. I think fleetingly of friends and family up in those alpine expanses, with their heavy packs and their wind-blown tents. Been there, done that, got cold and wet. Time for supper in the level, propane-heated, bug-free comfort of my borrowed home.

As I warm soup on the camper stove, I can't help but see directly into the long rig from Iowa parked next door. Its owners have just returned in a small SUV. Now he plays cards while his wife prepares supper.

On the lot, there's traffic. A Mobile Auto Services truck cruises, offering assistance to newcomers, checking on previous clients. A truck with "The Tree Man" lettered on the side pulls in and parks. No trees for him to doctor here. Turns out, he's from Outside, living on the lot while he sells his services in suburban Anchorage. He's home for the night. An elderly couple returns to their camper van from the Dimond Center Mall. He pushes her wheelchair slowly, steadily in the dying sunlight. When they reach their rig, he unlocks the side door and gently assists her inside. Then he folds the wheelchair and parks it. Tough to do in the back country.

Another couple, denizens of a 5th-wheel-style trailer leveled next to Rich's SUV, has family members in Anchorage whom they are visiting. Ed and Ruth were campground hosts at Cooper Landing, one of the busiest fishing spots on the Kenai Peninsula, all summer. "You know, there're lots of single

---

John McPhee took perhaps the most famous swipes at Anchorage in his bestseller *Coming Into the Country:* "Almost all Americans would recognize Anchorage, because Anchorage is that part of any city where the city has burst its seams and extruded Colonel Sanders…. It has come in on the wind, an American spore."

Anchorage still merits McPhee's late-1970s jabs. Poor planning has led to haphazard development and ugly architecture. Much of the city is an appalling mix of malls, fast-food restaurants, box-like discount stores, and massive parking lots. Yet for all this laying down of asphalt and mushrooming of boxy buildings, pockets of wetlands, woodlands, and other wild areas remain scattered throughout Anchorage, and the Chugach Mountains rise grandly on the town's eastern fringe. Those natural areas sustain a wide diversity of wildlife: Anchorage is seasonal home to Pacific salmon, 230 species of birds, and 48 different mammals.

—Bill Sherwonit

women traveling on the road, just having a good time," Ed
tells me. "Mostly the people in Alaska are really good: it's really
safe. But I've thought of getting a shotgun anyway, without
ammunition. People tend to get scared off if they hear you
cocking a shotgun inside your rig."

I didn't bring mine, but I feel comfortable as night falls,
even though I've never spent a night alone in a city parking
lot before. Bears and blizzards are more my style. So far, my
fellow campers display a detached sense of community—
keeping an eye out for each other, discreetly. A TV screen
flickers in one rig, its antenna raised like whale flukes, tiny in
proportion to the RV's behemoth body. I take a late-night
stroll around the lot, alone. Rich has departed for the evening
in his vehicle, leaving his small trailer behind. So has another
lone man, from Arizona. Have they gone dancing? Is that why
they park here in Anchorage, for the nightlife a city offers, a
respite from their travels in wilder Alaska? "No hookups" takes
on new meaning for me.

The sound of a generator wakes me Sunday morning, carried on a wind that rocks my camper gently. I need the bathroom, and the morning paper, another perk of pavement
camping. Returning from Wal⋆Mart, I bend to pet a dog that
nuzzles my knees, but her owner calls her back. He is Dick
Francis. He's talking with two other men, beneath a caribou
rack tied on his Montana camper-van. "We were just saying
that women don't like to hunt and fish," he says. "Do you?"

"Of course."

Three pairs of eyebrows rise simultaneously. In their collec-
tive experience, there are not enough women who enjoy the
outdoors. "You see those rigs coming up here," Dick says.
"He's driving and looking really happy; she's sittin' with her
arms crossed and frowning." Dick is in Alaska this summer to

hunt, fish, and work the busy construction season. Keith Campbell came north with Dick, and the dog, Lady. He's sailed the Inside Passage twice on small boats. This year he wants to see Alaska's mainland.

Tom Kelly, the third man, is having his great Alaska adventure. Introducing themselves to me, Dick and Keith also shake hands with Tom. "You haven't met?" I ask.

"Nah, we been talkin' for three days but we haven't met," Tom laughs.

An hour and three rain squalls later we're still chatting on the pavement outside Dick's rig. Dick's smile disappears into his tanned, seamed face when he laughs. Today is his last free day before a two-month job at Fort Richardson in Anchorage's east side. Keith's thick gray curls escape from under a blue corduroy Alaska cap. When I mention my mother, he asks, "Does she dance? I'm looking for a dancing partner while I'm here."

Most of Tom's forty years have been bound by what he calls a Midwestern mentality. "Same job, same people, same house. People expect you to be you. Change is not what's expected." But when his son said, "Dad, I don't think you are ever going to go up there," Tom quit his job and drove to Alaska. A month ago, he stalked bull caribou north of the Brooks Range and killed one with his bow. He kept the backstrap and rack, donating the rest of the meat to the Fairbanks food bank. He shows me a picture of himself with a fish hook through his chin and blood matting his new beard, grinning an impossibly wide grin, the happiest of men. "I kept right on fishing," he laughs. Then moans, "I gotta get out of this parking lot. It's driving me crazy!"

Other rig owners have "For Sale" signs posted. One battered truck and one classic black sedan look abandoned to the side of the RV parking area. "Is there zoning here?" I ask.

"Nah," the men say, "but if you got a bucket outside..."

I do, of course. Is that why my Iowa neighbors, who can see the gray water draining into the bucket from my sink, are so aloof? To each his own, I think. My camper drips, but their rig generator woke me up this morning.

I trek back to Wal★Mart for some research in the "Books" aisle. A new question has emerged. I pull out a copy of *Catch and Release: The Guide to Finding an Alaska Man*. Sure enough, it omits all mention of hanging out in Wal★Mart parking lots. I make a note to send an addition to the editors.

As the rainy day passes noon, I wrap up my expedition with one last stroll around my village. Ed and Ruth are gone for the day, their trailer locked. Bill and Terri plan to camp here all week, until their daughter flies in to meet them. Woody and Rose take off for Talkeetna, "unless the weather stays this bad. If it does, we'll camp at the Wal★Mart in Wasilla." The Chugach have disappeared under low clouds flowing like thick cream.

Dick and Keith invite me for a last cup of coffee, this time out of the rain, at the McDonald's inside Wal★Mart. Tom ambles by, observing that I'm in danger of becoming a "lot rat."

"Better than being a house rat," I respond.

After coffee, I take up my sink-drain bucket and lock the camper door. My restless spirit is primed after this weekend among road wayfarers. Now that the Alaska Highway is paved, I could just keep going, on to the next Wal★Mart and the next.... I jump into the truck cab, slide Dire Straits into the cassette player, sing "Sometimes you're the windshield, sometimes you're the bug" and head off down the road.

Ellen Bielawski is a co-editor of this book. She never camps at Wal★Mart unless looking for a story.

TOM DUNKEL

Taking on the Kenai

Alaska-in-miniature is just a quick drive
south of Anchorage.

ABOUT THE ONLY THING THAT ISN'T OVERPRICED IN
Alaska is advice. Folks still dispense it free just like in the
Lower 48, and right now I'm getting a friendly earful.

"Don't hesitate when you're here, 'cause you may not ever
be here again," says Eddy, who is urging me to push the tourist
envelope during my stay in Alaska. "This is wilderness fanta-
syland. There's nothin' left like it, unless it's Siberia, and it's
pretty hard to travel there."

We've never met before. Eddy just happens to be sitting
two bar stools from me at Ray's seafood restaurant in Seward,
which just happens to be one of the hot towns on the Kenai
Peninsula.... Eddy wears a big cowboy hat, smokes big cigars,
and has a small airplane. He lives in Wyoming and frequently
flies north to sportfish. He's crazy for Alaska, so much so that
he wouldn't mind dying here. Apparently, the perfect way to
go is to be devoured by a grizzly bear.

"That's *gotta* elevate you to a higher plane," declares Eddy,
smitten by the prospect of traveling first-class to the hereafter.

To each his own demise. I can appreciate the basic wisdom of Eddy's travel logic, though. Alaska is Big Country: Colorado on steroids. You can't let it intimidate you. Don't be spooked by tales of campers who get filleted by a grizzly. Don't be cowed by cold air or bug bites. Venture out of your car and off the tour bus. Get dirty. Break a sweat. Indulge your curiosity.

The Kenai Peninsula—know simply as "the Kenai"— couldn't be more user-friendly. It's the abridged version of Alaska: just an hour's drive south of Anchorage, packed with postcard views, seemingly endless riffles of snow-dusted mountains, rivers that roil with spawning salmon, an abundant supply of moose, bears, eagles, and those comical puffins that look to be wearing false noses, four active volcanoes, and one gigantic, otherworldly icefield.

I encountered Eddy the Advice Man five days into my trip. By then I was already immersed in the Kenai's many delights. In fact, I had just spent the day shoehorned into a kayak, silently knifing through frigid Resurrection Bay. Tom Twigg, an architect turned guide, took me and three other novices out for a ten-mile spin. We embarked from a sliver of beach on the outskirts of Seward under a blue, late-summer sky.

The beauty of a kayak isn't portability, but rather its idiot-proof buoyancy. Twigg gave us an orientation on paddle strokes and weight distribution, reminding us of the 50/50 rule for cold-water survival ("The average person has a 50-percent chance of surviving a 50-yard swim"). On that sobering note, we shoved off, Twigg in a solo kayak, the rest of us doubling up.

I hoped that a little low-key kayaking would provide an antidote to the assembly-line adventure I'd experienced the day before, when I cruised the bay on a 150-passenger sightseeing ship. It zipped along at twenty-three knots, looping into a fjord that dead-ended at the glistening lip of Holgate Glacier. The wall of ancient ice thundered as house-size chunks cleaved off and crashed into the water. Passengers gleefully shouted at the glacier in an attempt to induce even more calving. During the six-hour excursion, cormorants and red-necked phalaropes darted overhead, plump sea lions sunbathed on exposed rocks, and a pod of orcas cavorted in the boat's froth. Splendid sights all, but diminished by the cattle-car viewing conditions. I later learned that this ship had accidentally rammed a humpback whale a few months earlier.

Now, skimming around at sea-lion level, I felt sprung from a cage. In kayaks, we were part of the actual show of the bay, not gawkers holding admission tickets. Horned puffins gaped from nooks in the cliffs we paddled under, tucked tight in their holes like letters in post-office boxes. Bald eagles lazed overhead—they seem as common as crows here—riding the thermals and oozing majesty.

Twigg led us up a side creek that was barely knee deep, yet running heavy with pink and chum salmon. Hundreds of them, hyperkinetic as jumping beans, wiggled beneath us, driven by the strange hormonal explosion that propels them ever onward to spawn and promptly die, their bodies providing food for bears and other forest critters. "Dog" salmon the chum are called, suitable mainly for pet food, since their flesh degrades quickly as they near the coast.

"Once they hit fresh water," Twigg noted, "salmon are basically living off themselves."

While the creek reeked of death, life rolled merrily along out in the open bay. As we headed back at day's end, a lone sea otter did a slow float about thirty feet ahead of us. He was munching clams. We could hear the crack of shells breaking against a stone on his belly. Sea otters don't produce blubber; they depend on their thick coats for warmth. To keep the

hairs from matting and losing insulation, they groom constantly and execute barrel roll after barrel roll.

"Sea otters and kayaks have played a big role in Alaska,"
Twigg said, as we fought a slight headwind and our escort
kept easy pace, snacking away. "The Russians basically en-
slaved the Natives into hunting otters." After Vitus Bering's
voyage of discovery in 1741, the Chinese developed an insa-
tiable appetite for otter fur. Overhunted in the Kenai, sea
otters have since recovered and are as valuable today as they
once were, not for fur, but for Alaska's tourism industry. That
brings its own threats. At Seward, the marina has swelled to
550 slips and now accommodates jumbo cruise ships. With
more traffic on the bay, veteran guides admit it's getting
harder to find wildlife.

I dodge big tourism by begging off Seward's renovated Best
Western in favor of the Van Gilder Hotel, a Victorian-era rem-
nant listed on the National Register of Historic Places. Instead
of cable TV and in-room coffee, the Van Gilder offers a walk-
up room with antique furniture and lots of character. I half expect to look out my window and see gas lamps lighting the
way for sourdoughs as they stagger out of honky-tonk saloons.

Don Nelson, who gave up wildcatting on the North Slope
ten years ago and opened the hotel with his wife, says the new
breed of cruise-ship tourists are apt to hop on a day-trip char-
ter bus to Denali as soon as they hit shore. "It isn't like before,"
he says. "They used to rent a car and go off exploring."

I have done my own exploring by driving here from
Anchorage via Portage Glacier, then down seventy-five miles
of highway through a flume of mountains. Portage Glacier is
one of Alaska's top attractions, but more because of its prox-
imity to Anchorage than any inherent grandeur. Exit Glacier,
near Seward, has the knee-buckling grandeur.

I pull into the parking lot of Exit Glacier on a drizzly morning. The sun is straining to bust through the cloud cover—a "sucker hole," as local pilots call such tantalizing breaks in bad weather. Two short loop trails go to the base of the glacier; another winds four miles uphill. The latter parallels this protruding tongue of the Harding Icefield, a frozen desert that straddles Kenai Fjords National Park and Kenai National Wildlife Refuge. It sprawls over 700 square miles, blanketing the lower Kenai halfway to Homer.

I place my bets on the icefield trail, and it turns out to be a lucky day for suckers. The clouds lift. The panoramic views pull into focus. I've hit the hiking jackpot. The trail climbs through thickets of cottonwood and alder, then through clusters of red salmonberry and pink fireweed. Up and up. Subalpine meadow surrenders to alpine tundra. I bump into Don and Debbie Muggli, a Seattle-area couple who gave themselves an Alaska vacation as a twenty-fifth-anniversary present. Don's a hunter and bear buff. He points toward a sunny patch of green on the opposite mountainside, about a half mile away.

"There are two bears up there," he says. "Any meadow like that, they dink around up there."

I get out my binoculars. Sure enough. Two black bears are on their hind legs, locked in playful embrace. Dinking around. Don figures they're yearlings, since they don't have the baggy coats of adult males.

"They haven't got a care in the world," he adds. "Who's gonna bother them up there?"

Of course, the same could be said of us. As long as those dancing bears stay across the valley, who's gonna bother us up here? Not the pudgy marmots scurrying in and out of trailside burrows. Not the magpies swooping above. Certainly not those fuzz-ball mountain goats that I can occasionally glimpse sunning on an unreachable rocky perch.

It's three and a half more hours of hiking to where the trail tops out at about 3,100 feet in a moonscape of ice and rock. Harding Icefield appears to have no bounds. The whiteness unrolls like a carpet over the horizon. Earlier I met a ranger, Doug Lowthian, whose small 1996 expedition tried to cross the icefield in midwinter. A seven-day snow squall forced them to give up, and Lowthian huddled inside his tent reading a French allegorical novel over and over for three days, until they decided to brave the storm. "It was a very intense wilderness experience," he said.

"Intense" is how things can get in Alaska. It's wise, therefore, to assess your coping skills honestly. The tale goes around about a pilot who once dropped a hunter deep in the bush. The man insisted he knew the ways of the wild. He had his gun, his food, and his pepper spray to fend off bears. The pilot took off. Looking back, he was flabbergasted to see the guy squirting pepper spray all over himself as if it were insect repellent. He collapsed in a twitching heap. The pilot returned, loaded the "hunter" on the plane, and hauled him back to civilization, where he belonged.

The slang word *cheechako* is the Alaskan term for the tinhorn like that, however apocryphal. So as I drive Sterling Highway across the midsection of the peninsula, I resist any temptation to pass myself off as a fisherman. This part of Alaska is arguably the angling capital of the world. During high season, people "combat fish" shoulder-to-shoulder for miles along the banks. I pull into a boat launch site near the flyspeck town of Cooper Landing, on the Kenai River. Guide Josh Dougherty is tying lures on three clients' poles, making ready for departure. It's the tail end of a slower-than-usual coho salmon run. I ask what it's like in the height of summer, when sockeye fever strikes and fishhooks are flying.

"It's a good place to get pierced," Dougherty says. "That's why we go out in a boat."

I opt for a raft, though not for fishing. There's an adventure travel company just upstream that offers twilight rides on the river. I join five other customers; Vickie Burton, a British investment banker turned guide, takes the oars. "Will we see any bears?" everyone asks her. We see pine martens, silver salmon, bald eagles, Dall sheep in distant hills, and an abandoned miner's cabin. No bears.

"I understand they saw a bear earlier today," Burton says cheerily.

Sure. The ol' saw-'em-earlier-in-the-day line. We beach the raft after a three-hour glide and start unloading our gear. Suddenly,

The Kenai River's record-holding salmon is a 97-pound, 4-ounce king caught in 1985. Your chances of catching a trophy fish are reasonable, but so are your chances of catching a hook in the arm or leg, given the "combat fishing" crowds. The hospital in Soldotna displays a stuffed fisherman dummy decorated with hooks extracted from unlucky anglers who ended up in the emergency room.

—Andromeda Romano-Lax

there they are: three brown bears—a mother and two cubs—fishing directly across the river. They stare intently at the rippling water, swipe a paw at some target, and as often as not snare a wriggling salmon. All three bears appear to be well over this year's one-coho limit.

Most of my Kenai trip is pure improvisation. When I spot an inviting trailhead, I take a solo hike, clapping and hooting like a madman to scare off nosy bears. I like the looks of the log cabin restaurant at Gwin's Lodge, have lunch on a whim, and am rewarded with a terrific home-cooked meal. Gwin's rhubarb pie is so good that I want to take the crust home and have it mounted, Alaskan big-game style.

The highlight of my swing through the town of Kenai is driving down Broad Street and having to stop for three moose noshing on shrubs by a drive-in bank. I could bag them with a weed whacker. At the nearby visitors center I learn that 7,000 moose roam the peninsula. I also see the black sea otter cape that Miss Kenai wore in a 1967 beauty pageant.

Local museums are troves of such curios—an unsung joy of travel. On reaching Homer, therefore, I zeroed in on the Pratt Museum. It has a fine collection of whaling, mining, and Native-culture artifacts. The exhibit on the Exxon oil spill of 1989 includes tapes of radio transmissions and an account of the cleanup of 11 million gallons of oil—

> The Kenai Peninsula is a haven for big game, but it wasn't always so. At the turn of the century, one hunter noted that "there are so many sportsmen now coming in that the large game is suffering quite a slaughter." In 1941 President Franklin D. Roosevelt established the Kenai National Moose Range—later expanded to 2 million acres and renamed the Kenai National Wildlife Refuge. Managing the land for moose has benefited other animals as well. Wolves, formerly eliminated from the Kenai, have returned and now number about 200 animals. Caribou, also wiped out a century ago, have been reintroduced and now migrate across the Kenai in four distinct herds.
>
> —Andromeda Romano-Lax

enough, refined, to fill the average car's gas tank once a week for 15,800 years.

Homer is the artsy-craftsy cultural hub of the Kenai. The houses are cute, the art galleries plentiful. (Seward, by contrast, bills itself "the *real* Alaska.") Out on Homer's 4.5-mile-long harbor spit, you can sip espresso after charter-boat fishing for halibut.

Homer has everything going for it except convenience. All the real-deal mountains, lakes, and glaciers lie across Kachemak Bay. There is no road. You're at the mercy of bush pilots and ferry schedules.

A day trip by ferry to Halibut Cove—a quaint, self-governing community of artists and rugged homesteaders—is as *de rigueur* as hoisting a beer at the Salty Dawg Saloon. I'm lucky—retired state legislator Clem Tillion is at the helm. Tillion, age seventy-two, keeps sticking his head out of the wheelhouse to offer a running commentary on everything from the Gull Island bird rookery to the origins of glacier names. His wife, Diana, it seems, has mastered the art of painting landscapes with octopus ink.

When the ferry docks at Halibut Cove, passengers flock to her gallery. Meanwhile, I go have a cup of tea with Clem in the stately bayside house he built by hand. A shotgun rests on the piano in the foyer. Life is good at Halibut Cove, he says, but there's no sewer system, no school, and no grocery. His granddaughter died in a house fire some years ago. There was no hook and ladder to rescue her.

"After dinner don't forget to check the bioluminescence in the water."

Diana McBride issues that reminder as we twelve guests—a full house at Kachemak Bay Wilderness Lodge—dive into our nori-wrapped halibut with wasabi cream sauce. In 1969 Diane and her husband, Mike, boated over from Homer to this uninhabited, undeveloped peninsula. Twenty-nine years, one main lodge, and six satellite cabins (with sauna, solarium, and hot tub) later, they're still infatuated by their surroundings.

"There's so much stuff going on in this estuary," Mike exclaims as we move on to the summer berry cheesecake. "The water is just full of life."

The next morning he leads us on a low-tide walking tour of his beloved mudflats. It's like stepping into a nature movie, with McBride as narrator. All that we are oblivious to, he sees. An octopus's tunnel in the mud: "He's like a beaver. He's actually sitting in a pool of water down there." The thumbnail-size limpets that cling to jagged rocks: "These guys are little grazing animals. You can think of them as cows." A tangle of bull kelp: "Fastest growing plant in the world. This stuff can grow an inch an hour."

The McBrides have created a marvelous resort-cum-classroom. Mike is resident professor. A passionate polymath, he's on the board of the Smithsonian Institution and an elected fellow of the Royal Geographic Society. He's also a one-time bush pilot, deep-sea fisherman, and commercial abalone diver. With his survival skills, he could probably fashion an emergency shelter out of dust balls.

"This is a powerful place," Mike says of Kachemak Bay. "It's in the soles of my feet."

Chris Day feels the power, too. She's a naturalist from Homer who frequently takes McBride's guests on fly-hikes into the remote alpine zone of Kachemak Bay State Park. She and I spend an afternoon exploring Kinnickinnick Lake. It's another nature movie. Day points out the white reindeer moss and bright red bearberry that I'd normally stomp by. She examines the digested seeds in a splat of bear scat, then picks a willow-rose leaf and peels back the layers to show me where a wasp deposited its larvae for safekeeping.

"There's lots of neat country that people could get into," Day says, "but they don't know much about it, and they're afraid of it."

We scramble around the periphery of Doroshin Glacier for four hours. Like Eddy the Advice Man, Day is a big fan of grizzly bears. She thinks they're misunderstood and unjustly maligned. We don't encounter any on our hike, so I miss my chance to get elevated to a higher plane. All's not lost, though, as Day reminds me while we soak up the vista.

"You could be the first or last person on Earth in a place like this," she says. "It's a real good feeling."

Tom Dunkel is a contributing editor for National Geographic Traveler. *He lives in Washington, D. C.*

STEVE HOWE

* * *

Hell Can't Be Worse
Than This Trail

*One century later, a steep route to the gold fields
still tries men's souls.*

THE SNOW-FILLED GULLY REARS 500 FEET BETWEEN
granite buttresses, thrusting into a ceiling of clouds that hides
the pass above. Halfway up, I turn around to face the approaching storm. The air is thick and sits cold and heavy in
my lungs. Each breath comes hard, like sucking air through
wet wool. Fog roars upward through the pass, soaking every
windward surface and tinting the crags a hazy monochrome
reminiscent of turn-of-the-century photographs. Meteor-
ological mayhem and human epics have long been part of
crossing the Chilkoot Pass—the infamous weather caused by
its location (it sits between the moist Gulf of Alaska and the
frigid Canadian "Interior"), the insane human history result-
ing from gold fever.

For nine months, from September 1897 to May 1898,
roughly 25,000 aspiring prospectors stampeded through this
slot, chasing dreams of instant wealth they thought waited
along Canada's Klondike River. The thirty-three-mile trail
from the Gulf of Alaska at Dyea Inlet over Chilkoot Pass to

Lake Bennett at the headwaters of the Yukon River became a tumbling tent city of supply dumps, saloons, bunkhouses, whorehouses, and casinos. Stampeders who couldn't hire professional packers traversed each foot of the route thirty to forty times, ferrying the year's worth of supplies the Canadian Mounties required for entrance to the Yukon Territory.

The Klondike gold seekers who traveled the Chilkoot Trail bore little semblance to the frontiersmen mythologized in the novels of Robert Service and Jack London. They were raw beginners at wilderness travel, hence the epic tales. But what they lacked in experience, these dreamers made up for in optimism; they called this particular segment of trail that I'm hiking the "Golden Stairs." There had been gold rushes throughout the 1800s—to California, Colorado, Idaho, Montana, South Dakota, British Columbia, South Africa, and Australia—but nothing as large or frantic as the Klondike Stampede....

As I prepare to start out on the Chilkoot Trail, I look around at the tidal flats at Dyea, which bear little trace of the madness that occurred here almost a century ago. Only puffins and sea lions populate the once-hectic estuary of the Taiya River.

> I had a brief, rose-colored vision of one of those tough, surly Tlingit packers who hired themselves out to the Klondike stampeders to pack goods over the pass, who were known to sit down in the middle of the trail on strike for better wages, usually just before the summit. The Scales got its name because this was where the packers would re-weigh their loads and jack up their prices.
>
> Whatever they charged, it wasn't enough.
>
> —Dana Stabenow,
> "A Time Machine Called the Chilkoot Trail"

Despite this tranquility, at certain times the Chilkoot Trail is hardly a reclusive wilderness experience. Each July and August an average of 3,000 people backpack across the pass, following in the footsteps of the stampeders through Klondike Gold Rush International Historic Park, often referred to as "the world's longest museum."

As I check my pack contents one more time, I think about the gold seekers who hastily unloaded their supplies at Dyea Cove and Skagway Bay, about ten miles south, in early August 1897. The horses, skillets, axes, and food needed to survive the trip to the gold fields were dumped off the boats onto tidal mud flats. Thirty-foot tides claimed many of the beached outfits before the supplies could be moved to higher ground, and for months, knots of sobbing men lined the shore. Naturalist John Muir witnessed the chaotic scene and likened it to "a nest of ants taken into a strange country and stirred up by a stick."

The track before me plunges into a lush coastal rain forest of birch, poplar, spruce, and fir. Thick banks of dryopteris ferns and broad-leaved devil's club wall the trail as it winds past still, mirrored flood channels of the Taiya River. Common mergansers float beneath the first footbridge, nine downy hatchlings bunched around their mother's tail, each one perfect as a dandelion ball. Black bear scat is common and full of lush spring grasses.

Faint relics of the gold-rush insanity litter the Chilkoot today. Old beams, telegraph wires, and rusted flywheels are scattered amid the white flowers growing throughout the forest understory. Tall conifers appear, draped in green tendrils of blyoria lichen. The trail enters a glade at the confluence of the Taiya and Nourse rivers. A tent town called Canyon City sprang up here during the rush, only to disappear again when a railroad was completed over White Pass—a competing parallel route to the Yukon—in late 1899. Served by a blacksmith shop, several restaurants, and saloons, the population topped out at around 6,000.

Crossing the river on a suspension bridge, I find a large rusted steam boiler tucked among the firs and poplars. It helped power the most sophisticated of four tramways that creaked over the Golden Stairs by spring 1898. This one ran seven miles over the pass and contained the longest cable span in the world: 2,200 feet between towers. During its brief career, the tram pumped cargo into the Yukon at the rate of nine tons an hour—for those with the money.

The stampeders were a different breed from the experienced sourdoughs who initially struck pay dirt and triggered the rush. "They come from desks and counters; have never packed, and are not even accustomed to hard labour," wrote Tappan Adney, a correspondent for *Harper's Illustrated Weekly*. One veteran miner looked over the assemblage and shook his head. "They have no more idea what they are going to than that horse has."

No one who started out from the coast later than September 1897 could reach and float the Yukon River before freeze-up. Some gold seekers gave up, but most dug in and began relaying loads up and over Chilkoot Pass through the howling Alaskan winter, planning to have their outfit moved and their boats built when the frozen Yukon River broke apart in spring. The usual method was to haul the entire gear pile slowly up the pass in five-mile stages, moving about sixty-five pounds per trip.

The trail leaves Canyon City, climbing steeply past vistas of the rugged Nourse River drainage, with its ripsaw skyline and crenelated glaciers. I wander slowly up through the dark, shadowed forest and drift into Pleasant Camp at dusk, glad to find the site unoccupied. After the gloom of the Taiya Canyon, this open river-front camp must have impressed the stampeders— as it does me—with its pastoral charm. All night, meteorites streak across Ursa Major, the Great Bear.

As autumn gave way to winter in 1897, the Chilkoot Trail swelled with struggling packers, staggering horses, and howling dogs. Mixed in among the gold-crazed men were con artists, card sharks, and outlaws. Good bunco artists could make $2,000 a day. Shell games sprang up next to campfires, and the dark of night was particularly dangerous. Sunrise often revealed corpses along more remote portions of the trail, their pants pockets turned inside out.

My own dawn is more tranquil, marked by low clouds turning to rain. I dawdle the morning away, then strike out on the wet and squishy trail, its fern banks glistening. At Sheep Camp the terrain opens, offering views up through scrubby alders to a huge, convex shield of granite, stippled with snow and stunted trees. The pass itself remains hidden behind clouds.

Sheep Camp offered the last flat ground, shelter, and firewood before the pass. A traditional stopping place for Indian packers and mountain goat hunters, it mutated overnight into a stampede city of 4,000, and bad weather in the pass occasionally swelled its numbers to 8,000. Sheep Camp was the limit of livestock travel on the Chilkoot, and many prospectors simply abandoned horses or dogs here. Injured and starving animals wandered through the camps until the harried miners shot them by the hundreds and dumped them in the Taiya. Pneumonia and dysentery raged up and down the Chilkoot. One night there were seventeen spinal meningitis deaths in Sheep Camp alone.

A red-headed woodpecker busily forages on a poplar, hopping in a counterclockwise spiral up the trunk. Foaming cascades roar down the surrounding cliffs, braiding and sheeting over the rocks in a violent staircase effect. I come across Upper Sheep Camp Shelter, a log cabin with wood stove, table, and logbook. The entries are an amusing counterpoint to the grimness that occurred here years before: "This golf bag's getting filled with rainwater." "Beautiful trail! Now if I could just get this stinking Julie Andrews song out of my head." Then the words of a twelve-year-old boy from Calgary stop me cold: "The stampeders climbed the pass with thoughts of striking it rich. So why do we do it?"

I'm pondering the question when in bursts a young Swiss couple. Ursula and Markus spotted a black bear and are still wide-eyed and trembling after their encounter with what to Europeans is a nearly mythical creature. According to the hut log, Bigfoot, Elvis, and Liberace sightings are also common on foggy days near the pass. Ursula holds up her bear bell proudly.

I trudge on. Sheep Camp and treeline fall quickly behind. Snowfields must be crossed, willow thickets negotiated, and boulders scrambled. The Taiya bubbles beneath dangerously thin snow bridges. I don snowshoes and begin to climb up Long Hill into a massive glacial amphitheater. These broadening alpine vistas afforded the gold seekers a sudden overview of the phenomena that engulfed them: "We passed hundreds of prospectors moving forward singly and in small parties," wrote stampeder Edward Morgan, "some men staggering under packs loaded on their backs, others drawing or pushing small sleds laden with their outfits, still others driving sleds, moving sometimes, under dog power. The procession of toiling humanity thinned out as we climbed and many of them had ceased all attempts...seated themselves on their belongings, and hung up signs advertising: Outfit for Sale Cheap."

Women were also present in the long struggling line. Diarist William Haskell wrote that he "...could not fail to notice many

During the gold rush, scores of women—miners' wives, entrepreneurs, and prostitutes—climbed the Chilkoot's Golden Stairs alongside the men. Their hike was even harder. Socialite Martha Black conquered the Pass wearing a tight corset, long skirt, and bloomers. On top of that, she was pregnant.

Gold Rush Women by Claire Rudolph Murphy and Jane G. Haigh describes the travails of numerous other female stampeders, including Lucille Hunter, who gave birth on the trail, and Anna DeGraf, who reached the summit on a crutch, with her clothes in tatters and her feet wrapped in rags. DeGraf, 55, had headed north to search for her missing son, who had disappeared into Alaska two years earlier. She never found him, but her pioneering spirit prevailed. DeGraf wrote, "My mother used to say, 'You must howl with the wolves when you are with the wolves,' and so I made the best of things up there."

—Andromeda Romano-Lax

instances…in which the women showed a fortitude superior to the men. It was a revelation, almost a mystery. But after a while, I began to account for it as the natural result of an escape from the multitude of social customs and restraints, which in civilized society hedge about a woman's life…. Her nature suddenly becomes aware of a freedom, which is in a way exhilarating." About a dozen women became professional packers.

Intersecting mountain goat tracks flow down one side of the valley and up the other toward steep glacial seracs. In September 1897, these same ice fields developed into a temporary lake, and when the ice dam finally failed, a twenty-foot wall of water rushed down the granite aprons. Stampeders climbing Long Hill scattered as the flood crashed into a rest area beneath a giant boulder called the Stone House. Forty tents and outfits were wiped out.

I investigate the remains of old tram towers, then cross the valley and begin climbing a gully that looks like it has seen its share of snow slides. With the nonstop winter traffic pouring through this narrow valley, it was inevitable that an avalanche would occur. On April 3, 1898, the first good travel day after two months of heavy storms, stampeders were passing up and down this snowfield when it gave way. Within minutes 1,000 rescuers had arrived from Sheep Camp. For days, they dug trenches through the debris, locating many victims alive, some of them thirty-feet down. One ox was found chewing its cud. Victims and rescuers could hear each other. Last goodbyes were hollered through the snowpack. More than sixty people died. [Avalanche debris quickly hardens into a cement-like firmness and people buried by avalanches seldom survive more than a half-hour of burial.] The corpses were mushed down the valley to a makeshift morgue where Frank "Soapy" Smith declared himself coroner and stripped the bodies of valuables. When avalanche debris melted the following spring, undiscovered corpses floated on the surface of a pool alongside the trail.

Eventually I find myself at "the Scales," a hummock of polished rock where professional packers reweighed all loads, charging up to one dollar per pound to haul supplies over the summit. Old beams are scattered about, the wood as limp as soggy cardboard. Rusted iron straps and long rods drilled into the rock recall the elaborate cable ways that once clattered through here.

This is also the site of the Golden Stairs. Here an entrepreneur actually had a handrail installed and steps chopped into the ice nightly, which stampeders could use for a five-cent toll. One sourdough named Frank Berkeley counted

1,378 individual steps, and they constituted the biggest bottleneck between Seattle and Dawson. Everyone went the pace of the slowest.

I turn away from the soggy gales and kick my way through the snow toward the ridgeline as an approaching storm rises in intensity, squeezed to a frenzy by its passage over the Coast Mountains. Visibility becomes hopeless, and since the open bowls on the Canadian side have no landmarks and seasonal trail markers aren't yet in place, I decide to bivouac in the pass and hope for clearing weather. Klondike National Historic Park is a heavily regulated corridor and this isn't an approved campsite, but the conditions are worsening. This seems the best among undesirable options. Soon I'm inside my flapping tent while the storm rages.

I awaken to the chucking of rock ptarmigan. The storm has spent itself, leaving a leaden overcast. Red-breasted mergansers and red-throated loons flap past the tent, oodling with each beat of their wings. All through the dawn, waterfowl skim northward through the notch, their necks outstretched in labored flight.

As I finish packing, I'm hailed by a couple from Berkeley, California, who've climbed up Peterson Notch. Their jeans are soaked to the knees, but otherwise, they're game. Six rangers from Parks Canada appear, marking the trail over the open snowfields on the year's first patrol. Ho for the Klondike! The rush is on! We head into Canada in a loose group and pass a day-use shelter. During the busy season, hot chocolate and lemonade are sometimes dispensed here to passing backpackers. Nice, but not quite the same as the tent that once stood nearby advertising, "Hops beer, five cents."

We descend over mushy snowfields, traversing a steep, avalanche-prone hillside en route to the turquoise waters of

Crater and Morrow lakes. Most Indian packers descended these same slopes by simply hopping atop a sled full of cargo and launching. Since a six-foot cliff of snow usually surrounded frozen Crater Lake on the final run out of these sled rides, their sport required substantial abandon.

Below Morrow Lake, we pass Happy Camp, still deeply blanketed in snow. A narrow basalt gorge funnels the trail to Deep Lake, with its rock terraces, contorted shoreline spruce, and mountain goats wandering the cliffs above. The rangers and I pause to watch the snow-white scramblers. Christine, a nineteen-year Parks Canada veteran, shares her binoculars as we talk appreciatively about the local flora and fauna, but she also sees the trail in a sociological light.

"Midsummer here is not a wilderness experience, but the sense of community that builds between hikers is fascinating," she says. "People meet on the lower sections of the trail and maybe see each other again on or near the pass. After trading stories the whole way, by the time they reach Lake Bennett they're fast friends."

My new friends move on while I brew hot soup. In these high latitudes, the sun won't set until nearly midnight, so there's little need to hurry. Eventually, I amble down out of the snowbelt and along the rim of Deep Lake Gorge, a chasm of twisting, dropping waterfalls.

I turn a corner to find Lake Lindeman, best described by stampeder Julius Price: "Here lay stretched at our feet, though some distance below, a large, placid sheet of water, like a huge piece of rose-coloured silk spread between the mountains." Prospectors had used Lake Lindeman since 1880 as a place to build boats for their Yukon journeys. By spring of 1898, Lindeman City had swelled to 4,000 citizens as they waited for the river ice to break and the surging meltwater to carry their crafts down through treacherous Lindeman Creek, across the expansive lakes Bennett, Tagish, and Lebarge (the latter the scene of Robert Service's famous "Ballad of Sam McGee"), and another 550 miles of the Yukon River through Whitehorse Rapids to Dawson and its nearby gold creeks. It will be another 200 years before these forests fully recover from the boat building.

I'm coaxed into a layover day by the Parks Canada tent museum, a pocket-size treasure trove of old photographs and books on nature, Native tribes, and Klondike history. Again, the hut logbooks entertain. There's a satire on Robert Service called "Smell of the Yukon" based on drying socks. The entries list sightings of moose, bears, cougars, wolverines, and Bigfoot. Again, profundity is left to the young. "When I die," writes a ten-year-old girl from Whitehorse, "I want to be on a mountain with gold on the other side."

Steve Howe is a writer for Backpacker *magazine and co-author of* Making Camp: The Complete Guide for Hikers, Mountain Bikers, Paddlers and Skiers.

NANCY DESCHU

✴ ✴ ✴

Downtown Duel

Even in the big city, wild things reign.

I STRADDLE MY BIKE IN THE MIDDLE OF MCKENZIE Street and study the black dog lying unattended in the city playground, only a block away. I've been bitten by too many dogs in my life, so I'm extra cautious. But as the dog stands up and ambles into the street, I don't see the svelte body of a friendly black lab or the blocky head of a gentle Newfoundland. Instead, the animal takes on the distinct shape and gait of a black bear. Not what I was expecting to see this early Sunday morning in urban Anchorage.

At that moment, a woman walks out of a nearby house to pick up her Sunday newspaper and the bear charges toward her. Although she is overweight and wearing clogs, she sprints toward her neighbor's chain-link fence and vaults over it like an Olympian. But the bear's real target is not the vaulter; it is the dullard bicyclist who has been staring at him for the past minute. Before I know it, he abruptly shifts course away from the vaulter, straight at me.

In a split second, I process my entire brain-load of bear information and I decide the bear does not want to eat me, he just wants me to disappear from his kingdom. I choose the risky option to run, so I can hide and get out of his sight. I race my bicycle across the pavement like panicked prey, the bear snapping its jaws closer and closer to my rear tire. My intended cover is a slot between the garage door and an SUV parked in the driveway of a neighboring house. I dive under the front bumper and yank my bike towards me, though it's a poor excuse for a bear barrier.

After twenty years as a field biologist in Alaska, my first serious bear encounter is taking place two blocks from my home, as I'm riding to the coffee shop. I lie still and listen to the bear tap his claws on the driveway, like manicured fingernails thrumming on a kitchen counter. He tap-taps his way towards the garage door and I wedge closer to the SUV's left front tire.

Now I hear the bear's winded breathing and catch a glimpse of his furred feet. The slot is tight for him, so he turns and circles the SUV counterclockwise. The nature of the tapping changes and I guess that he has moved off the asphalt driveway, back to the rough-surfaced street. The clicking tempo quickens and finally fades as he gallops north towards the thread of forest that hugs the city's Coastal Trail. As I slither out from under the SUV, the last I see of the bear is his round, black butt loping up and down, disappearing into the coastal woods.

I walk over to check on the woman who leaped her neighbor's fence. She is still lying on the lawn, one blue clog inside the fence with her, the other lying at the edge of the street, and I worry she has had a heart attack. But she lifts her head and tells me she is O.K. After we introduce ourselves, she suggests that the bear had strayed from the comfort of Kincaid Park, a large stand of woods a few miles down the coast. We agree that he was not a bear-gone-bad from eating human garbage, just a lost teenager standing his turf. Even so, we think it is terrible how he bullied us.

Still flushed with adrenaline, I make the rash decision to continue my trip to the coffee shop. I peddle down Captain Cook Drive and cycle onto Anchorage's Coastal Trail at a spot where the forest thins out and there's a sweeping view of Cook Inlet's murky waters, an openness I think the riled bear might avoid.

I breathe deeply, taking in the August sea air. As I bike along I notice my tires are crossing giant brown paw prints on the black paved trail. I am pleased that the city has spent a few tax dollars to stencil grizzly bear prints on the Coastal Trail. How amused the summer tourists will be, to come upon the distinctive painted prints when they stroll this scenic route after dining at downtown restaurants. Long after they leave Anchorage, they will recall that this northern city has a love for its wildlife and a quirky sense of humor.

As I scan the inlet, I have a sudden sinking feeling. The bear prints are exactly the same color as the inlet's mudflats. I hop off my bike and quickly look around. No bears in sight. Leaning over, I lick my finger and run it across one of the prints. It smears like fresh, damp mud, not paint, and I realize that a grizzly bear has recently passed through. A grizzly so close to downtown is exceedingly rare. Feeling bear-hexed, I prepare for another encounter.

With my back against the seaward fence and my bike against my landward vital organs, I move stealthily over the next quarter mile, until reaching a busy street that leads into town. At the Downtown City Market's outdoor café I review my day so far: two bears, one black and one grizzly, in the same section of trail, within a short distance of downtown— and I had crossed both their paths? I do not share this tale with anyone at the café, because I do not fully believe my own story. I bike the two miles home along major thoroughfares full of traffic and free of bears.

Three days later, I read in the *Anchorage Daily News* that, on Sunday morning, a wayward grizzly thrashed repeatedly into its own reflection in the living-room window of a downtown house. The bear left a mess of slobber marks and muddy paw prints on the glass—and a terrified man inside.

I begin to believe my story's plot. A grizzly bear and black bear, both astray in the city, cross paths that morning. The grizzly bullies the black bear out of the coastal woods and then irritably pads his giant paws through the mudflats and up the bank to the paved trail. Meanwhile the black bear finds refuge in a playground, where he lies recuperating on the cool dirt beneath the red sliding board.

As the grizzly marches down the Coastal Trail, on his way to a duel with his own reflection, the resting black bear is disturbed once again, this time by a bicyclist taking an aggressive stance on McKenzie Street. Helmeted, hands on hips, she eyes him steadily, unknowingly challenging him to his second battle of the morning in the wilds of downtown Anchorage.

Nancy Deschu makes her living as an aquatic biologist, studying rivers and lakes. Besides technical writing for her science profession, she pursues an interest in creative nonfiction and poetry. Her scientific perspective and field experiences in Alaska and the tropics, where she spends winter vacations, are reflected in her prose and poetry. Although she has seen many, many bears in her twenty years in Alaska, she has had only one frightening encounter, just a few blocks from her house in urban Anchorage.

* * *

Point Retreat

The routine of guided tours yields its own mysteries.

AS A DECKHAND ON A JET BOAT TAKING VISITORS ON two-hour whale-watching tours, my summer is filled with rushing, always at the beck and call of captains, owners, staff, and tourists. I meet each load of passengers delivered to the dock by the company bus, walk them down the ramp, and help them aboard the red jet boat. "Watch your step please. Make yourself comfortable. Watch your head stepping down. Watch your step please. Make yourself comfortable." One after the other. Time after time.

When everyone is seated, I untie the boat and cast off at the captain's pleasure. Usually he is in a hurry: impatient, concerned about every minute, mindful that we are scheduled to return in exactly two hours for another load of tourists. Sometimes, though, he gabs on the radio or visits the head or compares notes with other captains on other boats while I stand smiling, waiting for his signal to cast off.

As we leave the harbor, motoring slowly through the no-wake zone, I stow the bumpers, close the hatches, and grab an

orange Mae West life vest for the requisite safety talks. I point
out the fire extinguishers and flare kit, demonstrate the floating device, and caution everyone to remain seated when the
boat is in motion. Children fuss and people who don't speak
English chatter loudly.

"Humpback whales from the greater Juneau vicinity are
known to winter in Hawaii, where they breed and give birth
but do not feed," I repeat to a new group every two hours.
"They return to our rich waters here in Alaska where they
feed on krill, herring, and other small schooling fish. They eat
a ton or more a day, every chance they get. Sometimes it seems
like they're eating all the time." I pause here to glance at the
ship's progress, timing my speech with the buoy marker past
which we can try our luck at accelerating, not always a sure
thing. "Captain says that's what it's like to be on a tour ship."
Pausing here, I get a sense of the group; the more they laugh
at my first joke, the better the crowd.

"The mountains around Juneau are only three thousand to
five thousand feet in elevation, but they appear much higher
because they're so steep," I brag. "Picture that many of these
islands are just as steep as the mountains, so the water is quite
deep even close to land." I gesture toward the coastline.
"Remember we're looking for a column of vapor. Be sure to
look right up against the islands, because there might be a
whale where we would normally consider the shore." I look
around again. "It's a beautiful day in the rain forest!" I exclaim,
no matter what the weather. "Let's go whale watching!"

I hold my breath, hoping that the captain will synchronize
the boat's acceleration with the end of my talk. And when he
does, the captain and I will both hold our breath and hope
that the boat will speed over the water, instead of dragging itself along, jets clogged, plugs misfiring, rpm on the starboard
engine only half what it is on the port side, while I stand

smiling, bagels and juice in hand, offering refreshments to visitors who have paid good money to see whales, and by God they expect to see whales.

"They told us not to let you go more than two hours without giving you something to eat," I shout over the jets, pausing again for laughter. The boat bounces and lurches over the waves while I brace myself and balance a platter of twenty bagels and twenty pouches of juice, waiting for some matron from Florida to decide just exactly which bagel she really wants (*They're all the same! Take one! Take one!*) and for her husband to decipher what a dadgummed pouch is—a bag of juice? Never heard of it. Juice? You sure this is juice? (*Yes, it's juice. Take one. Or not, I don't care. Just make up your mind. Please!*)

"On the port side in the far distance is Admiralty Island," I continue. "The original name for the island is Kootznoowoo, which

---

Harriet offered the last toast of the evening. She stood up, her pink chiffon dress flowing about her, only mildly wrinkled. Her hair was combed back and formed a tight curl along her neck.

"Well," she said, looking around and preparing to give her final verdict on the tour. "The dinner was delicious." I smiled with relief. "I feel like I know Alaska," she continued. "There were too many trees and mountains, I can see animals better at my zoo. That grizzly bear at Denali Park was so far away, it looked fake. But all in all, it was a good tour." She held her glass in my direction, indicating approval. Now I understood that Harriet's painful and relentless annual tours provided stories and memories for forty-eight weeks of a much quieter existence.

—Chris Klein, "Confessions of a Tour Guide"

---

means 'Fortress of the Brown Bear.' That's a good name for it, because the brown bear population on that island is thought to be one per square mile. At sixteen hundred acres, it has one of the world's greatest concentrations of bears." Another pause while I hold up my hands to show my silver bracelets. "The Native people of this area associate themselves with different animals that we then take as our crests. My clan—the wolf clan—considers itself related to the brown bear, so I'm always careful to point it out to you when we go by." For some reason, this never fails to make them laugh.

"When I was a girl, my grandmother used to tell me we don't eat brown bear meat, because to do so would be just like eating our own cousin!" The captain was surprised to learn that I still consider the brown bear my cousin, the Taku wind my grandfather, the spider my neighbor. After being brought the truths of virgin birth, resurrection, and walking on water, why would I now persist in believing a myth? But I let the passengers laugh, the captain preach, the jet engines clog. Every day is the same, every passenger is the same. Every captain is the same. Every moment is unique.

Just outside Bartlett Cove, a dozen humpback whales have surrounded a school of herring in the deep ocean water. Beneath the surface, one circles a spiral net of bubbles around the fish. The whale constructs the net of bubbles upward from the ocean floor, trapping the herring in smaller and smaller circles, nearer and nearer the surface. Then one humpback begins to circle the net, singing in a high-pitched haunting voice, frightening the herring into a huddled ball of prey that rises to the top.

We hear the song over a hydrophone that the captain has lowered into the water. We look in every direction, searching for telltale bubbles. Eagles and gulls fly overhead, circling, calling, searching. I watch the gulls. They will know before we do where the whales will come up. "There! Over there!" A dozen whales lunge out of the water, mouths open, pink tongues and baleen and splashing water, gulls diving, passengers gasping, hearts racing. Then they are gone. Back under the water, checking for herring, swallowing the last mouthfuls, yumming their dinner. They surface again, slow and graceful. Their breaths explode and their spouts are a loud wet sticky *whoosh*. They are powerful, graceful, gentle. They are so close to us, yet oblivious to our presence.

The whales begin to travel away from us, into Barlow Cove chasing herring. We all want to follow, but the captain has something else in mind. "Be seated, please." In a flurry of joy and disappointment, thrills and complaints, the passengers are seated. I close the hatches, the jets roar and we're steaming toward False Point.

We no sooner round Point Retreat than we are in the midst of two dozen or more boats: whale watchers, sport-fishing craft, commercial fishing vessels, private motorized skiffs. The late sun reflects off the almost calm waters of Lynn Canal. The lighthouse at Point Retreat catches a ray of afternoon sun, Eagle Glacier glistening on the mainland behind it. The beautiful Chilkat Mountains are capped in white and shrouded in patchy, summer-evening clouds. The captain slows the boat, I open the doors to the decks, we pile out onto the aft deck. All around the boats spread up and down the waterway are the dorsal fins of killer whales. There must be more than sixty. In the reflected sun, their fins are dark against the water, black signals rising from the water, moving fast and disappearing, running in the water. The wolves of the sea.

"It's very rare for us to see both killer whales and humpbacks on the same trip," I tell the passengers, "especially humpbacks that are bubble feeding, and especially so many killer whales. We're very fortunate." A few passengers are not yet satisfied, but they will never be happy; if nothing else, they'll complain about the bagels. Most are thrilled to silence, beside themselves with joy. They realize what I'm saying is the truth. This is a rare trip. This is a rare moment.

The air becomes still. We become quiet. Together, we witness a sight that few people ever see: we are surrounded by killer whales. We are surrounded by freedom.

Conventional teachings suggest that eternity is something that starts after death, and then goes on—well, forever. But I know that it is this moment that is eternal. One wave moves in a certain manner while that particular killer whale rises above the water and catches one ray of light against the flash of its singular fin, and I stand here on this particular boat, late in the afternoon of this certain day, with these people who have traveled distances near and far to stand here and be captured with me in this moment, which is gone before I blink and which will continue always to exist.

Before long, the captain gives the signal to be seated for our long return trip to the dock where we will off-load these passengers, refuel and clean the boat, radio the dispatcher for tomorrow's schedule, and be finished with our work for this day. I will limp home, feet sore, tired, hungry, sick of bagels. I will wash the saltwater out of my hair, lie down on the couch, talk on the phone, fall asleep. I will rise the next day to work again until the summer ends, and then I will return to the university where I am belatedly completing my education. I will see more whales and eagles, I will see rough seas and calm. I will grow older. I will die. And all the while, a part of me will be lost in one moment. Killer whales will surround me forever in an eternal moment that will never happen again.

Tlingit Ernestine Hayes belongs to the Wolf House of the Kaagwaantaan clan in Southeast Alaska. Born and raised in Juneau, she moved with her mother to California at age fifteen. She lived outside Alaska for twenty-five years, always longing to be home. Upon turning forty, she vowed to return home, or die trying. It took her eight months to move up the coast from San Francisco to Ketchikan. Along the way she lived out of her car, stood in food lines, slept in shelters. After settling in Juneau in 1989, Hayes enrolled at UA-Southeast as a non-traditional student. The mother of three and grandmother of four graduated magna cum laude, with a bachelor's degree in communications, at age fifty-five, and has since gone on to complete her M.F.A. in Creative Writing. She is now on the faculty of UA-Southeast and lives in Juneau.

PART THREE

GOING YOUR OWN WAY

PAM HOUSTON

The Blood of Fine
and Wild Animals

*A hunting guide stalks memory and ambivalence
in the Alaska Range.*

WHEN I WAS TWENTY-SIX YEARS OLD, I FELL IN LOVE
with a man who was a hunting guide. We didn't have what
you would call the healthiest of relationships. He was selfish,
evasive, and unfaithful. I was demanding, manipulative, and
self-pitying. He was a Republican and I was a Democrat. He
was a Texan and I was not. I belonged to the Sierra Club and
he belonged to the NRA. Yet somehow we managed to stay
together for three years of our lives, and to spend two solid
months of each of those three years hunting for Dall sheep
in Alaska.

I was always quick, in those days, to make the distinction
between a hunter and a hunting guide, for though I was indi-
rectly responsible for the deaths of a total of five animals, I
have never killed an animal myself, and never intend to. I had
the opportunity once to shoot a Dall ram whose horns were
so big it would have likely gotten my name into the record
books. I had three decent men applying every kind of peer
pressure they could come up with, and I even went so far as

to raise the rifle to my eye, unsure in the moment what I would do next. But once I got it up there I couldn't think of one good reason to pull the trigger.

I learned about bullets and guns and caliber and spotting scopes, and I was a good hunting guide simply because I'm good at the outdoors. I can carry a heavy pack long distances. I can cook great meals on a backpacking stove. I keep my humor pretty well for weeks without a toilet or a shower. I can sleep, if I have to, on a forty-five-degree ledge of ice. I know how to move in the wilderness, and because of this I understand how the sheep move. I'm a decent tracker. I've got what they call *animal sense.*

When I was hunting Dall sheep in Alaska it was one on one on one. One hunter, one guide, one ram that we tracked, normally for ten days, before we got close enough to shoot it. My obvious responsibility was to the hunter. It was my job to keep him from falling into a crevasse or getting eaten by a grizzly bear, to carry his gun when he got too tired, to keep him fed and watered, to listen to his stories, to get him up at three in the morning and keep him on his feet till midnight, to drag him fifteen miles and sometimes as much as four thousand vertical feet a day, and if everything went well, to get him in position to shoot a sheep to take home and put on his wall. My other job, though understated, was to protect the sheep from the hunters, to guarantee that the hunter shot only the oldest ram in the herd, that he only shot at one animal, and that he only fired when he was close enough to make a killing shot. A hunter can't walk a wounded animal down across the glaciers in Alaska the way he can through the trees in the Pennsylvania woods. A bad shot in Alaska almost always means a lost ram.

I describe those months in the Alaska Range now as the most conflicted time of my life. I would spend seventy days testing myself in all the ways I love, moving through the Alaskan wilderness, a place of such power and vastness it is incomprehensible even to my memory. I watched a mama grizzly bear feed wild blueberries to her cubs, I woke to the footfall of a hungry-eyed silver wolf whispering through our campsite, I watched a bull moose rub the velvet off his bloody antlers, and a bald eagle dive for a parka squirrel. I watched the happy chaos that is a herd of caribou for hours, and the contrastingly calculated movements of the sheep for days.

I learned from the animals their wilderness survival skills, learned, of course, a few of my own. I learned, in those days, my place in the universe, learned why I need the wilderness, not why *we* need it, but why *I* do. That I need the opportunity to give in to something bigger than myself, like falling into love, something bigger, even, than I can define. This did not have to do with shooting an animal (though it would have, of course, in its purest form, had we not packages and packages of freeze-dried chicken stew) but with simpler skills: keeping warm in subzero temperatures, avoiding the grizzly bears that were everywhere and unpredictable, not panicking when the shale started shifting underneath my boot soles in a slide longer and steeper than anything I'd ever seen in the Lower 48, finally riding that shale slide out like a surfer on a giant gray wave.

I listened to the stories of the hunters, the precision and passion with which the best among them could bring the memories of past hunting camps to life. I understood that part of what we were about in hunting camp was making new stories, stories that were the closest these men ever got to something sacred, stories that would grace years, maybe even generations, of orange campfire light.

But underneath all that wonder and wildness and the telling of tales, the fact remains that in payment for my

Alaskan experience I watched five of the most beautiful, smartest, and the wildest animals I'd ever seen die, most of them slowly and in unspeakable pain. And regardless of the fact that it was the hunter who pulled the trigger, I was the party responsible for their deaths. And though I eat meat and wear leather, though I understand every ethical argument there is about hunting including the one that says it is hunters who will ultimately save the animals because it is the NRA who has the money and the power to protect what is left of America's wilderness, it will never be O.K. with me that I led my hunters to those animals. There is no amount of learning that can, in my heart, justify their deaths.

So when I remember that time in my life, I try to think not only of the killing but also of the hunting, which is a work of art, a feat of imagination, a flight of spirit, and a test of endless patience and skill. To hunt an animal successfully you must think like an animal, move like an animal, climb to the

---

If outfitting has a spirit, it seems that spirit must be a bit of an eccentric, enjoying the contrast of hours or days of waiting with minutes of frantic stuffing and packing. Years before, I noticed that if everything in camp was ready to go, the airplane would be late. Consequently, I had started leaving my sleeping bag unfurled and noticed a marked improvement in planes arriving as scheduled. Clients often seemed bewildered when I told them to pack up everything except their bedroll and not touch it until the airplane was on the ground. It didn't always work, but it did seem to help my clients' craving for some harmless idiosyncratic behavior in their guides—and better stories when they returned home.

—Steve Kahn, "The Hard Way Home"

top of the mountain just to go down the other side, and always be watching, and waiting, and watching. To hunt well is to be at once the hunter and the hunted, at once the pursuer and the object of pursuit. The process is circular, and female somehow, like giving birth, or dancing. A hunt at its best ought to look, from the air, like a carefully choreographed ballet.

French psychoanalyst Jacques Lacan believed that men desire the object of their desire, while women desire the condition of desiring, and this gives women a greater capacity for relishing the hunt. I believe that is why, in so many ancient and contemporary societies, women have been the superior hunters. Good hunting is no more about killing an animal than good sex is about making babies or good writing is about publication. The excitement, even the fulfillment, is in the beauty of the search. While a man tends to be linear about achieving a goal, a woman can be circular and spatial. She can move in many directions at once, she can be many things at once, she can see an object from all sides, and, when it is required, she is able to wait.

Occasionally there is a man who can do these things (most of the guides I knew were far better at them than I), and he is a pleasure to guide and to learn from. But the majority of my clients started out thinking that hunting is like war. They were impatient like a general, impatient like a sergeant who thinks he should be the general, impatient for the sound of his own gun and impatient for the opposition to make a mistake.

But the sheep didn't often make mistakes, and they were as patient as stone. So it was my job to show the hunter that he could choose a different metaphor. If hunting can be like war it can also be like opera, or fine wine. It can be like out-of-body travel, it can be like the suspension of disbelief. Hunting can be all of these things and more; like a woman, it won't sit down and be just one thing.

I wore a necklace in my hunting days, a bear claw of Navajo silver. The man I was in love with, the hunting guide, had given it to me to make amends for one of our breakups, one of his affairs. He gave it to me in a tiny box, wrapped elaborately, like a ring, and I shook it, heard it clunk, thought, *Oh my God, Oh my God, he's really doing it.* When I opened it, saw that it was not a ring but a pendant, I was not disappointed. I simply wore the pendant like a ring, confusing the symbolism of that pendant just enough to carry me back into the relationship, and back into hunting camp one last time.

It was late August, and much too warm in the high mountains. I'd been dropped, by airplane, 100 air miles from Tok with two bow hunters from Mississippi. We'd made a base camp and climbed from it, up the valley of the Tok River to the glacial headlands. The sheep would stay high in the warm weather, higher, probably, than we could climb. But we tried anyway, crossing glacial rivers normally small but now raging in the heat wave, knowing after each crossing that we wouldn't make it back across until the weather turned again and the water began to subside. We had our packs, of course, a tent, sleeping bags, a change of

---

The next day my Athabascan companions and I traveled some seventy miles out on the tundra in search of caribou. One small skittish herd startled and sprinted into white land and sky, vanishing where there was no horizon. Only one turned our way and gratefully we took her. Dinner and breakfast and dry meat. Land food for the spirit as well as the body.

—Ellen Bielawski, "Diamond Diary," *Connotations*

clothes and enough food, if we didn't shoot anything, for a little better than three days.

When we got to the glacier at the head of the valley we hadn't seen any recent sheep sign, and this told us that the sheep would be higher still, lying with their bellies in a snow-field, not even needing to eat until the weather cooled down. We were wet and tired, hot and hungry, but we dropped half our gear, the tents and bedding, and climbed higher up the rocky moraine that flanked the glacier. We climbed through tangled forests of alder that grew, it seemed, horizontally out of the rocks, climbed over the soggy mounds of tundra, squeezing into it with our boot tips and fingernails when it got too steep. Our socks got wetter, our breathing more labored; for hours we climbed and still no sign of the sheep.

The hunters—I forget their names now, but let's just call them Larry and Moe—were nervous. We were all nervous. The packs were too heavy, the air was too thick, the sun was too hot, and we'd come too long and too far not to have seen any sign of the sheep. We collapsed on the top of a rocky out-cropping surrounded by tundra. Larry amused himself by shooting arrow after arrow at a ptarmigan (a fat bird with fuzzy white après-ski boots on) who, as slow and stupid as that particular bird can be, let the arrows whiz by his head. Larry couldn't hit him, and the bird refused to fly away. Moe poked at a hole in the ground with a long stick, worrying whatever was inside. I went into my pack, looking for food, and found, buried between the cans of tuna and dried apricots, a rock—quartz, I believe—weighing six or seven pounds.

"You sons of bitches," I said to Larry and Moe, who had been watching me, smirking.

That's when the ground hornets finally got angry enough to come out of the hole in front of Moe. Maybe wasps know who in the crowd is allergic to them; these wasps seemed to. Four of them, anyway, came straight for me, and stung me on the hand. The first-aid kit, the shots of epinephrine, had made it as far as the mouth of the glacier and no farther, and that was at least four hours away.

I sat quietly and listened to my heartbeat quicken, my breathing accelerate into a frenzy. This is how it's all going to end, I thought, hornet-stung, and trapped on the glacier with Larry and Moe. Then self-preservation took over. I ordered Larry to carry me on his back over to the glacier, ordered Moe to scout ahead and find a place where the ice had melted and the water had pooled. I tried to exert no energy as Larry climbed with me across the moraine and onto the glacier. Moe whistled that he had found a pool several inches deep, and Larry laid me in it while I did my best to breathe through the ever-smaller opening that was my throat.

I lay in that glacial pool until I was so numb I wasn't sure I could feel my torso. Eventually, the adrenaline subsided and my throat eased back open. My hand, my whole arm, was swollen to five or six times its normal size. I wrapped myself up in what remained of our dry clothes and tried to chew on a granola bar but I had no appetite. The late Alaskan summer night was bending on into evening, the sun rolling sideways along the horizon and threatening to go below it. It would get cold soon and the night wind off the glacier would start. No one wanted to say what we all knew: that we had to get back down to the mouth of the glacier by nightfall, had to get to our sleeping bags before it turned cold. Larry couldn't carry me the whole way. And I wondered, if I couldn't make the climb back down through the tundra and rock and alders to where our gear lay, would it be the right thing for them to simply leave me behind?

"Let's give it a try," I said. "If we go now we can go slowly." This wasn't true, but I spoke with authority and the boys believed me. We'd be climbing back through those alders at the worst time of day. Our range of vision would be cut way down, the rocks and tree trunks would be slippery with dew, and the grizzly bears would be moving. "You guys sing real loud now," I told them. "Let's give the bear the opportunity to do the right thing."

We moved across the tundra and back down into the alders. With every step, every tightening of muscle, my arm exploded in pain and my head swam. My pulse increased, my throat tightened, and I had to drop back a little and rest until it began to open again. Eventually the fall got so steep and the alders so thick that there was nothing to do but lower ourselves through the branches with our arms, like children on a jungle gym. The pain in my arm reached a certain level of excruciation, and then moved on into numbness, the way a blister will if you keep walking long hours after it has popped. We could hear animals moving near us in the alder, big animals, and every now and then we'd get a whiff of dark musk.

"Sing louder, goddammit!" I shouted ahead to the boys, who were scared into silence by the noises beside them, and bent on getting back out in the open to the relative safety of the place on the glacier where we'd left the tent. They broke into a halfhearted round of "King of the Road," and I could tell by their voices they were moving much faster than I could, and would soon leave me out of screaming range.

That's when the heavy chain on which I wore my bear claw caught on an alder branch, just as I bent my elbows and swung my legs down to the next-lower set of branches, and my head snapped up and I was nearly hanged there, by the strength of that chain and the weakness of my arm and the force of gravity pulling me down. I gasped for breath, but there was none, and so I lifted my good arm up to the branch above me and did something I never could do in gym class, a one-handed chin-up, and repositioned my feet and unhooked my necklace from the alder branch.

I took the bear claw in the palm of my hand and felt the coolness of the silver, and I felt my strong heart pumping, sending blood to every part of my body, including my misshapen arm, and I realized I'd had it wrong all along about the necklace. That I had relied on somebody else's set of metaphors to understand it. That it had nothing to do, finally, with an engagement ring or the man who gave it to me, that it had, finally, nothing whatsoever to do with a man. And that whatever role that man had played in taking me to the Alaskan wilderness in the first place, he had nothing to do with why I stayed, nothing to do with all the things my seasons with the hunters, with the animals, had taught me, nothing whatsoever to do with the strength and tenacity that was getting me, bee-stung and frightened and freezing, down that near-dark Alaskan hill.

I wore the necklace differently after that, and years later, when the clasp on it wore paper-thin and the pendant fell one day into my coincidentally open hand, I replaced it with pieces of eight from the seventeenth century that I found near a silver mine in Bolivia, and I wait now to discover the meaning of this new/old silver I wear.

It's been years since I've guided any hunters, though I have returned to the Alaskan wilderness, with a camera or a kayak or a pair of cross-country skis. I am a far better outdoorswoman for my years guiding hunters, and even more important, I have a much deeper understanding of my animal self. I also have the blood of five fine and wild animals on my hands, and I will never forget it. And this is perhaps why, like the hunters, I need to keep telling my story, over and over again.

Pam Houston is the author of Cowboys Are My Weakness, Waltzing the Cat, *and* A Little More About Me, *from which this story was excerpted.*

HEATHER VILLARS

✷ ✷ ✷

On the Pack Ice

Everyone helps when a whale is harvested,
even strangers in town.

THERE IT LAY: THE BOWHEAD WHALE. A CREW OF INUPIAT hunters had killed it. A trailing line of Barrow's community had pulled on ropes as thick as wrists dragging the whale onto shore like some great tug of war on track-and-field day. The tail and fins were lopped off. Long scorings lashed the whale's slate gray skin, perpendicular to the length of its body, as if the crew were slicing a large loaf of bread. The hunters had pressed lines into whale skin like a baker might press her knife into a pan of brownies, estimating where her final, even cuts will be.

I arrived on the back of my friend's snowmachine. A resident of Barrow, Jeremy maneuvered the machine across five miles of frozen ocean left from winter. Ahead of us, leading the way, was Jeremy's cousin Craig, a biologist who studies bowhead whales for the North Slope Borough Department of Wildlife Management. My friend Toby brought up the rear, a loaded rifle slung over his shoulder.

Toby and I were in Barrow for three days. A bargain airline

fare brought us from Anchorage for the spring whale hunt. In May, Inupiat whaling crews camp on the edge of the Arctic Ocean as they have for thousands of years, waiting for the spring migration of bowhead whales. Captains and crews harpoon and harvest the bowhead to feed their community for another season.

Barrow sits at the northernmost point of Alaska, some 350 miles north of the Arctic Circle. At this latitude, Barrow's 4,500 residents are kept in the dark during the winter; for three months each year, the sun never breaks above the horizon. My first night in Barrow, May 10, marked the new season of light. The sun would not set again until August 2.

When Toby and I first arrived, Jeremy took us on a walking tour of the town. I wanted desperately to run out onto the pack ice, to touch the ice cubes that stood tall as storage sheds, wide as my outstretched arms, pointed and randomly placed like rubble from a collapsed building. I hiked around the coastal edge of town, my footsteps piercing the snow's icy layer with a satisfying crackle, until Jeremy told me I

A n icy glossary: floe—a large piece of floating ice; fast ice—ice attached to the shore; ice-blink—a pale yellow reflection on the sky, indicating ice at a distance; ice pack—large body of near-solid ice extending across the whole sea; lead (leed)—a strip of navigable water opening in the pack; pressure ridge—formed when ice under pressure rises up, breaks apart, and forms a jumbled barricade of fractured ice pieces, difficult and often dangerous to travel through.

—Ellen Bielawski

---

wasn't allowed. Polar bears, he said. We shouldn't be out on the ice without a rifle. In all that whiteness—white sky, white snow, white ice for miles—it would be too easy for a bear to sneak up on us. Plus, he explained, with the whale hunt on, people were cleaning out their underground storage of last season's muktuk. With all that whale meat lying around town, waiting for garbage day, the polar bears were in picnic fervor.

On the second day of our visit, Craig got the radio call that a whale had been landed. We all headed out onto the ice— that giant, forbidden playground—three snowmachines in a loud humming line. The frozen Arctic Ocean seemed endless. Ice lay in large chunky piles across the landscape, glowing in the morning sun. From town the ice field looked like a giant meringue ladled out upon the state's edge, one huge baked Alaska waiting for the end of dinner to make its debut on the dining room table. I had never seen anything so rare and sparse and beautiful. Every few moments I saw trails of arctic fox footprints in the snow, the only sign of life except for the loud squawk of sea gulls overhead.

After an hour on the snowmachine, with the tracks of other machines our only guide, we came to one of several whale camps along the edge of the ice. The Arctic Ocean was a glistening blue sheet stretched taut against the floe edge.

The shoreline teemed with activity. Men cut through the segmented scorings on the whale's skin to slice strips of whale skin and blubber, each a foot wide and up to six feet long. The skin was thick, a pencil-lead gray, the fat beneath rosy pink, mottled with blood. The Eskimos call this muktuk. It's a very healthy food, rich in niacin, iron, calcium, even vitamin C.

The crew harvested the muktuk like this: one man flung a hook as big as my hand into the scored flap, and pulled on the connected rope. The skin and fat, eight inches deep, peeled off as smoothly as a nonstick Band-Aid. Another man, standing on top of the whale, wielded a long dowel-handled blade, cutting behind the strip of muktuk as his partner yanked it away. Their actions reminded me of skinning chicken breasts. With a bit of tension on the skin, and a bit of slicing from underneath, it comes free easily. When enough of a strip was free, one or more men grabbed the muktuk with their hooks, dragging the giant slice off to the side. A pile of slices, each as big as a man's leg, grew high.

A group of women carved some of the blubber from a piece, leaving the dark gray half-inch of skin and two inches of fat. They boiled this, cutting it into four-inch strips, the fat turning a pale white. They call this *unalluq*. When it was ready, the women offered large steaming pots of the boiled whale to the crew: the first warm taste of the successful hunt.

Jeremy, Toby, and I tried to stay out of the way. I felt like an outsider, a white person and one of the few not from Barrow. I was there to watch, not to judge, not to interview. Jeremy had given Toby and me a lecture on not being too overeager with our cameras. I tried to be respectful. And to keep my mouth from dropping open in awe.

Craig and two colleagues were busy measuring the whale—tail length, fin length and width, body length—each measurement penciled onto the clipboard in Craig's rubber-gloved hands. One of the scientists sliced a six-inch stripe through the wall of the whale's stomach, dipping her specimen cup inside. When full, the cup steamed with the whale's partially digested lunch.

Craig told us this whale was a runt, small for its age, though it was the biggest animal I'd ever seen, bigger than a VW bus. It was probably only five years old, a baby, Craig said. Scientists think bowhead whales don't become sexually mature until they're eighteen to twenty years old. But they're not certain. Scientists, it turns out, don't know a lot about bowhead whales. With each specimen cup, each list of statistics about a harpooned whale, they were excavating the natural history of these mammals, piece by steaming piece.

Meanwhile, Toby and I stood quietly, eyes wide, taking it all in. After a half hour on the sidelines, Toby chatted up one of the crewmen working to harvest the whale. A longtime Alaskan fisherman himself, Toby respects Inupiat whaling customs. He, unlike me, has seen blood and death. He knows that we are often kept alive by killing our animal cousins. Toby asked the man if it would be O.K. to take pictures. The man said yes, don't get stepped on.

The crew butchered the entire whale in a matter of hours. The snow steamed red with lost life. The hunters rejoiced, their white *parkys* stained the color of cherries. I watched a group of women perched amid the pile of small intestines. They wore rubber gloves with elongated plastic sheeting stretched to their elbows and secured there with elastic, like a shower cap. One woman used a knife resembling an ulu—a half-moon shaped Inupiat knife that I had associated more with tourists than with Native food preparation. This knife's blade measured about a foot along its curved edge, with a characteristic wooden handle sprouting from its center of the straight edge. The woman wielding the knife cut apart the thin membranes that connect the intestines' sausage-like casing to itself in accordion folds, a beautiful, if gory, tangled embrace. Another woman fed the recently freed tube of intestines into the hands of a third woman, who piled them neatly into a plastic bag. I thought back to the lessons I learned in history class about Native peoples, how they use every part of the animals they kill, how they respect what they take from the land. Hints of this surfaced there on the pack ice: of community, of challenge, of respect for the animal—these centuries-old customs being carried out before me. After the scientist collected her data from the stomach, the Native women flopped the organ into a plastic bag.

While the adults worked, kids circulated among them with thermoses of coffee and stacks of Styrofoam cups. Other kids passed buckets of fried chicken, then bowls of steaming fry bread, then kettles of tea. Toby, Jeremy, and I declined. We were not there to eat these people's food. We weren't really even invited.

Small children climbed around on the pack ice, playing king of the mountain. An orange flag on a long, wooden stake flapped in the cold wind coming off the Arctic Ocean, its center a white and red symbol resembling the Mercedes trademark. Jeremy told me the flag belonged to this whaling crew and marked this camp as its own. Later, at other camps, I saw different flags, with different symbols and colors, each announcing a team's territory.

> What I've learned— what I grew up with and maintained—is sharing. You don't get the whale. It comes to you. That's what I've been taught. There's just so much respect for the whale. Once it's landed everything is taken. Things like, you put the whale's skull back into the water. That, in itself, asks for the spirit to come back next spring. And you still do that to this day. A lot of things we do are not written, but passed on.
>
> —Rex Allen Rock, Sr., Whaling Captain, Pt. Hope in *Growing up Native in Alaska*

The sun blazed down on us, pushing the temperature to a high of 8 degrees Fahrenheit. Weeks of camping along the floe edge, where ice, snow, and water all reflect the sun, had darkened the whaling crew's faces to the color of rich soil. The crew's fur-lined hoods waved in the wind. Sun gleamed off their reflective sunglasses.

Watching, I noticed the odd convergence of history and

technology on the ice. We traveled by snowmachine. Inupiat no longer need a dog team to pull their muktuk-laden sleds back to their village. Many whaling boats are still lined with sealskin, and many whalers use paddles instead of outboard motors. No longer do the whaling captains use hand-carved stone arrowheads and harpoons. Instead, they use more accurate and lethal shoulder guns. But the tools used to butcher the whale are not tools from Home Depot. They have the customary dowel handles of hoes and shovels, but each is tipped with rounded metal blades, some with pointed tips like scythes, others round and symmetrical like ulus. Even with the ease that modern technology provides, the hard work of spotting and landing the whale, then cutting and loading the meat still remains.

And now, of course, the Department of Fish and Game keeps track of the whole hunt. Though the Inupiat have hunted bowhead whales for over 2,000 years, though Barrow and other subsistence whaling communities have an enormous stake in the health of the bowhead whale, the International Whaling Commission has been keeping its nose in their business since the mid-1970s, when it placed a ban on Inupiat whale harvesting. In response to the ban, Native Alaskans formed the Alaska Eskimo Whaling Commission, to work toward compromise. Now the Inupiat work in conjunction with biologists like Craig to learn more about the stock of bowhead whales, and each season they set a limit on the harvest. Watching Craig and his colleagues at work, I saw that the scientists and whaling crews have a friendly relationship. Whaling captains contact the scientists once they've landed a whale. Then it is the scientists' responsibility to get to the camp in time to take measurements, samples, and photographs. Afterward, the scientists and the whaling crew eat *unullaq* together, celebrating in the successful hunt.

While I visited Barrow, I sensed a spirit of joy and expectancy. I can only compare it to harvest time in rural Minnesota, my home state. Barrow's high school practically shuts down during whaling season, explained Jeremy, because the kids must be ready to help with whales if a family member, a neighbor, or a friend takes one. At the grocery store, women collect boxes for hauling the muktuk back to town. They stockpile coffee, Styrofoam cups, and food to cook at their whaling camp. Everyone carries a VHF radio, Barrow's version of the cell phone. Word spreads quickly when whales are landed, and workers gather to help haul and clean the kill.

For our second full day, Jeremy arranged a dogsled ride for us with Geoff, a friend of his who keeps a team for travel and sport. When we got to Geoff's house, however, his wife, Marie, told us that her whaling captain brother had just landed a whale. She bubbled with joy. This was his first year as a captain, she told us, his first whale!

The dogsled ride could wait. I hitched a ride with Geoff and Marie; Jeremy and Toby followed behind. Geoff pulled a long, wooden sled behind his snowmachine. Marie stood at its far end, her fur-lined *parky* hood flying in the wind. I sat in the sled and hung onto its plywood edges when we bumped over chunks of ice in the path.

On our way, we got lost among the many tracks leading to different camps. Geoff kept stopping to radio the crew and ask for directions. We couldn't see more than a hundred feet in any direction because huge chunks of ice blocked our view. Yet when we drove on to a next stop, everything looked the same, ice and snow for miles. Geoff asked, "Do you turn left or right at the first fork?"

The voice on the other end of the radio asked, "Did you hit the Christmas tree yet?" We thought he was kidding, until we actually passed a small evergreen tree, planted in the snow as if it actually grew there. Everyone laughed, and I didn't get the joke until I realized that there are no trees in Barrow. Permafrost does not allow landscaping.

When we arrived, the crew was still in boats, towing the whale toward shore. Two crewmen stood on shore and pulled small ropes threaded through the points of the tail fin. Once the fin emerged, they attached the block and tackle's wide yellow strap around its base. As the line of people grew along the yellow ropes of the block and tackle, I stayed out of the way, ready to take photos of the whale emerging from the water. I stood near two Inupiat women, watching, just about to snap my last photo, when the whaling captain spotted us. He yelled, in a deep authoritative voice, "You didn't come here to take pictures! Get in line and help!" I felt like a child, castigated in public, ashamed. I really did have the best of intentions: staying out of the way, not intruding on the communal activity. *This isn't my culture,* I thought. *It would be rude to jump in and act like I belonged.*

But I had it all wrong. There was work to be done. I looked to my left and made an embarrassed face at the women who were scolded with me. Their bronzed faces mirrored my own. We scrambled to fall in line and help. The whaling captain and his crew stood near the waterline, watching the whale come up. Someone screamed for people to run to the next camp over, to have them come help.

The process reminded me of what I know about giving birth. There is pushing, and in between pushes, there are small breaks to check the position of the emerging infant, to verify that the mother is O.K. Then the pushing resumes. Bringing a whale to shore, this midwifery of death for the mammal and life for the village, happened in these same fits and starts. The captain would yell "PULL!" and the message would get relayed, telephone-style to the end of the line, as people along the way yelled in agreement, "PULL!" We all pulled, some people slipping and falling on the ice, and then the captain ordered "STOP!" and his command would come back to us through the series of intermediate yellers, and we would all let go of the rope, readjust our hats and mittens, and bounce up and down to keep warm. The whaling crew would readjust the position of the whale's body, to make sure it was landed correctly. And again, the message to pull.

The whale slowly emerged from the ocean in a long, graceful tube of soot-toned flesh, its fins easing out from its sides like wings. I couldn't actually see it come forth, standing so far down the rope line, but I could feel it emerge in my hands through the rope, in a vibration of beckoning; it answered our communal call, sliding gracefully out of its watery home. Once the final pull had secured the whale far enough onto the pack ice, our tug of war complete, the whaling crew ran joyfully to take photos with their catch. They stood, proud men in white *parkys*, baring shocks of white teeth against caramel skin.

I felt an urge to run my hand down the length of the whale's body, to caress the newly departed, to thank the gentle creature for offering itself to us humans. Before I could move from my place in line, a woman from the whaling camp nearby came to offer a huge stew pot full of *unalluq*, a gesture not only of nourishing calories to help the crew as it dismantled the new catch, but of community between whale camps, an acknowledgement of the shared goal of food for the entire village.

This time, Jeremy, Toby, and I each took a slice, and toasted one another gaily, banging our *unalluq* against each other's in a salute of friendship, of commonality, of a job well done. It tasted sweet and salty, like warm sushi. Marie and Geoff, Craig, and the other scientists celebrated with us, the warmth from our smiles almost palpable enough to melt the ice from our eyelashes.

Heather Villars was born and raised in the flat, featureless Midwestern United States. Upon relocating to the snow-capped allure of Anchorage, Alaska, where she recently completed an M.F.A. in creative writing, her mouth hung open for several months. She has since grown used to writing under the mountains' startling presence, but tries daily to remind herself of their treasure.

NILES ELLIOT GOLDSTEIN

★ ★ ★

In God's Back Yard

A young rabbi finds renewal on a dog sled's runners.

AFTER MY FIRST YEAR AS A RABBI, AS WELL AS MY FIRST experiences working in the professional Jewish world, I felt a deep need to return to Alaska. I wanted to reignite the spark that had originally propelled me into rabbinical school with so much zeal and idealism. As a young rabbi I had longed for a religious community that was bursting with pride, joy, passion, and vitality, that held as its eternal mandate the loving commitment to a sacred covenant between its members and God. What I discovered was something else: a cult of woe, a reactionary community that seemed to be obsessed with its own degeneration, with intermarriage, assimilation, anti-Semitism, and the Holocaust. I was losing my faith.

I had to get away, to return to a place where I could once again find inspiration for my soul. I made arrangements to fly to Fairbanks, where I had worked for a summer three years before as the student rabbi for the town's Jewish community. My friend Dave had been working up there as an environmentalist and wilderness guide and raised dogs on the side. We decided to meet in the early spring for a dogsledding adventure north of the Arctic Circle, our second mushing trip together. I spent most of March trying to find the appropriate gear in Manhattan for a trip to the Last Frontier, but by the end of the month I had everything pieced together and I'd arrived in Fairbanks. Dave met me at the airport in his rusty shambles of a truck, and within fifteen minutes we were back at his cabin, unloading the sleds from the vehicle's roof and hooking up our dogs to their tug lines for a practice run through the dark and icy night.

It had been two years since I'd last stood on a dogsled. On our first trip, a five-day foray into a starkly beautiful area known as the White Mountains, everything was a challenge for me: putting harnesses on the team, learning the verbal commands for my lead dogs, making turns without falling off the sled into the snow. This time most of it came back to me within minutes. It was night, but because I had to be back in New York the following week, we didn't have much time to wait for me to regain my bearings. It had been warm that past week, so by the time we got onto the trails the daytime melt had frozen and they were rock hard. We wore headlamps to make our way through the darkness. Whenever the dogs looked back toward me, their eyes flashed in the beams like blue moons. It took us just half an hour to mush around the outskirts of Fairbanks to Hidden Hill, a small Quaker community where some of Dave's friends lived. They served us fresh salmon and homemade pumpkin pie.

Sated from my meal and anxious to get back to the dogs resting outside, I thanked our hosts and put on my boots. The air that had stung my face during our run to Hidden Hill was refreshing as I walked out of the cabin. (If you dressed warmly enough, the cold months in the Alaskan interior were bearable—unless you had to deal with wind.) Stars filled the sky, an immense swath of blackness. It was a different world from New York. It seemed a more *real* world. A dozen pairs of eyes stared at me silently. My feet crunched into the snow as I walked toward our sleds. Suddenly the dogs erupted into a frenzy of barking and lunging. The vague animal forms grew clearer as my vision adjusted to the night. There were our two teams, thrashing and howling in wild expectation of the trail. I recognized only a few of them from our last trip; Dave had borrowed several of these new dogs for me from a friend....

Mushing through a cold Alaskan night was unlike anything I had ever experienced. The sensation itself, similar to skiing or surfing, is not what is remarkable. It is the *scene*. You stand alone on a sled in darkness. Other than your headlamp, only the moon lights your way through the woods and over the streams and rivers. Frigid wind blasts your face. A team of animals, silenced by their exertions, pulls you forward over snow and ice with a focus that makes it seem as if nothing in the world but running

---

All of us in Alaska think of our state in different and personal ways, but somewhere in most of us there is love, an appreciation, an affection, for the land, for the wild, and for the raw beauty of this frontier. It is what drew many of us here, what keeps us here, what makes us Alaskans. Nothing touches this chord more strongly than sled-dog racing. Something in the sight of the powerful, eager, finely tuned animals mastering the wilderness, touches the romantic in us, expresses so vividly this kinship with the land.

That's why, come March, thousands of us listen for every scrap of information on who is where in the 1,100-mile Iditarod Trail Sled Dog Race from Anchorage to Nome.

—Lew Freedman,
Iditarod Classics

ultimately matters to them. Little matters to you, either, but the moment.

The following day, while Dave took care of some last-minute errands related to our sleds and camping gear, I drove around Fairbanks buying food for our trip. Dave had prepared two long lists for me, one for us and the other for the dogs. First I went to the supermarket. I got the basics for a cold weather journey: rice, beans, butter, cheese, meat (for him), fish (for me), and crackers that were hard enough to survive the rough and tumble of the trail. We would have to pack all of it, labeled by type of meal, tightly into our sleds. They would double as freezers. Liquor was a trickier issue. Beer did not have enough alcohol content to hold its liquid form, so unless we wanted to drink ice we had to purchase harder stuff. The spirit we settled on for our Arctic excursion was rum. When I was finished gathering our supplies, I concentrated on our teams. Dog food had never seemed so complicated. Because of all the energy the dogs would burn during the trip, Dave spelled out very carefully what I needed to buy in order to replenish them: beef fat (for a quick jolt of energy), dry dog food (to be mixed with warm water to help rehydrate them), and several fifty-pound sacks of ground and compressed meat with a bold label on them that read CONDEMNED CHICKEN CARCASSES: NOT FIT FOR HUMAN CONSUMPTION.

After my tasks were completed, I had a couple of spare hours to see some of my former congregants. I'd been in touch by telephone with a few of them over the past three years. I visited Leah and Mike, who proudly showed me their new house—and I used a flush toilet for what I knew would be the last time in a week. I also met with Richard and Margot, who gave me a tour of the very first synagogue the Jews of Fairbanks had owned, which they had just bought (when I lived there in 1992, we held our Sabbath services in the chapel at Fort Wainwright, the town's sprawling army base). Richard wept as he walked me through the building. While it was nice to catch up with old friends, seeing everybody again felt somewhat strange. The context was completely different. In my time of need, I wasn't turning to the Jewish community for spiritual revitalization. I was turning to the wilderness....

We left Fairbanks the next day. After several more hours of loading a dozen barking dogs one at a time into the transport track above the truck, and then hauling and securing our two sleds over that, we headed north up the Dalton Highway, a relatively narrow road that extends all the way to the hulking oil-drilling rigs at Prudhoe Bay on the edge of the Arctic Ocean. Our destination was the Brooks Range, a majestic wedge of mountains that cuts across the northern half of the state. In three or four hours we reached the Yukon River and stopped for coffee at a small truck stop run by an elderly Christian fundamentalist couple. The only traffic we saw was an occasional tractor-trailer on its way to or returning from Prudhoe Bay. The air was much colder than it had been in Fairbanks, so we both put on additional layers of clothing and checked on the dogs, who looked out at us from their wooden cubicles (which they had begun to gnaw apart). As we drove on into the night, ice fog began to set in, frosting the tundra and imparting a ghostly hue to the landscape. Near midnight, over ten hours since we had left Fairbanks, we pulled into another truck stop at the "town" of Coldfoot. The place was a genuine frontier outpost: miners, trappers, and other assorted adventurers mingling over burgers and beer. Dave and I ate dinner, bought a new headlight for our vehicle, and got directions to Nolan, an active gold-mining camp about thirty miles north of Coldfoot and the site of our starting point....

It was numbingly cold when we reached Nolan. I tried
(and failed) to sleep in the truck's enclosed cabin, while Dave
slept outside underneath the transport track. My sleeping bag
did little to protect me from the frigid air, which turned my
breath into white smoke: the truck's windows frosted over
within minutes. Our dogs slept quietly to the side of the road,
each one attached by his collar to the picket line that linked
them together. At dawn we got started. Before we had a
chance to put food into their metal bowls, the dogs started
barking. Endlessly. Only their breakfast shut them up, which
gave us a few minutes of relative silence to take down our
sleds, check the gear, and move our truck into a more secluded
area. The trailhead was on the outskirts of the camp, a few
hundred yards away from us. Our plan was to make a giant
loop through a section of the Brooks Range and return to
Nolan and the truck in a week.

After I gathered the bowls, Dave and I put on the dogs' harnesses and hooked them up to their respective sleds. They
were fresh and excited—so excited that they lunged forward
and jumped into the air in anticipation of the run. Sled dogs
like it very cold, so they are at their strongest early in the
morning. I learned that the hard way. When we were both
safely on our sleds, we removed our anchors and raced down
the road. Dave led the way to the trailhead and called for his
lead dogs to turn right into the park. My team followed. We
careened off the road, barreled ahead another couple of hundred yards over taiga, then entered a wooded area. As the dogs
dragged me helplessly around a spruce, my sled began to tilt
precariously onto one runner. Suddenly it flipped over, and I
skidded face first into a pile of snow. Luckily I had held on to
the sled with one hand, and the weight of my body forced the
team to come to a stop (if I hadn't, they most likely would

have sprinted on without me for miles). The dogs turned back and stared at me with expressions of befuddlement.

We were mushing in Gates of the Arctic National Park, and the Brooks Range was just one region within it. Dave had selected one of the more remote and spectacular chunks of Arctic Alaska for our trip, but after thirty minutes of mushing we ran into a major challenge. Because we had decided to make this trip in early spring, we knew that we risked encountering overflow, even in the colder areas north of the Arctic Circle. Overflow occurs when, due to rising temperatures, the upper layers of ice melt over their frozen foundation, leaving up to several feet of slush hidden beneath a paper-thin, icy veneer. [Overflow may also occur on rivers throughout the winter, when water flows through a hole or crack in the ice onto the ice's surface.] What looks like a frozen river can quickly crack under the weight of a sled, ruining supplies and sometimes drowning dogs.

Wiseman Creek, which we needed to cross at several points during the first few days of our trip, was filled with overflow. It was not very deep, but because no other mushers had used our route in several weeks, we had no idea about the present condition of the creeks and rivers ahead. That left us with two alternatives. Either scrap the entire trip and return to Fairbanks or push on with the clear understanding that we were taking our chances, that when we tried to make our way back to the truck the following week we might be stranded. Dave was ambivalent. He wanted to mush, but he was worried that we could run into trouble or that I could be trapped and miss my flight back to New York. He left the decision to me. I thought about why I was there, about my self-imposed mission. And when I reflected on just what was at stake for me, the decision was easy. We moved on.

Overflow turned out to be a constant annoyance but never bad enough to force us to turn around. In the early mornings the upper layers of ice were sufficiently hard to support our sleds, but by noon they developed the consistency of a Slurpee. The two of us had to run (or often, like our teams, slip and slide) along the side of our sleds; our weight, coupled with the drag caused by the overflow, would have made the sleds too heavy for the dogs to pull. It was grueling work, and we had to repeat it whenever we had to travel over hills. At the end of each day my arms had new bruises from breaking so many falls, and my boots were usually soaked with water. The routine was the same whenever we made camp. Remove the harnesses and connect the dogs to the picket line, away from the wind (though they are comfortable in temperatures well below zero, a bitter wind can harm them). Look for dead wood to saw into small pieces for cooking and heating. Melt snow for drinking water. Feed the teams. Set up the tent. Eat dinner, drink some rum, try to go to sleep. The mornings were miserable, with temperatures five or ten degrees below zero, even at the beginning of April. Any piece of clothing that so much as brushed against water the day before was frozen stiff when we woke up. My bare fingers were so numb (our heavy mittens were too awkward and cumbersome for the task) that hooking our dogs back onto their tug lines took ten times as long as it did later in the afternoon. But after the teams were taken care of and we'd had our hot coffee, the rush of air that refreshed my face as our sleds raced out of camp made the morning's travails a distant memory.

The strenuousness of our trip made reflection difficult, but there were moments when I was mushing through a valley or over a small inland lake that I was able to absorb the beauty and achieve an almost meditative state. My worries about the Jewish world washed away. My anxiety about feeling out of place as a rabbi didn't seem to matter. I was a child of God in God's back yard, and everything was going to be all right. Taking care of my dogs was like taking care of six screaming babies, but I loved them. Even though their ceaseless barking and fighting with one another often drove me to the point of madness, I trusted my team. They were my lifeline, my link to the outside world. And I owed them my gratitude and respect. I also owed Dave. Despite all my adventures, my encounters with jail cells, grizzly bears, and mountaintops, deep down I was just another Jewish intellectual, and I knew it. Once again I was dependent on others for my well-being. I could not have made the trip without the guidance and experience of my friend. And neither of us could have made it without our canine companions.

Several days into our trip, on a Friday night, I

Suddenly, the rowdy sounds of the pandemonium drop away as the dogs burst free, you and they adrenaline-pumped partners sailing through a snow-filled forest, no colors but the white of the snow, the shadowy green spruce, and the blue sky brightening your way through the dark woods. Today, my thirteen-year-old daughter Devon rides in the basket, entranced with the speed, the beauty, the strength of those sweet, sturdy dogs drawing her further into the unknown. I haven't ridden behind a dog sled in twenty years, but a familiar thrill surges through my veins as my heart picks up the steady rhythm of the dogs' gait, my body aligning with the curves of the trail in a fluid rolling motion that sends the balky sled arcing smoothly along its icy trajectory.

"Do you see, Devon?" I ask my daughter. "Do you understand why I had to come back to Alaska?"

—Pat O'Hara,
"The Great, Big, Broad
Land Way Up Yonder"

tried to observe a makeshift Sabbath beneath the Endicott
Mountains. Judaism in the rough. I took out two candles that
I had packed back in New York and stuck them into the snow.
Since it was spring, the midnight sun had just begun to
emerge, and our campsite was draped with long shadows. I lit
the candles. After I said the appropriate blessings, Dave and I
ate dinner and talked in the tent about wild country and wild
women until it grew dark outside. Cody, my wheel dog and
Dave's pet, was with us, lying between our two sleeping bags.
Dave was ready to go to bed. I told him that I wanted to go
for a walk down to the river but that he should go ahead and
put out the fire. The dogs, silent but watching my every step,
were curled into balls to insulate themselves from the cold. I
was cold, too. And tired. I had been so busy dealing with the
day-to-day chores of handling my team that I had forgotten
what it was that had brought me to this spot on the Earth. But
as I stood there alone on the ice and looked over the peaks
into the purple sky, I remembered.

The dark night erupted before me. Waves of white-green
light scrolled across the heavens. It was the aurora borealis, the
Northern Lights. I had seen them before, years ago, but never
from this perspective. They seemed to be directly in front of
me, hovering over the mountains. Almost beckoning.
Pythagoras, the early Greek philosopher, claimed that the
cosmos itself could speak, that the motion of the celestial
bodies was so great that the reason humans could not hear it
was that it had been with us from the moment of birth and
we could not distinguish it from its opposite, silence. Yet I
swear I heard something that night. Not with my ears. But
with some other part of myself. I watched the pulsations of
light the way you watch panthers in the wild, with awe and
amazement. I knew then and there that I was in the presence

of something untamed and untamable. Transcendent and mysterious. Something that warmed my blood and made my soul tremble with new life.

I'd found what I had come for. Alaska was my Sinai.

Niles Elliot Goldstein is the founding rabbi of The New Shul in Greenwich Village, New York. He was the voice behind "Ask the Rabbi" on the Microsoft Network, is the National Jewish Chaplain for the Federal Law Enforcement Officers Association, and is the author or editor of numerous books, including God at the Edge: Searching for the Divine in Uncomfortable and Unexpected Places, *from which this story was excerpted.*

✦ ✦ ✦

Seeking Paradise

*The rough beauty of an alpine fishing trip
soothes a family's growing pains.*

I CHOSE THIS REMOTE, APOSTROPHE-SHAPED LAKE, AND the cabin that shares its name, just because I liked the sound of it: Upper Paradise Lake. *Paradise.*

After a long, difficult pregnancy and three weeks of sleepless new-baby nights, I needed some paradise. I'd heard how easy the fishing was up here: friends visiting this same Forest Service cabin had caught and released 500 grayling in a weekend. I'd never caught a fish in Alaska, but surely I would manage to catch one here. I would hold it firmly in one hand, and marvel at its iridescent, sail-shaped fin, and feel a part of the alpine wilderness. I would feel strong and able; whole again.

There is also a Forest Service cabin at nearby Lower Paradise Lake, but that didn't sound as good. Upper versus Lower is simply a geographical distinction, but the terms reminded me of Dante's levels of heaven and hell. And if I was going to fly my nineteen-day-old baby, mischievous four-year-old son, and unhealed body into heaven for a weekend, I wanted a suite in heaven's top floor, not in the lobby.

We drove to Moose Pass, two hours south of Anchorage. The highway ends just south of Moose Pass, in Seward. But this was not the end of our trip, because any serious summer road trip in Alaska must extend far beyond roads. To escape, to feel that traveler's high of pushing beyond what one knows—sometimes toward what one fears—one must take to the air.

At the shore of Trail Lake, our pilot and a teen-aged assistant loaded our luggage into the floatplane that would take us to the cabin. They studiously avoided seeing the final item left on the dock: a bassinet-like infant carrier. Beneath the hood peered two small round eyes, as grayish-green as the glacial lake surrounding us.

Finally, the pilot faced me squarely. "Baby's going, too?"

"Yep."

The pilot lifted his eyebrows but said nothing more, and then helped me straddle a pontoon and heft my baby daughter Tziporah and her carrier into the plane. There wasn't enough room. My husband Brian and the pilot occupied the front two seats. Aryeh and I squeezed into the rear two. The narrow tail of the plane was packed with fishing rods, bedrolls, backpacks, and duffel bags. Finally, I managed to make space at my feet, jamming the infant carrier with all my strength, wedging it tightly behind my husband's seat. I waited, tensely, expecting the pilot—or the baby—to protest.

Instead, the floatplane's engines roared to life, interrupting my fretting. Our earphones crackled with static. Even Aryeh had a pair, the earphones as big as coconut halves, clamped to either side of his head.

"You doing all right?" I asked him.

His posture was so stiff with excitement that he barely turned his head to answer me. "Roger," he said, beaming, pressing his lips together to force a swallow.

I'd spent the morning snapping at my son, rushing him into the car, reprimanding him when he poked at his newborn sister or woke her up from a nap. We'd all been sleep-deprived and crabby for the drive to Moose Pass. It was a relief to see him happy at last.

And then we were off. The small airport lake fell away and a misty, emerald-colored valley spread out beneath us. Within minutes, we could see no towns or roads, only more milky-green lakes and gray, braiding streams. The plane tilted toward the mountains, fighting blasts of wind. Out the window, just over my son's head, narrow waterfalls spilled down the steep flanks of glaciated peaks. We passed close enough to see animal tracks stitched into the snow on nearly vertical mountainsides. And then close enough to see mountainsides where there were no footprints—no signs of life, past or present. We'd flown only ten minutes, but this was farther from roads and trails than I'd ever been in Alaska.

At Upper Paradise Lake, our pilot wordlessly unloaded our gear with disconcerting speed, dumping our bags on a narrow gravel beach next to an overturned rowboat. Then he hopped back into the cockpit, started up the engine and sped away from shore. The plane's roar softened to a whine, and the whine to silence, interrupted only by the asthmatic huffs of an unsteady northerly wind. Then we were alone—more alone than I'd ever felt on the Kenai Peninsula, since we knew the terrain was too difficult for bushwhacking back to civilization if the plane didn't return, if an appendix burst, or if someone dropped an axe on his foot. We had no radio, no way to communicate with the outside world. That was the cabin's chief flaw, and also its allure.

The one-room log cabin that would be our home for three days was crafted of dark-stained timbers, fitted together like aged Lincoln Logs. It sat forty feet from the lake shore, surrounded by wind-stunted dwarf evergreens and shrubs. Songbirds darted over the shrubs, tossed about by gusts. Snow-streaked peaks rose in all directions, blending into the grayish-white sky. The largest, just in front of us, appeared to lean to one side. The soft moan of a distant waterfall, spilling down the peak's face was occasionally audible over the wind, giving the mountain a voice.

The calendar said July, but at this elevation, it felt like spring: temps in the low fifties, wind smelling of snow. I hurried to the cabin

> From the Panhandle to Interior Alaska, public-use cabins can be rented from the Forest Service, the Bureau of Land Management, Alaska State Parks, the National Park Service, and the U.S. Fish and Wildlife Service. Modest prices ($15 to $75 per night) make these cabins among the best vacation bargains in Alaska.
>
> —Bill Sherwonit

to get my bearings and nurse the baby. As soon as I lay down on the hard, wooden bunk, tiredness washed over me. I had intended to rush right back out and explore our surroundings, but then my uterus clenched suddenly, like a flower closing its petals for the night. With Aryeh, pregnancy had been easier, and I had healed so much faster. This time around, I felt like all my organs had dropped about six inches, like my insides were only barely resisting the pull of gravity. I hurt worse now than the morning after I'd given birth.

The baby fussed, and I tried to bundle her more tightly against the unheated cabin's chill. If I could just settle her down, I thought, I could sleep. Brian started building a fire in the wood stove, but the heat didn't spread quickly and I felt cold. All my muscles ached. Aryeh kept running around the cabin, and then veering toward the baby and me with a

menacing, maniacal giggle. "Touch, touch!" he'd screech, causing Tziporah's sleepy, lavender-veined eyelids to jerk open
nervously.

"Be quiet!" I yelled. "Be gentle!" But my son only giggled
more hysterically.

The baby's nerves were frayed by so much mischievous
noise and poking. So were mine. This had been the problem
at home, too. Why did I think it would be better on the road,
and better yet away from all roads, in a cabin in the Alaska
wilderness? At home, I didn't dare leave Tziporah unattended
for even the thirty seconds it took to leave the living room
and throw away a diaper. Every time I rounded the corner
from the bathroom back into the living room, I would hear a
sound like the bleating of a goat—Tziporah's fragile newborn
wail. Proof that she had been jostled or frightened. And I
would spot Aryeh tugging on the baby's hand, or pushing his
face into hers too roughly, or moving a pillow so that she was
no longer guarded from rolling off the couch.

"Don't you realize you can hurt her?" I'd growl protec-
tively. "Don't you even know what gentle means? Can't you
be sweet to your sister?"

Maybe it's just hardwiring, I told myself, trying to be reasonable. *Maybe little boys can't help it*. But then I'd catch a malig-
nant gleam in my son's eyes. Even when I was doubled over
in pain, he begged for me to pick him up, or to run to another
room and fetch him something. *No compassion*, I thought. And:
Where did we go wrong? And even when Tziporah was crying,
Aryeh giggled and shrieked louder, delighted by the chaos,
though he said over and over and over that he loved her. We'd
started a reward chart on the refrigerator: one sticker for every
day Aryeh didn't actively menace his sister. But he couldn't
make it through a single day. He couldn't earn a single sticker.
I agonized: Hadn't we taught him that people can hurt, that

living things can hurt, that he is not at the center of the universe, the only thing that wants or feels?

At home, there was simply no escape from Aryeh's volume and motion—his tireless pinball-like trajectories, which made every room seem too small. Here in this dark log cabin in the Kenai mountains, there was only less room, fewer places to hide. But I hoped the simplicity of this primitive lodging, and this location—no phone or email, no visitors at the door every hour, no work demands—might help us sort things out.

Within an hour of our arrival, the wood stove was popping and hissing, a steamy warmth was saturating the cabin, and the baby had faded into slumber, wrapped in a tight cocoon of blankets. I urged Brian to take Aryeh outside so that I could nap, too.

Sleep rejuvenated me. When Aryeh pushed open the cabin door two hours later, cheeks patchy red from the cold, I couldn't even imagine why I'd felt impatient or angry, today or ever. He stood in the open doorway—gusts of wind whipping his blond curls—chattering about fish and grayling and how he'd caught one and sixteen inches and could I come down to the rowboat to see.

I wrapped myself and Tziporah in more layers and we all headed out again in the rowboat. Brian and Aryeh had caught three grayling, enough for dinner, but now I'd get my chance to catch a fish, an easy fish, my first fish. Brian rowed us north along the shore, toward the leaning mountain and the waterfall.

"Can we stop and cast here?" I asked.

"Wait," Brian said. "There's more of a cove up there. It will be better."

The wind plastered my bangs against my eyes, my gloved hands were cold already, and I knew the baby might not tolerate this outing much longer. Minutes passed as Brian slowly worked the oars, battling small, choppy waves. The rowboat seemed to stand still. The waterfall at the head of the lake was no closer. The wind battered our ears and snatched at our words.

"How about here?" I called out.

"This isn't a good spot," Aryeh said, mimicking his father. "Around the curve. I know how to do it. I'll show you."

Finally, we gave up and set the anchor along a straight stretch of scrubby shore, and I took one of the two rods we'd brought. I tried to remember how this worked, how far back to pull my arm, how to avoid nailing innocent bystanders with a sharp hook.

I cast once, enjoying the simple feel of it, and the sound— a sharp whizzing through the air before the satisfying *pa-lunkkk* of lure hitting water. I cast again. No bites yet. Then Aryeh started reaching. "Can I try? I know how. Can I try?"

"Let Mom do it," Brian said. "You caught your fish already."

I tried to cast again, but Aryeh kept reaching, waving and pulling at the air. He insisted on using the smaller rod I was holding.

"Just one more time," I said. "Let me." But then, worrying as he reached toward me that he might stand up in the boat and fall into the icy water, I relented, handing the rod to him.

Brian, from his seat in the stern, reached precariously over the bundled baby to hand me the other rod. But Aryeh and I were seated too close together to both cast. I needed all my attention to duck and throw my gloved hands up to my face every time Aryeh's hook came arcing wildly through the air.

"Maybe this just isn't a good spot," Brian said finally, as the wind pushed at us. The baby's face looked pink and chapped from the wind. Red pinpricks were appearing around her al-most-invisible hairline as she slept—tiny bites from bugs we'd never seen.

"That's all right," I said. "I'm cold, too. Forget it."

Next day, I was determined to spend more time outside, and to get an earlier start fishing. We spent part of the morning taking photos, wandering a small bog behind the cabin, and exploring the lake shore. About a foot back from the waterline there was a uniform band of gnarled, pinkie-sized, weathered wood pieces, like a bathtub ring of driftwood. Just beyond this were patches of knee-high grass, sprinkled with wildflowers so small and delicate that we hadn't noticed them the day before. But on hands and knees, they came into view. I counted a dozen kinds

---

It is July, but we are in the Arctic and it snowed overnight. We are camped on a gravel beach, just above sea ice jumbled along the shore. My son, age five, wakes in the frigid tent. "I have to pee, Mom." "Put your parka on," I say sleepily. "No," he replies automatically. I wait, knowing the Arctic is about to teach him a lesson no words of mine can. By the time he undoes the double canvas doors of the tent, stands outside briefly, comes back, does up the doors, and crawls into his sleeping bag, his small body is practically blue with cold. But he's never done that again.

—Ellen Bielawski

---

within a few yards: columbines and lupines, geranium and Jacob's ladder, cinquefoil and monkshood. Of all these, my favorites were the palest blue forget-me-nots, bending and blinking in the wind.

I was marveling at this miniature alpine world of fragile beauty when I looked up and caught sight of Aryeh methodically sprinkling sand and gravel on top of his baby sister's head. In two breathless strides I was next to them, seething. Tziporah looked up at me with round, green-eyed innocence, staring up at her brother, then staring up at me. Her long eye-lashes were covered with sand—it was a miracle none of the dust had blown into the eyes themselves—and there were tiny bits of gravel in the corners of her eyes, just above the pink rims. I gasped and stuttered and swept a hand over her face, which started her crying, since now the sand was in her eyes. In one motion I swept Tziporah into my arms and stomped away, fuming.

"I can't believe him!" I ranted to Brian for the next few minutes. "He's hurting her! He doesn't care about anyone or anything!"

Brian smiled. "He'll learn. He'll figure it out."

"I don't think so," I said, rocking the baby back and forth. I soothed the baby and Brian soothed me, and finally we called to Aryeh and all got into the rowboat.

"Let me have the stern this time," I grunted.

With my back to my family, I took the oars. I rowed as hard as I could, enjoying the work of it, the strain against my shoulders and biceps. Never mind my wasted body from the stomach down; my shoulders and back were still strong. Stronger, even. I pulled hard, exhaling roughly, pushing my lips together, toiling against the wind. We moved slowly along the shore, past rounded humps of glacier-scoured bedrock, and more stunted spruce trees, bent into gnarled bonsai shapes.

For every three rows I had to correct our course with a one-oared row on the right side. I liked the rhythm, the sheer effort of it, with no one to see my contorted face as I strained and pulled. Row, row, row; correction. *This is the best part of the trip,* I told myself. *Who cares about fish anyway?* Row, row, row; correction. We had another day until the floatplane came. Maybe I'd just spend it rowing.

Finally, we rounded a small peninsula and we were in a

protected cove, where the water was clearer and smoother, with views of deeply scored glaciers overhead, spilling from the encircling mountains. We could hear rushing water. We rowed a few yards more and anchored just in front of the stream, where we could see the water quicken and funnel around a bend, draining the lake. Our anchored rowboat swung lazily around its tether, pulled by the stream, and we could imagine fish swimming under and around us, dancing in the same cold currents.

Brian cast. Immediately, he pulled a grayling into the boat, slipped the hook out of its mouth and then released it. He cast again. Another catch. Another effortless release. Aryeh was squirming in his seat. So was I.

"Hand me a rod!" I called out. "Let me try!"

On my first cast, I felt a gentle tug at the end of the line. On my second, I felt a tug again, but this time it kept pulling. I reeled the fish in, and it came easily, it's sail-like fin slicing and sparkling through the water. With a few more reels, I lifted the fish into the air. I pawed at its thrashing body, suspended from my line, and pulled the fish down into my lap. It was small, maybe eleven or twelve inches.

"Too small to keep," I announced, trying to sound nonchalant. Brian handed me his needle-nosed pliers while Aryeh twisted and jumped in his seat.

I still couldn't believe my luck. I alternately smiled and winced, breathing fast, trying inexpertly to work the hook out from where it was firmly embedded. Two of the hook's three barbs had pierced the grayling's delicate mouth, a tiny, smooth, muscle ring, opening into a pink cavern. I tried to be matter-of-fact, digging the pliers into the mouth, trying to do it one fearless motion. But time passed, and decisiveness turned into hesitant surgery.

"Darn it," I muttered.

"What? What?" Aryeh demanded, trying to sit higher in his seat and peer over my shoulder.

"Nothing, it's just…not working."

I went after one barb, then the other. The mouth tore. The fish fought the clutch of my hand. I winced and tried again.

"Are you getting it out?" Aryeh asked.

"Almost," I said. But I wasn't.

My heart raced along with the grayling's. I was shocked to notice that I could feel its pulse, through my glove, against the palm of my hand. Looking down, toward the steady thrum, I noticed that in my excitement, I had been squeezing too hard. On the black cotton palm of my glove, there was a rainbow of sequins—fish scales, rubbed off the side of this long-suffering fish. I stared at this for a long moment. And then I stared at the grayling, this torpedo-shaped, speckled tube of flesh and blood, its once-beautiful fin now collapsed against its body, its iridescence fading.

"It's not working," I said. "I think I'll have to kill it."

Aryeh shrieked: "Don't kill it!"

But this reaction didn't make sense. Why should he have cared? He and Brian had caught three fish yesterday. They'd killed those fish, too, but evidently more swiftly.

I turned the pliers around, intending to use the red, rubberized handle to deliver a solid knock on the grayling's skull. But my grasp slipped, and the pliers delivered only a timid thump. The grayling started thrashing even more. The violence of all this startled me. The casting and reeling had been so satisfying, and now this part was clumsy and confusing and awful. And what about the part that I'd imagined for weeks: where I would just hold the fish, and feel happy, and able, and whole?

"I've got to do it," I told Aryeh. "It's bleeding."

"It's bleeding!" he shouted back, panicking now. "Don't kill it, Mom! Don't kill it!"

"Oh, for heaven's sake."

All this had happened in two minutes, maybe three, but it felt like forever. Now I rested for a moment, staring at the still-thrumming fish in my palm, and at the red, rubberized pliers handle.

Brian was silent. Aryeh hadn't spoken since his last shriek. I didn't want to raise the pliers again. Everyone was waiting. I felt suddenly heavier, bolted to the seat of the rowboat, and weak.

Then Aryeh spoke up, his voice an octave lower, steady and reassuring. "If it's hurt, kill it," he said. "We'll just have to keep it."

His switch from panic to smooth calm was so sudden that it startled me.

"That's O.K., Mom," he said again. "It's bleeding. Kill it. Go ahead."

And at that moment, I stopped worrying. At that moment, for a moment, I knew that Aryeh understood more than I'd ever given him credit for: about gentleness, and violence, and the subtleties of both. I'd misjudged him. I'd let my own body's wounds—the cramps, my exhaustion—color a whole weekend needlessly red and raw. *Tziporah will be safe with her brother,* I told myself. We'll all keep learning from each other.

I raised the pliers more forcefully this time, and delivered a death blow. Then I set down the grayling in the blue-gray bottom of the boat, just inches from Tziporah, sleeping in her blanket cocoon. And I sat with the rod in my lap and stared out at the lake. Behind me I heard the gentle whir and dunk of Brian casting again, and then Aryeh taking a turn with Brian's rod.

"Are you feeling sad for the fish?" Aryeh asked finally, addressing my back.

"I am," I said, not turning around, not wanting him to see my wet eyes and cheeks. "Isn't that strange?"

It didn't seem right bringing this too-small grayling back to camp, with its missing scales and mangled mouth. I felt some pride for having caught a fish, my first Alaska fish, but I didn't want to eat this one, though I knew it would be a waste not to.

Suddenly, an eagle appeared in front of us. It spread its wings, lowering itself daintily into the tip-top branch of a skinny spruce tree guarding the stream's mouth. I watched it, and it watched us.

Then unexpectedly, I stood up in the rowboat, surprising even myself, and with all my strength lobbed my dead grayling into the air. The eagle swooped as the grayling arced and splashed down into the water. But the eagle stayed on course, and just as the lake's riffled surface closed over the grayling, the eagle's talons splashed down into the water, spearing it. The bird rose and circled us, wagging the grayling over our heads. It landed on the lake shore, just beyond a small rise, to eat the sacrifice in seclusion.

"Thank you," I mouthed toward the eagle, for having removed this indelicate reminder of my rough, ungraceful errors.

And then, a little louder, to myself: "O.K., O.K. All right. O.K., O.K. All right," the same rhythm as casting and reeling, or watching a child grow up, or rowing a boat, making a few corrections here and there to stay on course.

Andromeda Romano-Lax is a co-editor of this book and the author of several books, including Searching for Steinbeck on the Sea of Cortez: A Makeshift Expedition Along Baja's Desert Coast.

PHILIP CAPUTO

✶

The Last Road North

*A father and son seek "the true wild" on a drive
through the Arctic. What they discover is both
frightening and exhilarating.*

WE WERE TWENTY MILES NORTH OF THE ARCTIC CIRCLE
and alone on the *Jim River*, three of us floating on one-man
rafts under a sun that never set. Tony Oswald, a photographer
and former Alaskan fishing guide, was in the lead, my twenty-
two-year-old son, Marc, was behind him, and I, feeling the
miles we had rowed as well as the effects of the late hour,
brought up the rear. If I had judged the time by the sky, I
would have said it was late afternoon, but my watch told me
it was midnight. We'd been on the river for more than ten
hours, making frequent stops to catch grayling, from gravel
bars littered with driftwood and printed with the tracks of
moose, wolves, and grizzlies. We hadn't seen any bears or
wolves, but we had passed a cow moose and two calves grazing on weeds in a slough. They raised their heads to eye us,
then trotted off with hardly a rustle into a stand of tall, leaning spruce. Every now and then, we'd caught the faint, distant

165

rumble of a truck on the Dalton Highway, the dusty supply road for the Prudhoe Bay oil fields and the Trans-Alaskan pipeline. Otherwise, we hadn't heard a man-made sound nor seen a sign of our own species—not a single boot print.

That was welcome but not surprising. The Jim, a tributary of the Koyukuk River, itself a tributary of the mythic Yukon, flows through a wilderness bigger than California: Arctic Alaska, the last frontier of the state that calls itself the Last Frontier. The nearest human settlements to us were two tiny villages: Coldfoot, thirty-odd miles north on the Dalton, and Bettles, fifty miles to the west.

The trip was a graduation present for Marc, and for me the fulfillment of an old dream. In 1959, when Alaska was granted statehood, I was a restless high-school senior, a bit intoxicated by Jack London and Robert Service. I wanted to quit school to be a fur trapper in the land where, in Service's words, "the mountains are nameless and the rivers all run God-knows-where." I never went, and the dream went into a long hibernation. It was finally awakened by the news that the Dalton Highway had been opened to public traffic.

The highway runs for 414 unpaved miles from its starting point at Livengood, north of Fairbanks, to the town of Deadhorse, near the Arctic Ocean. It was named for James W. Dalton, an oil explorer who played a major role in the discovery of the Prudhoe fields and died in 1977, only three weeks before the last weld on the 800-mile-long pipeline was completed. In those days, the road was restricted to service crews hauling supplies and equipment to Prudhoe Bay. In 1981, a section of it became accessible to the public, and on December 2, 1994, the whole length was opened.

The Dalton is the only major road in Alaska north of the Arctic Circle, a region of some 150,000 square miles. It bridges the Yukon River, climbs the Brooks Range, and crosses the Arctic coastal plain. Along the way, it passes through or near three refuges and a national park whose total area almost equals that of the six New England states combined: the Arctic National Wildlife Refuge and Preserve (19.8 million acres), Gates of the Arctic National Park and Preserve (8.4 million acres), the Yukon Flats National Wildlife Refuge (8.6 million acres), and the Kanuti National Wildlife Refuge, a postage stamp at 1.6 million acres.

Maps now show where Robert Service's rivers run; yet many of them remain nameless, and are still highways for the epic migrations of salmon and Arctic char that grow to twenty pounds. Most of the mountains also remain nameless, and beneath them, caribou wander across fenceless ranges in numbers recalling the tides of bison that once inundated the Great Plains. Above all, there is the grizzly, the incarnation of all that was wild in the Americas before the arrivals of Cortez and the Massachusetts Bay colony. As many as 40,000 range through British Columbia and Alaska; by comparison, only about 1,000 roam the U.S. Rocky Mountains.

I was stirred by the idea of driving a road that is a modern equivalent of the Oregon Trail. Perhaps I would get an idea, however faint, of what America looked and felt like to the pioneers, who called the Rocky Mountain West "the Big Open." Having hiked, camped, canoed, fished, and hunted in many parts of the continental United States for more than half my life, I had come to the melancholy but inescapable conclusion that the Big Open is all but closed. Vast cattle ranges are being carved into ranchettes for refugee Californians. Most "protected" wilderness areas, when they aren't being clear-cut, are becoming wilderness simulacrums—defanged, declawed, domesticated Disneylands, teeming with video-recording tourists.

Even in relatively uncrowded national parks, there are enough bureaucratic regulations to make you consider joining a citizen's militia. You must reserve campsites as if they were hotel rooms. You have to obtain permits. You have to stay on marked trails, and, in some parks, you are not allowed to have ground fires.

John McPhee, in his 1976 classic about Alaska, *Coming into the Country*, observed that our society has "an elemental need for a frontier outlet, a pioneer place to go—important even to those who don't go there…all we have left is Alaska." He was right. At 586,000 square miles, it's so sparsely settled that if its population density were applied to New York City, only 250 people would live in the five boroughs. And one of the biggest, most open parts of Alaska is the Dalton region, where there are no marked trails. In fact, there are virtually no trails of any kind, and no permits are required. You can walk or camp wherever you choose. Of course, there is a yin to that yang. If there are no rangers to hassle you with red tape, neither are there any to pull you out of trouble. No first-aid stations around the bend, few search-and-rescue teams. Suffer a broken leg or some other mishap, and you will have to do what the prospectors and explorers did in the old days: send for help and hope you don't die before it comes.

The isolation and wildness were a little daunting, but they were the reasons we had come to Alaska's far north. There can be no true freedom without wilderness and no true wilderness without freedom, and neither comes free. A toll is levied in sore muscles, sweat, and, occasionally, as we would find out, fear.

Late in June, Marc and I joined Tony and his friend Jennie Chandler in Fairbanks. For the next three days we bought supplies and gear and worked out a rough itinerary, poring over topographic maps in our motel rooms. We would float and fish the Jim and Koyukuk rivers for grayling and salmon, trek across the tundra to photograph caribou and musk ox, and hike the Brooks Range in the footsteps of Robert

Marshall, the naturalist and explorer who had mapped some 12,000 square miles of those mountains in the late 1930s....

We headed north on the Elliott Highway. It was a somber, rainy afternoon, and we were happy to get out of Fairbanks. Urban Alaska, what little there is of it, is remarkably drab and ugly—as if the overwhelming landscape suppresses the human impulse to build things that try to match nature in beauty or stupendousness. Seventy-three miles later, the Elliott ended. Ahead was a small green-and-white sign:

JAMES W. DALTON
HIGHWAY
YUKON RIVER 56
ARCTIC CIRCLE 115
COLDFOOT 175

The Yukon River! The Arctic Circle! Coldfoot! Other names beckoned from farther up the road, some given long ago by gold-fevered prospectors,

My first view of the pipeline was at the Bureau of Land Management's visitor stop north of Fairbanks, where you can pose for photos with the pipeline, read about its history, buy t-shirts and magnets made from chunks of scrap metal (the magnets, not the t-shirts), and become one with the pipeline as much as allowed by federal law and corporate private ownership restrictions. Young wo/man, that pipeline is not a toy! Do not climb on it! Don't even think about climbing on it! Thinking about climbing on the pipeline constitutes Thought Crime #1784-B, and you know who you are! The funny part is that if you get on the Internet and find people's diaries of traveling the haul road—a lot are available—they almost all include a photo of the participants standing on the pipeline at some point. Come get me, coppah! You'll never take me alive!

—Robin Cerwonka, "Paris! Rome! Deadhorse!"

some more recently by oil men, some by Eskimos and Athabascan Indians in a time beyond recorded history. Bonanza Creek. The Sagavanirktok River. The Sagwon Uplands. We were headed up a raw and open road into the Far North's far north.

The rain had stopped by the time we crossed the Yukon on a steel-and-plank bridge, the only span of the river in all the 1,400 miles it flows through Alaska. Half a mile wide and six fathoms deep, gleaming like liquid brass in the evening sun, the river wound westward between high, wooded bluffs toward its meeting with the Bering Sea, where great whales breached and blew.

We fueled up at a ramshackle gas station, where we got a look at two very different types of American traveler. One was a lonesome adventurer: a middle-aged biker whose Harley was so mud-caked it looked like a clay model. He had ridden across most of the Lower 48, up the Alaska Highway, then up to Dalton to Deadhorse, and was heading home to Ohio—a round trip of 8,500 miles. The other type—too many of them—climbed off a Princess Tours bus and walked into a café with the stiff gaits of people who spend too little time using their legs.

The sight of them in their sneakers and bright synthetics got me down. If tour buses plied the Dalton, could it really be called a modern Oregon Trail? Worse yet, could concession stands, RV parks, flush toilets, and Best Westerns be far behind? It was hard to imagine them on the Dalton, but who could have imagined in the 1890s what Yosemite would look like today?

Indeed, the opening of the Dalton has caused some conservationists to worry that it will draw ever more tourists and leave wild places like Gates of the Arctic as crowded and tame as some other national parks. One cause for worry lies in the conflicting mandates federal agencies have over the Dalton region. The Bureau of Land Management (BLM) controls a five-mile-wide "recreation corridor" on either side of the highway and is already drawing up plans to develop visitor facilities and campgrounds. The National Park Service manages Gates of the Arctic, while U.S. Fish and Wildlife oversees the Arctic National Wildlife Refuge, and both are committed to preserving the "unimproved," pristine nature of those areas.

In Fairbanks, I had talked to Dave Mills, the superintendent of Gates of the Arctic, and Steve Ulvi, who manages the Nunamiut Eskimos' subsistence hunting and fishing in the park. Ulvi makes a brief appearance in *Coming into the Country*. McPhee describes him as a "cinematically handsome" man of twenty-three, who was then pioneering near the Canadian border. He's forty-four now, but still as handsome, with pale-blue eyes and an extravagant mustache that gives him the appearance of a gold-rush prospector.

He prefers to describe himself and others like him as "representatives of the landscape, senators for the wilderness." He had told me that park officials hope to maintain Gates of the Arctic as a "black-belt" park, meaning that it is not for the unfit, the unskilled, or the timid.

> No sight or sound or smell or feeling even remotely hinted of men or their creations. It seemed as if time had dropped away a million years and we were back in a primordial world. It was like discovering an unpeopled universe where only the laws of nature held sway.
>
> —Robert Marshall, *Alaska Wilderness: Exploring the Central Brooks Range*

"The idea is to give hikers and campers a chance to feel like Bob Marshall did when he was exploring this country—a sense of discovery and adventure, and of solitude," Ulvi had said. "Gates of the Arctic gets three thousand to five thousand recreational visitors a year. That's less than the number of people who ride the elevator in the Statue of Liberty in a day. We have people who go in there on real expeditions, sometimes for six weeks. We don't need to spend money on visitor facilities. We're at the point in management of this area where Yellowstone might have been in 1900. Hopefully, we've learned from places like Yellowstone how to do things the right way. But now there's this raw road into this incredible wilderness. Open a road and you open a Pandora's box."

Mills, a balding man of medium build, had interjected: "I don't think the road itself is a threat to Gates of the Arctic. It's possible to develop reasonable access, but we hope the BLM manages its corridor as a buffer. If we do this properly, we'll preserve the park's integrity."

I reflected on those comments as we drove northward through mile after mile of taiga and tundra fells, ridges, and hills that occasionally crowded close to the road but mostly opened up and stretched away forever. On the Dalton Highway, all worries about the relentless pressures of modern civilization seemed unfounded. The only visible works of man were the road and the pipeline, zigzagging alongside on five-foot stilts....

By the next day, we were camped on the Jim River at the end of a rough track, about a mile off the Dalton. Nearby were two big beaver ponds, where nesting yellow-legged sandpipers went into noisy panic whenever we approached. The campsite was hard used by bowhunters (hunting with firearms is prohibited within the pipeline corridor, for the obvious reason that a stray bullet could pierce the pipe) and showed it: a fire-ring, a couple of huge cable spools, a table jury-rigged out of scrap lumber. But the frequenting by humans had not affected the wildlife in the area. There were wolf tracks, moose droppings, bear trails. And mosquitoes, which exist in Alaska in numbers as incomprehensible as the diameter of the known universe measured in miles.

At midday, we trucked the rafts to a crossing eleven miles north of our camp. Jeannie would drive the Tahoe back to camp and wait as Tony, Marc, and I floated downriver.

Tony took Marc and me to a quiet slough and showed us how to handle the rafts, called Water Otters, which consisted of a seat mounted on a platform and two rubber pontoons belted to an aluminum frame. You face the bow instead of the stern, and row by pushing rather than pulling the oars—except when the current threatens to sweep you into a rock or some other hazard. Then you turn the raft and row conventionally, tacking across the stream.

"That's about it. You turn, face the danger, and row *away* from it," Tony said, wreathed in the smoke of a Swisher Sweet—a thin, utterly foul cigar that was our most effective bug repellent.

After the lesson, we strapped our fly rods to the Otters; loaded rope, fly boxes, and essential survival gear into watertight compartments beside the seats; and launched into a stretch of calm water. Tony had told Jeannie to expect us between eight and ten that night. The Jim is an easy river with only a few short whitewater stretches, so we wouldn't be delayed by frequent portages around rapids. Besides, it was a fine, warm, cloudless afternoon. We weren't thinking about the fact that even easy rivers can be dangerous when you're north of the Arctic Circle and the water is somewhere between ice and forty degrees.

After traveling about a mile, we made the first of our fishing stops. Behind us, tiers of spruce climbed toward a mountain far to the northeast, its peak white against the unblemished sky. For a while, I was content to admire the scenery and watch Marc, a novice fly-fisherman, cast some very pretty loops. He made six presentations with a streamer and hooked three grayling, which were striking any fly we cast at them. When each of us had caught and released at least two, we rafted on. The float went like that, hour after hour, until midnight, when we realized that the solitude and the perpetual Arctic daylight had bewitched us. We were hours overdue, with three or four miles to go. We decided to row hard for home.

As the Arctic dusk fell, the mosquitoes boiled out of the woods and muskegs. I paused to apply a varnish of Alaskan cologne—100-percent DEET—and to light up a Swisher Sweet. Ahead, Marc and Tony prepared to negotiate a tricky passage. Just beyond, the river drew into a bottleneck between a high bank and a gravel bar, then picked up speed and curved in a frothing rush past an undercut bank, where several big spruce had fallen; their roots still clung to the soil, causing them to stick out in the current in long sweepers. A few yards downstream, more fallen spruce formed a nasty looking jumble of snags.

Tony rowed bow-first into the bottleneck; then, as the accelerating current drew him toward the sweepers, he turned his raft and paddled cross-current to stay clear of the trees. He sailed easily into quieter water below. Marc followed. I was positioning my raft when I saw Marc suddenly spin broadside into one of the fallen trees. His right oar jammed under it and, acting as a lever, flipped the Otter onto its side. The raft careened into the snags downstream, where it stuck with one blue pontoon in the air, the other caught in the trees. Marc, pitched overboard, was clinging to the sweeper, water rushing over him. I could see only his head, the top of his orange life vest, and part of his right leg, flung over a branch.

Tony beached his raft and ran to Marc's aid. That was the sensible thing to do, but when it's your son clinging to a log in an Arctic river, you don't think about what's sensible. I rowed straight into the fast water, back-paddling hard to avoid capsizing myself on the sweeper. Bumping into it bow-first, I sculled into a back eddy strong enough to brake the main flow. The raft slipped against the bank and was moored there by the currents.

Straddling the sweeper, I inched toward Marc. My plan was simply to grab him and pull him to safety.

The river was golden brown beneath me and then dark brown. It must have been seven or eight feet deep, and the current was stronger than it had looked from upstream. While I knew things were serious, I didn't think they were critical. Then I realized that Marc's left leg was trapped underwater, probably in the crook of a submerged branch. His waders had filled, despite his cinched wading belt.

"Dad! I'm frozen! I can't hang on much longer!" he yelled above the rush.

Carefully, I stood and put all my weight on the tree trunk. It sank an inch or two, enough for Marc to free his leg. I inched farther out, almost prone as I reached to grab him. The standing waves sloshed over me, the cold numbing my fingers within seconds, but I somehow got a grip on Marc's arm with one hand. I couldn't budge his 180 pounds, not with the added weight in his waders, not against that current. For a second, I thought to tell him to let go and let the river carry him into the quieter water. Then I could pull him ashore without fighting so much current. But he could be drawn under by his flooded waders; if that happened, he could be swept into the snags and trapped. And the chance of drowning was just the half of it; the other half was exposure. Anyone up to his neck in forty-degree water can survive for only ten or fifteen minutes. I had to get him out quickly.

"The rope!" Marc hollered. He was the one in trouble, but was thinking more clearly than I.

I backed down the log and got the thirty-foot painter stowed in my raft. I made a loop with the bitter end, while Tony crawled back out onto the sweeper but could get the loop only to within inches of Marc's hands.

"I can't! Fingers…frozen! I'm going to let go!"

"No!" I screamed. "Grab it!"

Marc reached for the rope with his left hand and willed his fingers to open and grasp it. When he got hold with both hands, I scrambled to the bank. Tony took up the slack and we hauled him in. He lay shaking, spent.

We pulled off his waders—gallons of water spilled out—then helped him out of his drenched clothes and told him to walk around, to keep moving. Mosquitoes leapt on him ravenously. He was shivering violently. He was on the cusp of severe hypothermia, when the body begins to lose its ability to warm itself. It can be reheated only by an outside source—hot liquids, a fire, or another body. I was wet and chilled myself, but had more body heat then he. Stripping to the waist, I embraced him tightly, and almost cried out from the sting of what felt like a thousand mosquitoes biting me at once. Tony later said my back was almost black with them.

I held Marc for several minutes in what I like to think of as a life-giving embrace, but the truth was that it helped only a little. We tramped through the woods to a gravel bar about a hundred yards downstream, gathered a pile of driftwood, and got a fire going. Marc huddled beside the blaze. He was still shivering uncontrollably, and he was getting drowsy—a dangerous sign. We told him to get up and gather more wood—anything to keep his body moving, his mind alert.

For the next two hours, we sat by the fire, the flames leaping and falling as the evening dusk blended seamlessly into the dusk of the Arctic dawn. As Marc began to recover, Tony and I went back to the logjam and retrieved the two rafts, but we couldn't find Marc's oars. Both had been sprung loose from their locks and sent downriver.

"They're probably halfway to the Yukon by now," Tony said as we returned to the gravel bar, where we found Marc ready to travel.

"Dad, Tony, I'm sorry," he said. "I was rowing away, but…"

"Listen," Tony said, "there's no fault-finding out here."

"Well, thanks, you know, for saving my life."

Tony shrugged it off, and I said, "Glad you're still here, son," and then we set about solving the problem of how to get home with three rafts and only two sets of oars. Tony volunteered to tow Marc's raft, and that is how we went down the Jim—Marc's and Tony's rafts tethered, mine in the lead. When we were nearly back to camp, we swept past a great bald eagle standing on a jutting gravel bar. His head, white as cotton, turned toward us, his dark wings spread to the breadth of a tall man's arm span. He rose with his talons extended because he was flying only to a high poplar at the end of the bar. There he perched, gazing down, looking for fish. Behind him the spruce forest stood silent in the shadows of the morning.

In the following days, Marc came to recognize his mortality, so alien a notion to a healthy young man. As for me, I had wanted the true wild, and almost had got it in spades. In the wilderness, a small mistake or a moment of blind, bad luck can have grave consequences, and there is neither anything nor anyone to rely on but yourself and your skills, your friends and their skills. Not that we came to look upon the wilderness as heartless or hostile. Nature and her creatures are neither cruel nor compassionate. They are complete unto themselves, and therefore indifferent to human fate and emotions, to human ideas of right and wrong. Curiously, Marc's close call made us feel more a part of the world we had entered, because it humbled us. In the wilderness, where things die every day, we're merely creatures, subject to nature's laws and deserving of nothing. I knew I never would forget the look on Marc's face as he clung to the log, nor my own thought that I was going to lose him; yet, if the worst had happened, the rivers, forests, and mountains would not have acknowledged my grief and loss no more than they would the she-wolf's loss of a pup.

Thus endeth the lesson. We put the mishap behind us and went on....

M.M. 235—JUNE 29. We passed the northern limit of the tree line, marked by a short white spruce and a sign that said LAST SPRUCE TREE—DO NOT CUT. From there to the Arctic Ocean, 180 miles away, the tundra would be as barren as a desert. In fact, the coastal tundra, receiving an average of only eight inches of rain a year, would be a desert if not for the permafrost.

M.M. 240, THE CHANDALAR SHELF—JUNE 30. A grizzly's tracks led across the tundra and down the bank of a nameless mountain stream that fed the Chandalar River. The tracks were old, but I was apprehensive. The night before I'd seen a couple of square yards of tundra mat gouged to a depth of three feet, excavated not by a psychotic backhoe operator but by a grizzly, probably pursuing some small, burrowing animal; you could almost feel its savage determination. The bears of southern Alaska, fattening in rivers thick with salmon, have so much to eat that they've grown selective and wasteful, just like humans. They often suck the roe out of female fish and toss the rest away. But on the Chandalar, nature's shelves are not well-stocked; here, even the fiercest predator in North America has to settle for prey fit for a house cat, and work hard to get it.

Yes, I had come to be where the grizzlies roam in great numbers, but I did not want to run into one at close quarters. That led me to wonder if Marc and I should push into the thickets across the stream. The age of the tracks was no guarantee that their maker was not lurking about; and a bear so famished that it had exerted tremendous efforts to capture a tiny animal would probably *welcome* an intrusion by two well-fed human beings. If I had to subsist on crackers, wouldn't I welcome a porterhouse delivered to my door? I was petrified of the grizzlies.

Tony, a veteran of hundreds of bear encounters during his years guiding out of King Salmon, had a deep respect for the creatures, but they didn't terrify him. He told us it is mannerly, as well as prudent, to make noise if you think a grizzly might be near. Talk, sing, ring bells. Marc and I started chattering and bantering and thrashed through the alders like a troop of urban Boy Scouts on their first outing.

We passed through without any ursine confrontations and tramped on to a ridge, where we scanned the valley for caribou. The big migrations take place in the fall and spring, herds of 100,000 or more surging over distances of 1,000 miles. But in the summer, in flight from the tormenting mosquitoes and flies, smaller bands of, say, 100 or 200 move from the valleys and coastal tundra into the high ranges.

Late the day before, after passing the last spruce tree, we'd backpacked into the Chandalar hoping to spot a summer caribou trek. After hauling our forty-pound packs over the tussocks for three full hours we had seen a pair of shed antlers but no caribou. And we had covered just three miles. I felt as if I were walking on a waterbed with a sack of rocks on my back.

A thunderstorm, building up over the Brooks Range, had given us an excuse to pitch our tents on a desolate wind-swept meadow.

Marc and I scanned the valley below with binoculars. It was empty of game, as were the mountains on the far side, their slopes green at first, then black with scree, then white. The silence was dense and primeval, a silence that had never been sundered by the clatter of industrial or post-industrial civilization.

After the storm passed, Marc opened our tent door and said, "Look at this." A rainbow, its colors so vibrant that it appeared solid, arched over the river. It must have been 1,000 feet across and 1,000 feet high, and we were looking down on it. No caribou, I thought, but this is enough. More than enough....

M.M. 414, DEADHORSE—JULY 3. This was it, the end of the road. We voted Deadhorse the strangest and ugliest town any of us had ever seen. Every structure, whether warehouse, office, or airplane hangar, looked the same, built of extruded steel or aluminum and set on pilings (to avoid melting permafrost and causing the buildings to collapse). There were no churches, schools, bars, banks, or shops—we did find one general store, where a box of Triscuits went for $5. Deadhorse exists solely to house and feed the 1,500 men and women who work in the oil fields.

Since we hadn't seen any caribou on the way up from Galbraith Lake, Tony chartered a bush plane in Deadhorse. "No guarantees on seeing caribou," an insouciant flyboy named Rick told him. "Those animals were born under a wandering star."

Marc, Jeannie, and I got an unofficial tour of the oil fields from twenty-year-old Teddy Westlake, who knew his ethnic makeup down to the fraction: 13/16 Eskimo, the rest white. My friends in the eco corps would have drummed me out: I *liked* the oil fields. I liked seeing caribou trails and even bear tracks within sight of the wellheads; I liked seeing eiders, tundra swans, and red-throated loons nesting in thaw lakes below drilling rigs. Most of all, I liked being in a place where real people worked at real jobs.

The tour finished, Teddy drove us to the northern limit of North America. We got out of the truck and dipped our toes in the Arctic Ocean.

M.M. 188, WISEMAN—JULY 4-8. Three miles off the Dalton down a gravel track, Wiseman is a helter-skelter collection of mud-chinked log cabins, sled dogs barking in kennels, rutted dirt lanes, and a general store. It was founded in 1907 as a supply depot for miners. Robert Marshall used it as a base for his explorations, and described it as a village "Two hundred miles away from the twentieth century." The opening of the Dalton has brought it closer: In a few cabin yards, amid the

---

In 1969, I came home from high school in Anchorage to join my mother in watching the first big North Slope oil lease sale on TV. She said, "Alaska will never be the same." Twenty-nine years later, Mom and I drove up the pipeline haul road, a.k.a. the Dalton Highway, so she could see Prudhoe Bay. Now she stares grimly at the scarred gravel landscape, with its construction camp structures and industry logos, marching off into the fog. "So, Mom," I ask, "what do you think about drilling in the Arctic National Wildlife Refuge?" She peers into the distance towards the Arctic Ocean, then beyond. "Well...I think that if we keep destroying places, there won't be any left. But I won't see it...you will. And your kids will have to deal with it."

—Ellen Bielawski

huskies' cages and oil drums and battered pickup trucks, satellite dishes point skyward, seeking the signals of *Oprah* and *Monday Night Football*.

Eleven miles from Wiseman was the Silverado Mine. It would be our jumping-off point for a four-day hike into the Brooks Range and Gates of the Arctic. Despite its name, the Silverado is a gold mine, and it is a big outfit: thirty miners and Cat skinners whose huge bulldozers had removed half a hillside.

We backpacked into the bush, following a dogsled trail westward toward the Glacier River, ten miles away. About two miles in, we crossed into Gates of the Arctic. Around us, mountains soared, patched with dark-green spruce and the lighter greens of alder and willow swales. After five miles, we took a break beside a lake where a wigeon hen swam with her ducklings in tow.

"Howdy!"

The voice startled us. Up the trail came a man of about thirty, with a blond goatee. He wore a floppy hat, and an old Stevens side-by-side shotgun was in a scabbard strapped to his backpack. A gold pan shone from underneath the pack's top flap. Beside him trotted a mongrel carrying a saddlebag of dog food.

We invited him to join us for lunch. He declined food but sat down. His name was Doug, and he was a body-and-fender man from Homer, Alaska. He was camped near Wiseman, on the Koyukuk, where he was waiting for his partner to arrive from California.

"We got a little gold claim we work up at Wild Lake," he explained, gesturing vaguely at 100,000 acres of wilderness. "Summer's my slow season, so I take some time off to work it. My partner's late, and I got restless, thought I'd wander for a bit."

He noticed me eyeing the shotgun. "Only a twenty-gauge, but with rifle slugs, it'll penetrate a bear's skull." He patted his cartridge belt. "Birdshot in case I run out of food. I wouldn't shoot one of those wigeons, unless I got real hungry."

We chatted for a while, then Doug shouldered his pack, saying, "Be seeing you around." Off he went with his dog, his gun, and his gold pan, as free as anyone can expect to be.

It was 10:30 P.M. when we crested a 600-foot ridge, from which we looked down on the Glacier River, shimmering in the soft Arctic glow. We pitched camp on a bluff across the water from an abandoned cabin and built a crackling fire. There were wolf tracks in the river bank below, and the rocks in the riverbed were coral-hued and laid like the tiles in a terrazzo floor.

We explored the Glacier River Valley the following day. If we hadn't seen Doug, we would have thought ourselves the only people within fifty miles. He visited again, telling Marc that he had spotted a grizzly. Marc asked him what he liked most about Alaska. "The greatest thing," he replied, "is that you only have to dig down a foot to keep your beer cold."

For me, it was the country that went on and on, the absence of marked trails and fences, and the presence of bears and wolves. It was the bald eagle on the Jim River, the golden eagles soaring above the high, windy Atigun Pass, and the Dall sheep in the Atigun's meadows. It was the lone caribou bull whose rack rose like a king's crown as he trotted across the tundra while we were heading back south from Deadhorse. It was the beautiful yellow blossom that's called the tundra rose, and the fireweed that blazed on the mountainsides with a violet flame. It was nameless mountains and lakes.

And it was watching Marc hike out of the wilderness on his own. He had grown impatient with our plodding, middle-aged pace and declared he would push on ahead, out of Gates of the Arctic. Still a bit shaken by the accident, I was reluctant. I thought about the grizzly Doug had seen, the fresh tracks we had spotted by a nearby creek, and the ten miles of Alaskan bush that lay ahead. But he was twenty-two. Robert Marshall had been in his twenties when he mapped the Brooks Range. Time to let go. Past time.

"Well, take off, then," I said and watched him stride across a broad tundra valley, his figure growing smaller until it was gone.

Philip Caputo is a contributing editor for National Geographic Adventure *magazine, and the author of numerous books, including* A Rumor of War, Horn of Africa, *and* Means of Escape.

✳ ✳ ✳

Everything's Oishi

*Who needs the Love Boat
when you've got the sushi boat?*

THE GREEKS HAD HELEN OF TROY, WE HAD TETSUYA
Sato, Ted to his friends. His was the face that launched our
ship, the thirty-two-foot diesel cruiser *Spring Song*, chartered
bareboat out of Juneau, Alaska, for a one-week cruise.

The face did it a year earlier, when I was prospecting for
boatmates. Up in Ted's office in a Japanese commercial agency
in Chicago, on business that had nothing to do with the trip,
I knew he was the one. He looked susceptible to beauties as
mighty as Alaska's, and he looked like he wouldn't be a pain
in the ass. His wife, Reiko, when my wife, Sue, and I met her,
looked the same way, but less pumpkinish and more like a
classical-period woodcut. If Ted is folk art, Reiko is fine art.

And there, at *Spring Song's* table, was the face—round and
boyish and lightly purpled from postprandial Chivas Regal.
Ted ho-ho-hoed like a Ginza department-store Santa. Reiko
smiled upon her husband's hilarity. Sue and I enjoyed the af-
tershock from Reiko's medium-spicy pork curry, served with
rice made in a Panasonic computerized electric rice-cooker,

part of Reiko and Ted's field kitchen. Japanese cooking was their end of the deal we'd struck back in Chicago, where we all lived. I would be the skipper, splitting with Sue the general responsibilities of keeping *Spring Song* afloat and everybody alive, comfortable, and entertained.

"Mike, this is great!" Ted said, waving his arms around the boat. "This is our dream!"

You had to love his attitude. All the four of us had done so far was shop and haul supplies in cold rain heavy enough to melt the paper bags. We were free to shove off by late afternoon, but thirty-knot southeasterlies meant the trip down Stephens Passage would be frightful. The marine weather forecast said the next day would be better, but still probably seasick-making. So we stayed where we were, in Juneau, tied up to F-Float in Aurora Harbor, across a four-lane from the high school. Lesser boatmates would have been bitching already. I'd heard them do it, having twice before chartered cruisers out of Juneau, where Sue and I used to live. On both trips, toxic group chemistry had fogged up what should have been a transforming look at Alaska.

Veteran boaters know all about hell cruises. Nonboaters should imagine a bad date that lasts a week or more and costs in four figures, and on which you can drown. By the time I got to Juneau for Alaska Cruise III with the Satos, I feared tension and ill will more than submerged rocks, icebergs, early autumn gales, tides, hypothermia, drowning, marooning and the claws and teeth of grizzly bears—all of which were, to varying extents, real hazards. Fear reduced me to looking for omens. Send me, O Lord, a sign that this trip will be better than the last one, and the one before that. Send me a sign that I wasn't the jerk.

The signs that had been showing all day were good—so good that I tried not to credit them, for fear of a jinx. Maybe

Sue and I had finally found the right pe
in the bays and coves at the south end of
own elysian wilderness. We'd been to *I*
but we had yet to get there in a happy

Million-acre Admiralty Island is by far the
disfigured of Southeast Alaska's large islands. You can cru
day, alone in what John Muir, who coasted Admiralty in a
canoe, called "this foodful, kindly wilderness." Our plan, if you
could call it a plan, followed Muir's words. We wanted to eat
whatever the island's streams and tidewater provided and generally let it be as kind to us as it was in the mood to be. We
wanted to deepen our old friendship with Admiralty Island.

From the first night on, we'd be where we wanted to be, in
flawless maritime wilderness. We had a full day's travel to
Gambier Bay on the south side of Admiralty, our first anchorage. Then we had five days to poke around Gambier and
neighboring coasts and bays. We'd move as often as we felt the
need, taking time for hikes and tide-pool-poking, fishing, and
whatever else came up. On the way back to Juneau we
planned to stop in Tracy Arm, a deep mainland fjord with a
tidewater glacier. We weren't cruising so much as sauntering
around the continent's grandest wild coast.

Rain pattered like mice in the ceiling. While we slept, the
tide lifted us nineteen feet and then dropped us thirteen. The
rain was still falling when Ted and Sue threw off the lines and
Spring Song burbled away from the dock. Reiko doing her
molecular post-breakfast cleanup, missed the commotion of
casting off. "Oh," she said, "we are moving."

Moving was the least of it. We were undergoing a change a
state, ascending from pavement-plodders to beings glorious
and free. The pitch of idiot glory went up with the howl of
the 170-horse Yanmar diesel. *Spring Song* passed downtown

...u eye-to-eye with fishing boats, tugs and barges, and ...rk crews' floats. Vessels that earn their livings dominated the waterfront, and their company made everything saltier and more real. The cruise ships were another cause for self-congratulation. We were nobody's passengers—we were captain and crew, with sovereign privilege to screw things up and sink. If something horrible happened, it would be our fault. No, it would probably be my fault. That knowledge gave tremendous comfort. Ted and Reiko, who had never been boating before, swaggered around like Gregory Peck on the *Pequod*. "This is great," everybody shouted. "Isn't this great?"

Juneau's saltwater egress is Gastineau Channel, a ten-mile-long glacier-dug ditch banked by mountains. That morning clouds wrapped and unwrapped the summits, and scraps of cloud littered the mountainsides. The bigger ones plumed like smoke from cold, wet forest fires; the smallest floated like the ectoplasms in Madame Blavatsky's séances. It was, of course, still raining, but the rain didn't matter. Once we passed town and

---

A small private boat may be more luxurious, but the state ferry can get you to Admiralty Island more cheaply than either yacht or cruise ship. The Marine Highway system connects Bellingham, Washington, and Prince Rupert, British Columbia, with the southeastern ports of Hyder/ Stewart, Ketchikan, Metlakatla, Hollis, Petersburg, Wrangell, Kake, Sitka, Angoon, Pelican, Hoonah, Tenakee Springs, Juneau, Haines, and Skagway. Vessels carry from 210 to 625 passengers. Some have overnight cabins and room for vehicles, but you can save even more money by leaving your car at home and pitching a tent on the deck.

—Andromeda Romano-Lax

the end of the road system, the vile weather became a Wagnerian atmospheric, so gloomy it was sort of fun.

The channel took us to the junction of Taku Inlet, a big mainland fjord, and Stephens Passage, which wraps around the eastern and northern sides of Admiralty Island. This was our crossing into the huge hell-and-gone. The wind rose and pushed up steep little rollers, the tops of which bucketed against the pilothouse windows. The boat started a hoglike rooting in the wave tops. Comfort and morale, not to mention our breakfasts, were in imminent danger, witness Ted and Reiko's verdigris skin tone. My own stomach and balance organs opened disturbing lines of communication. "I think," I said, studying the sky and whitecaps and trying to sound captainly, "it's going to get really rough." If the wind and seas got up to the high end of the marine weather forecast, we'd be taking five- and six-foot chops right on the nose, and *Spring Song* would be bucking like a Brahman bull. The boat, I knew, would do fine, but we'd be over our limits. It was time to ease over to the mainland side of the passage so we could duck into a bay if the ride got too rough.

But then, almost instantaneously, the wind dropped, and Stephens Passage smoothed and shone like polished pewter. *Spring Song* eased into a motherly rise and fall. "Oh, we are very lucky," Ted sing-songed, as he would every now and again for the rest of the trip. He was right. This was the first of September, which in some years is already deep into Southeast Alaska's season of wet, wind, and gloom. The weather could go down the tubes for weeks, even months. Every clear hour was a gift.

The spasm of foul weather put another mental barrier between us and Juneau, which itself was retreating toward Chicago. The only thing close now was Admiralty Island. From its northeastern corner, about a dozen miles from Juneau, we

followed the eastern shore southward. The island looked dark
and implosive, intent on its own comings and goings.

Admiralty's Tlingit natives have always recognized a non-
human suzerainty over their island. They called it
Kootznoowoo, Fortress of the Bears. The Russians named it
Ostrov Kutsnoi, Island of Fear. Their fear probably had more
to do with the bellicose Tlingit, whose village of Angoon,
which is still the island's only year-round settlement, was later
flattened by American gunboats. The least relevant island
name, and the one that stuck—Admiralty—is owed to polit-
ical logrolling. In 1794 Captain George Vancouver surveyed
the island and named it after his employer, the British
Admiralty.

For 180 years white people did little damage to Admiralty.
The British just looked. The Russians wiped out the sea otters, then made a halfhearted try at coal mining. Yankees made
their bid with whaling stations, mineral prospecting, salmon
canneries, fox farms, and some spotty logging. Only logging
became a threat to the wild entirety. When it did, the island
became again Kootznoowoo, Fortress of the Bears.

A bear-killing human and a human-killing bear first made
Admiralty a wilderness *cause célèbre*. In 1927 professional
hunter John Holzworth publicized threats to Admiralty's huge
population of grizzlies from overhunting and development.
Two years later a bear killed a forest ranger on the island. One
newspaper in Juneau called for the extermination of grizzlies,
to make Southeast more logger-friendly.

Thus began the bear-flavored logging argument over
Admiralty that lasted half a century. The island was finally saved
in 1978 with the creation of Admiralty Island National
Monument, to be managed by the Forest Service, which had
been about to welcome industrial-scale logging with, among
other things, lavish outlays of federal money. There is a handful

of unwild enclaves—the village of Angoon, a native-owned parcel that's being clear-cut, a mining operation at the island's northern end, a peninsula outside the national monument boundary that may yet be logged—but these are lost in the million acres. Admiralty, which falls within the Tongass National Forest, is by far the greatest intact tract of the Northwest's ancient coastal rainforest.

Bears are a chief reason that Admiralty was spared from the Forest Service's War on Trees. The island has one of the densest populations of grizzlies on earth—almost a bear per square mile for 1,709 square miles. This is more than ten times the grizzly population density of Yellowstone National Park, eight times that of Glacier. Still, unless you're around salmon streams when the fish are running or are otherwise seeking them out, you probably won't see bears. When you do, the island makes them small. In giant old growth, an adult grizzly can look like a raccoon. Of course you, the looker, are more like a ground squirrel. The only colossus is Kootznoowoo, the Fortress.

Late on our first day out we got a look at what could have happened to Admiralty Island. The forest near Hobart Bay showed enormous off-color patches, as if badly woven and faded synthetic had been sewn onto the dark natural fabric of old growth. Stumps and old downed tree trunks shone in the cheap green. Sue and I could see that the land was being spectacularly "nuked," as they say in Southeast. The locals, who also call logged-over country "hammered," still seem to be searching for the right word for such wreckage, which spreads 100 to 200 acres a day in logging season in Tongass National Forest, half again as much in native-owned forest.

The forest along Hobart Bay happens to be Native-owned. From the non-Native non-Alaskan point of view, this was trickier moral ground than the nuking and hammering of Tongass National Forest. Still, we loathed the defilement. Sue and I acting like weekenders driving past a wreck with dead and dying still in the road. We looked away and tried to will it out of consciousness.

If the Satos noticed the off-color swath across the passage, they didn't know what it was or what it might mean for Southeast Alaska. They were, at that point, in wonderment overload, gawking at things grander and wilder than they thought possible. Trouble couldn't be part of the picture. I toyed very briefly with using Hobart Bay as a talking point. We could get serious for a minute, do some environmental proselytizing. Subsequent discussion would be especially piquant because the Satos are from Japan, number-one destination for the timber and forest products being stripped out of Southeast.

We could, yes, have gotten heavy. But to hell with it. Nobody was in the mood.

The mood on the way into Gambier Bay, our first overnight anchorage, was downright hilarious. A humpback whale and a troupe of Dall porpoises at the bay entrance celebrated the late afternoon's calm and improbable sunshine. Maybe this was our welcoming committee. Maybe, for that matter, there are sound scientific reasons for a thirty-ton-plus humpback to roll on its side like a house cat and for porpoises to make like kittens in a tear-around mood. The boil of whitewater and huge and tiny flesh and fins had me momentarily flummoxed. It never occurred to me, until I saw it, that whales and porpoises socialized.

A whale acting goofy, when you're that close and there's nobody but you and your friends looking, is way too much for decorous standing and observing. We carried on like a crowd in a sports bar. The whale fed the frenzy by lifting a flipper, giving us a good look at its chalky underside, then smacking it down. The whale lay on its side and washing-machined its tail. All this happened next to a low-tide rock at the end of a line of little islands. A swimmer could have pushed off the rock and grabbed the whale without taking a stroke....

The next day we took the dinghy ashore and hiked. Only Sue and I went, because an old skiing injury of Ted's was acting up. Our first major venture was exploring and stream-fishing at the mouth of what seemed to be the largest river coming into Gambier Bay.

The rising tide followed us across the river's gravel-and-mud flat. Off the boat I went on brain vacation, so it was up to Sue to keep us moving away from rises that would shortly turn into islands. When we were up in waist-high grass she went on bear alert, staring down rocks and stumps and every other dark disconti-nuity in the meadow, which was strewn with

Paddling my kayak, I could hear the orcas long before seeing them. On the flat waters of Southeast Alaska, sounds skim along like a stone. I was stretching out my leg, to rid it of a cramp, when I heard the familiar *whoosh*. Then I saw the large black dorsal, coming right at me. I heard a second *whoosh* and a third. Suddenly whales were blowing all around me.

I happened to be opposite a cliff face. Dozens of orcas converged on this wall, driving salmon ahead of them. In their panic to escape, the salmon were ramming head-first into the rock, knocking themselves senseless. The orcas zipped left and right, picking off the dazed salmon. Dorsals sliced through the water like so many black knives. Many came close enough to touch, but I was not about to stick out a hand while ten-ton carnivores were feeding.

—James Dorsey,
"The Whales' Gift"

dead pink salmon. With no river in sight, fish in the grass had a Magritte creepiness, as if a trawler had been upended over a hay field. The tide table explained all: A couple of days earlier, spring tides had floated the carcasses in from the flats.

Bears explained the bigger mess at the riverbank, which was trampled and littered with heads, tails, once-bitten fish, and fish without so much as marks from birds. Everything four-legged or flying had gotten all the pink salmon it could stand. Fish still wriggled and slapped in the river, but they were late-run zombies, more rotten and dead-looking than the corpses in the grass. We had been hoping for a fresh run of silver salmon, which mob other rivers on Admiralty at that time of year, but found only spawned-out pinks. Sue thought she saw Dolly Varden in a deep pool, but nothing bit.

The river mouth felt freshly abandoned, tired from festivity just ended. The festivity was summer. Out on the boat, the warmth was like June or July, but on shore we could see green going to yellow and feel the rush of autumn. The year was going around the corner.

No, we didn't see any bears. But they surely saw us. We inferred a large and active ursine community from tracks, trails, beds, droppings, and rotten logs torn to pieces among the gargantuan spruce. *Spring Song*, anchored a few hundred yards offshore, looked homier than ever. Nights in a tent on shore would have made us very nervous.

Ted and Reiko were surprised to see us fishless. When we set out, catching something had seemed like a foregone conclusion. No fish wasn't a problem, though. Just that morning we had hauled in the crab-pots with five keeper-size Dungenesses, which were boiled and buttered within the hour. Breaking open claws and legs and pinging bits of meat at the ceiling, we averred that fresh Dungeness shamed the frozen king crab back in Chicago. Reiko made surprising cat growls. "*Oishi*," she said. The English "delicious" didn't say enough.

No fish still wasn't a problem at that afternoon's high slack tide, when we anchored across the bay in 110 feet of water and lowered huge hooks baited with herring for halibut. The silence was almost continuously broken by sea mammals. The whales out at the bay mouth *whooshed* and *chuffed* like antique steam engines. One spouted with a very distinct whistle. Sea lions made shorter breath blasts, and seals plopped heads up and down. Most of the animals were out of sight in the scattering of small islands, but the sounds crowded around us.

After an hour and a half we gave up on halibut fishing. Taking *Spring Song* out to try some trolling for salmon, I saw one of the heavy breathers, a Steller's sea lion. It was alone, and it seemed to be working on a routine. When the boat drew abreast it inverted itself and wriggled the tips of its hind flippers.

Trolling didn't get us any salmon, but it got us whales. We pulled the lines in and idled alongside passing singles and small groups, which didn't seem to notice or mind. I thought back to my uncle's dairy farm in Minnesota. The humpbacks grazed their sea pasture like Holsteins, giving the same sort of dreamy, honest comfort. We watched the ridged black backs rising and falling, now and again a flourish of tail. There wasn't much clowning, no lunge feeding or whole-body breaching (the ultimate humpback trick), but we were enthralled for more than an hour. We would have kept on watching except we needed to get to an anchorage before dark.

"No fish," I said.

"The whales!" Ted said, looking a bit crazed.

He was right. The whales were better than catching fish. They were better until supper, when we started joking about the sashimi and tempura supplies that the Satos had brought to prepare the huge authentic Japanese fish lunches and dinners we were all counting on—because this was Alaska, world capital of fish.

No fish was getting to be an embarrassment. Everybody, you could tell, was feeling it, but Sue and I were feeling it more because we were the hosts. Sue took it harder than I because she came up north with a big, bad fish jones. Fishing was high, if not highest, among her reasons for cruising on *Spring Song*. I don't altogether understand her deep need to connect with gill-breathers via hooks and monofilament, but it's very bracing.

We found our focus in the morning, when the crab pots came up empty. The gauntlet had been thrown. Fresh seafood wasn't the issue. We would fish to remove shame from ourselves and *Spring Song*. We got ready to troll the way *The Prince of Wales* got ready to chase the *Bismarck*. But of course grimness of purpose does not impress salmon. Hooking seaweed, which did a briefly convincing imitation of big fish, hurt worse than nothing on the line. Something down there was laughing at us.

We were still fishless at slack tide, halibut time. We anchored on a hundred-foot flat, which seemed neither promising nor unpromising. We had a no-nibble half-hour and were starting to talk about moving when a rod wagged. "They're heeeeeere!" Sue sang. For a while the fish pulled on the bait, and nobody managed to set a hook. Sue finally talked one in. "Come on come on come on," she said, as if she were hand-feeding it. Then, "Ha! Gotcha!" She hauled up on the rod, which hauled back down. Sue's fish turned out to be a twelve-pounder, at the small end of the size range the locals call chickens. Big guys run up beyond three hundred pounds. Chickens, though, are much more delicious than the trophies.

Reiko's catch of number-two chicken halibut was amazing. "Yes! Yes!" she said. "Yes! Yes!" Then, when the fish was banging around the boat, she was talking to a parakeet. "Pretty boy, pretty boy." I gave her the gaff and told her to hit her fish on the head. "Really?" she said, then, "Jesus Christ!" and whacked it between the eyes. She went on Jesus Christing and whacking until the fish lay still except for a dying fin-quiver. Then she started saying, "I'm sorry. I'm sorry." She caught another and went through the whole business again.

That evening we had the first sashimi followed by tempura fish and vegetables. This was Ted and Reiko's big production number, which included special bamboo serving plates. Reiko held her sashimi slices up to the light and made lusty growls and *mmmmmm*s which didn't sound so surprising now. The fish let light through like lightly frosted beach glass. Clarity, Reiko said, is freshness. The sashimi tasted as clear and unlike fish as it looked. Warmed by wine, the group was suffused with gooey, familial friendship, which nobody, thank heaven, tried to speak. The sublime food became our proxy recipient of praise for one another and *Spring Song* and the trip.

Mike Steere is a frequent contributor to Outside.

DAVID ROBERTS

Shot Tower

Face to face with rock, a climber
opens up to the world around him.

ALREADY WE'RE MAKING EXCUSES. "YOU PROBABLY WON'T have to wait around too long," I tell my wife, Sharon. "We may back off right at the beginning." Ed Ward voices similar doubts; the tower looks hard. The date is only June 22, but it's too warm—hot, almost, at six in the morning. In the last few days, we have run into mosquitoes as high as 6,000 feet. And I am worried about lightning: even as far north as the Brooks Range, you can get it on a warm afternoon.

The peak itself: for Ed, a discovery of that summer. But I remember Chuck Loucks describing it, as he'd seen it in 1963; maybe the best peak in the Arrigetch, he had said. And I had glimpsed it, obscure but startling, from an airplane in 1968, and again, from summits a few miles north in 1969. Not an obsession yet; but something under the skin, part of my dream wilderness.

We take our time sorting hardware and food. Still down on our chances, we pretend to Sharon that we feel more casual about the peak than we do. At least I haven't had trouble sleeping the night before, as I have often in the last few years And I feel good about going up there with Ed.

We get started. The first three pitches initiate us gently: clean, easy pitches on a sharp-edged spine. Old plates of granite, covered with scratchy black lichens: then fresh-cut blank plates of almost orange rock. Sharp cracks, good for nuts and pins alike. Gradually we get involved, as we discover the quality of the climb. "Pretty fine rock," says Ed. "Yeah, the best we've seen."

For me, this is what climbing has become: a question, always, of how much of myself to give to the mountain. As I get older, it becomes increasingly hard to give, to surrender to the novelty of risk and cold and tiredness. You can't really give to the mountain itself, of course, to unfeeling rock in the middle of an empty wilderness. So the giving you do, perhaps, is to your partner, and that too gets harder as you grow older. Instead you hedge with easier climbs, or talk yourself out of hard ones, or back off prudently. But now and then a mountain teases you into commitment.

On the fourth pitch things get hard. Ed leads it, and I can tell by how slowly he moves that it's tricky. "Not so bad," he shouts down. "It's neat." Above him, the rock stretches dully into the sky. Way up is the "Mushroom," the first crux, we guess.

I feel the first half-pleasant gnawings of fear. What if the next pitch doesn't go? What if I get psyched by all these left-hand flakes? And what if there's no good belay ledge? The sun is sliding around from the south. Soon we'll get it directly. My God, it's hot already—what will it be like then? To be sweltering here, north of the Arctic Circle—absurd!

The fifth pitch, my pitch, goes, but it is hard and devious. I overprotect it, and the rope drag makes me shaky. Standing on a skimpy ledge, I bring Ed up, and notice that my toes are starting to ache, my arms to feel tired.

The obverse of commitment—and this, too, I always feel—is doubt. About whether the whole thing is worth it. About why I have to do something artificial and dangerous to feel content. About whether I haven't used up the impulse—can anyone really go at it year after year, climb after climb, without deadening his openness to other things? And about the danger, pure and simple—I want to stay alive. I can't understand why I must eventually not exist: that makes no sense at all. But I can easily believe that I could fall and be killed.

Or that Ed could fall now, leading the sixth pitch. It looks as hard as mine. He pauses on an awkward move. A simple slip, a twelve-foot fall, a mere broken ankle…and then what do I do? Or if it happens higher, after we have gone farther into this labyrinth of inaccessibility—what could I do for him? And supposing I had to leave him? Is it all worth it, and why do we both feel it matters so much?

In the valley below us flowers are blooming, hillsides of tundra creeping out from under the nine-month smother of snow. There are birds reconnoitering the willow thickets, and butterflies, and bumblebees—a beautiful part of the earth, wild, and for a month, all ours. Why is it not sufficient?

The climb eases off. A bit of lunch, but we are mainly thirsty. Sips from the water bottle, then, from a cake deep in a crack, a few blessed chips of ice. We are both tired, and it's well into the afternoon. The clouds are building up in the southeast, over the Alatna Valley; wasn't that thunder just now?

The climb gets hard again, harder than it looks, complicated. I lead the ninth pitch, all nuts in a left-handed crack. We're under the Mushroom, which looks especially rough. We talk about going straight over it—but a ceiling bulges ominously, and that new-cut rock on the right is sheer and frightening. Ed leads left. We've brought a single fixed rope. Here's the place for it; no hope to rappel the delicate traverse he's doing now.

Little things preoccupy me. How many shots left on my roll of film? Should I save some for the descent? Do we have enough hardware? Already—I curse our clumsiness—we've dropped two pins and had to leave one. If the lightning comes, could we get off quickly? Or better to hole up somewhere? My arms are tired, my knuckles have raw, scraped places on them. How should I string out the fixed rope?

I realize that I haven't thought for quite a while about Sharon waiting below. The climb has indeed teased me into commitment. For some time now I have been acutely aware of each crack in the plated granite, of the grain of the rock under my fingers—and of little else in the universe. On the one hand, it is all so familiar; on the other, utterly new. This is the way the Romantic poets saw the world, it seems to me; no wonder mountains were for them so primeval a presence, comparable only to the open sea.

But just as Keats could not see a nightingale without seeing a Dryad, so, on a climb, it is almost impossible for us to encounter nature directly. We dare not descend to the simplicity, the banality of rock itself: we keep those touchstones of sanity safely packed in our minds—the awareness of time, and the abstract thread of a route. What becomes precious to us on a climb is not the mountain itself, in all its bewildering intricacy, but the things we bring to it, the cheese and the candy bars in our pack, the invaluable metal things dangling under our arms, the quarter-inch of rubber under our feet. More than fear, more than self-consciousness, it is thirty centuries of acquisitive, aesthetic Western culture that stand between us and any unfiltered contact with what is there.

Ed has done the pitch, bypassed the Mushroom. Seconding, stringing out the fixed rope behind me, I am absorbed by the delicacy of the pitch, the nicest yet. On the ridge Ed has found a platform. More lunch, a patch of ice to chop up and add to our water bottle. But above us the going, which we had thought would be easy, looks tough, and the vertical wall below the summit shines unrelenting in the afternoon sun.

Pitches eleven and twelve go slowly; meanwhile the lightning is flashing southeast of us. We're too high to get off fast now. If it hits us, we'll simply stop somewhere and wait it out. It's still hot, too hot, sweaty and weird. The thirteenth pitch uncovers an incredible "moat," a slash across the ridge, as deep as a chimney, with a long patch of ice for a floor. We suck greedy mouthfuls of water off its surface, while the thunderstorm passes just east of us. A friendly place, this moat.

Evening now. The real crux is just above us: a sixty-foot wall, quite smooth, overhanging by a degree or two. From below, a week before, I had thought I saw a bypass on the left, over the north face. Now it simply vanishes, was never there. Nor any hope on the right. A single shallow, crooked crack splits the wall. Ed's lead. He goes on aid, the first time we've had to. The pins are lousy, tied off, bottoming. He doesn't like it. I belay in a trance of tiredness. Halfway up, Ed says, "We just don't have the pins to do it." I know it, too, but I urge him to keep trying.

He climbs doggedly, nervily. Two tiny nuts in shallow rivulets of rock. A cliff-hanger, even, which he'd brought along as a kind of joke. A nut in an overhanging groove comes out; Ed falls three feet, catches himself on a lower stirrup. I'm not frightened any more; only afraid that we will fail.

Ed persists. Pins tied off, the wrong size, one wedged in a shallow hole. He edges toward the lip of the wall. At some point I realize he is going to make it. I feel almost matter-of-fact; "Way to go," I shout, but not with the enthusiasm of half a day before. It is approaching midnight. Sharon has gone back to base camp, we are alone. We have twenty-two pins and nuts; I use one for an anchor, Ed uses seventeen on the aid pitch, and three bad ones to anchor the top.

We are at the pole of inaccessibility of our climb; it is the day after the solstice, and the sun hovers low and smoky in the north. The world is empty, alien, and we have never been more alone nor more self-sufficient. "Really fine, Ed," I say. "An incredible lead."

Two pitches to the summit, almost walking. A big place, unspecial; yet special to us, cozy in its barrenness. The best rock climb of our lives, for both of us. We look at each other, shake hands, self-conscious for the first time, as if we had not really known how little we knew of each other. It is almost midnight.

And all the long descent. Our tiredness builds, we seem half-asleep. The sun wheels east again, the heat and the mosquitoes conspire to make us miserable,

As soon as the plane departs, we throw on head nets to ward off swarms of mosquitoes. We will quickly adjust to wearing head nets almost all the time. One of the great ironies of the Arctic is that while nearly a desert in terms of rainfall, much of it is wetland tundra. Snow and water cannot drain out of ground hardened below by permafrost. Full of lakes, sloughs, and ponds that attract millions of migrant birds, the tundra is also one huge breeding ground for mosquitoes. July, the peak month for wildflowers, is also the peak month for mosquitoes. On long hikes up the mountain slopes to photograph the pink plumes, mountain avens, saxifrage, and dozens of other flowers blooming above the serpentine river, we look like camouflaged beekeepers in our green head nets.

—Karen Jettmar, "Deep Inside the Wilderness"

and, in our ragged fatigue, urge us to the edge of carelessness.

As I belay Ed below me, two birds land on my ledge, mocking, in their unthinking grace, our whole enterprise. I want only to be down, off the climb, alive again. And it hits me now how indifferent the mountains are, and therefore, how valuable: for on them we cannot afford to be relativistic. The terms of our combat are theirs, and if we discover on them nothing we can take back to show others, still we discover the utter alienness of the Not-Self, of the seemingly ordinary world all around us.

Running short on pins; we have used too many for anchors. The rappels now are just reaching, our single 180-foot rope forcing us to stop on ledges we hadn't found on the way up. We are so tired: all our conversation, all our thoughts, seem directed toward safety. We rehearse precautions as if they were lessons we had half-forgotten: check the anchor, check the clip-in, check the bottom of the rope. I want only to be off, free, able to walk around unroped. My arms, fingers, palms, toes ache.

The mosquitoes are everywhere, horrible. But we are getting down. It is full morning, another day: at base camp the others have slept and are waking to wonder about us. At least we have the luxury of knowing where we are. Down to seven or eight pins, we descend the easy first three pitches. Never too careful; take your time; don't think about the mosquitoes. Something about it is hectic and petty; something else seems tragically poignant. At last I step off Shot Tower onto real earth, and belay Ed down.

We're safe, and again it is over—the whole thing in the past already, though our arms ache and our fingertips are raw. We take off our klettershoes and wiggle our toes wantonly in the air, laughing as if we were drunk. Sharon has left us a full water bottle. We seem to be falling asleep with our eyes open, going off in short trances. Everything seems good, but the climb is over, and already I anticipate the long ordinary months stretching into our futures, the time to be lived through before life can become special and single-minded again.

David Roberts is a writer and mountaineer who went on thirteen expeditions to unclimbed peaks in the 1960s and '70s. His first two books, The Mountain of My Fear *and* Deborah: A Wilderness Narrative, *are about two of those expeditions. This story was excerpted from his book,* Moments of Doubt and Other Mountaineer Writings. *He lives in Cambridge, Massachusetts.*

PART FOUR

IN THE SHADOWS

✦ ✦ ✦

Hairy Man Lives

A mysterious biped roams the bush.

It could be said that Ted Angasan believes in Hairy Man. But that would be misleading and unfair, rather like saying that you or I believe in whales, or Northern Lights, or Jupiter. To Angasan, an Aleut who lives in the Bristol Bay region, the Hairy Man is as much a part of the natural landscape as bears, birds, and trees. Angasan requires no proof and offers none. But he has stories to tell that speak of the creature's existence.

In the late 1950s, one of Angasan's teenage pals reported seeing a hairy, humanlike creature near the village of South Naknek. The friend, named Peter, had surprised the animal as it lay on some fifty-five-gallon fuel drums. Panicked and alone, Peter grabbed his gun, shot—and missed. The creature, in turn, screamed loudly, then took off running.

Peter ran too and didn't stop until he'd reached the village, where he told of his meeting with Hairy Man. Most people remained skeptical. "They thought he'd seen everything but a Hairy Man," Angasan recalls. "But I believed; you can tell when a guy is lying or not. He was scared to death." Angasan pauses a moment, as though sorting through memories, then adds, "I know the story is true, because I've seen it, too."

Angasan saw Hairy Man in 1985, while on a commercial flight from Kulukak Bay to Dillingham, the region's largest town. Passing over forested mountains near the village of Manokotak, he noticed an unusual form below. "There was this giant thing sitting in the trees," Angasan says. "He looked like, not quite like a gorilla, but dark and full of hair. I'd say, from the trees around him, he's between seven and ten feet tall."

Angasan rejects the suggestion it might have been a bear. "Uh-uh," he says, shaking his head. "I'm color blind, so I look for shapes. I could see his eyes and his head, his whole body. He was looking at us, watching us fly by; he didn't seem bothered at all. But he was a Hairy Man, all right."

Rather than announce his discovery, Angasan remained quiet for the remainder of the flight. "I didn't want the pilot to go down there and scare the daylights out of him. I figured it would just make the thing go crazy, so I kept it to myself. But he exists, the Hairy Man. And he looks exactly like he's called."

Angasan tells his stories in a dispassionate, matter-of-fact manner. There's no attempt to convince the listener, or sensationalize the experience. If anything, he seems reluctant to say any more than necessary. Yet the fact that they're his stories makes them all the more believable.

Angasan is a respected leader within his culture. Among other things, he has served as the Bristol Bay Native Corporation's executive director and represented the region on Alaska's Inter-Tribal Council. From a Western perspective, he's articulate, politically savvy, sharp. In both worlds, Native and Western, he's a credible witness.

And he's not alone. Many people throughout Alaska—mostly Native and mostly rural—acknowledge the existence of a large hair-covered, two-footed creature that is human or ape-like in nature. The Hairy Man.

Nearly every region on earth has legends of a mysterious "hairy biped" that inhabits wilderness areas. The best known are the Himalayan Yeti, or Abominable Snowman, and the Sasquatch, or Bigfoot, of Canada and the Pacific Northwest. Over the years, thousands of people have claimed to have seen these creatures. More rarely, their footprints reportedly have been found, or their pictures taken. During the 1970s, Canadian journalist and author John Green studied 1,000 reported sightings of Sasquatch. What he discovered was "a consistent picture [of] an upright ape…a remarkably inoffensive creature" that is solitary, omnivorous, largely nocturnal, forest-dwelling, and much larger than humans."

Still there remains no documented proof of their existence. Or at least none that Western science is willing to accept. As anthropologist Grover Krantz (a believer in the possibility of Sasquatch's reality) explains in his 1992 book *Big Footprints: A Scientific Inquiry into the Reality of Sasquatch*, "Science requires solid evidence for the existence of a new species…. Nothing of the kind has been recovered for the Sasquatch; therefore it does not exist in the eyes of science."

Scientists and other researchers have so far shown less interest in Alaska's hairy bipeds than in Sasquatch or Yeti. Of the half-dozen Sasquatch/Bigfoot books at Anchorage's public library—books aimed at a general audience—none mention Hairy Man. From an academic perspective, the anthropologists who've documented Alaska Hairy Man stories have tended to treat them as Native mythical beings, rather than real creatures—not surprising, given their scientific bias.

The Alaska Department of Fish and Game has not undertaken a Hairy Man study, says Jim Fall, an anthropologist with the state's Subsistence Division. And yet he's often heard Dena'ina Athabascans speak of *Nant'ina*, large, hairy creatures that "are fairly malevolent and dangerous. One of the themes is that they steal children and raise them in the wild." From a Western perspective, Fall says, "One could speculate that the origins of these stories might come from outcasts or social misfits not subject to traditional norms, and therefore dangerous.

"The thing you have to remember about Native beliefs," he adds, "is that boundaries between humans and other creatures are often blurred. There's no question the *Nant'ina* is part of Dena'ina reality."

Like the Dena'ina, most of Alaska's Native groups include some version of Hairy Man in their worlds. To many southwestern Eskimos, this being is *Urayuli*. To Lake Iliamna's Athabascans, it is *Get'qun*, to southeastern Tlingits, *Kushtaka*, and to Bristol Bay's Yup'iks, *A-hoo-la-huk*. For some, the Hairy Man is gentle; for others, menacing. But whether dangerous or harmless, human or ape-like, the creature most often seems to be dark-haired, larger than people, reclusive, solitary, nocturnal, and a forest- or mountain-dweller. He doesn't speak, but may scream, whistle, or imitate animal sounds.

Sam Stepanoff has always been comfortable in wild places. An Aleut resident of Perryville and, later, Chignik Lake (villages on the lower Alaska Peninsula), he learned wilderness survival skills from village elders; even as a young boy, he would often go camping alone. "I was never afraid of anything," he says, "not even in the dark." But once, at age fourteen, he lost his usual cool.

Out harvesting sea urchins with friends one night, Stepanoff heard a dog barking in the nearby mountains.

Recognizing it as his dog that had run off four days earlier, he followed the howls into the hills and tracked it down. As he stooped to pick up the dog, "the alders made some noise right beside me, and I saw a person. I thought it was the boys; we used to play around, scare each other. I said, 'Knock it off, I know who you are.' But it didn't move, so I shined a flashlight, and it was a man, his face just pure wrinkles. I said, 'Who are you?' but got no answer. He's just looking straight at me, not speaking. I got so scared, I dropped my dog and went down the cliff. I ran to where [the others] were gathering wood for a bonfire, and told them what I'd seen, and they took off running, too."

Back in Perryville, Stepanoff shared his story with the village elders, who searched the hill but found nothing, not even tracks. The elders told him other "hairy guys" had been seen in the hills; occasionally they'd come into the village and rob fish from smokehouses.

"I've read all about the Abominable Snowmans and

B athing with fire is an ancient tradition among Southwest Alaska's Yup'ik people and often precedes an evening of storytelling. In the old days, a village's men and boys lived together in a large log structure covered with sod, called a *qasqig*. In the center of the *qasqig*'s floor was a large pit. Directly over the large pit was a smoke hole in the roof. Most of the time the pit was covered with planks. When it was time to bathe, the planks were taken off and the men built a fire in the pit. Once the fire was burned down to hot coals, the smoke hole was covered. The trapped heat intensified. The men crouched and rolled on the floor of the *qasqig*. When the heat became too much to endure, the participants would dash into the snow or a nearby stream, to gain relief.

—Tim Troll, "Steambath"

Bigfoot," Stepanoff says. "But the guy I seen was little, smaller than me. I never could figure it out; he just looked like a real old man, all wrinkled. He had a beard and was kind of hairy, but he was human."

An aside. There are numerous Native stories of "little people" who dwell in Alaska's mountains. But they tend to be leprechaun-sized beings, whose bodies are not covered with hair. John Gumlickpuk, a Yup'ik elder in New Stuyahok, has described an *iircingarak*, or mountain spirit, that he saw many years ago. It resembled a regular person but was much shorter, carried a stick and wore a tall, pointed hat. When Gumlickpuk approached, the *iircingarak* vanished without a trace. "Most of the time they're invisible," he explained through a translator. "But occasionally they allow themselves to be seen."

Gumlickpuk also once encountered a Hairy Man near Togiak, where he was born in 1906. Then in his early thirties, he went outside at sunrise and met a man covered with long hair. "He was as big as us, but hairy all over," Gumlickpuk says. "The only place he didn't have hair was his face." Startled by Gumlickpuk, the man quickly ran away.

Speedy exits are characteristic of many Bristol Bay Hairy Men. "I've talked to lots of people in the Nushagak and Togiak drainage, and the stories they tell have many similarities," says state wildlife biologist Larry Van Daele. "One thing that's consistently said about Hairy Men, is that they can run incredibly fast. Another is that they can jump long distances, over large rivers or trees."

Case in point: John Gumlickpuk's wife, Elena, tells of a Hairy Man who was spotted by a woman washing clothes. When confronted, she says, "he jump off, way far. He could jump over high bushes and really run fast."

Numerous Hairy Man sightings have been made in the Lake Iliamna area east of Bristol Bay. During the mid-1970s, one was reportedly shot and wounded at the Athabascan village of Iliamna. Bush pilot Tryg Olsen recalls, "The thing was supposed to be as large as a moose standing on its hind legs. Jim Coffee said he shot it, and when they checked where it apparently bled, they found what looked like red transmission fluid. There was quite a fuss; a story got written in the newspaper, and a TV crew even got sent out. But they never found it."

Though it didn't receive any media attention, an even more remarkable encounter with hairy bipeds occurred nearly two decades earlier in Iliamna. Myrtle Anelon, a lifelong resident, was seventeen when two "hairy things" visited her home in October 1957.

One night, after everyone had gone to bed, the family's cat began meowing loudly, then scampered up a ladder onto the roof. Shortly after, there was a loud crash, "like something had fallen through the ladder's steps," Anelon says, "and while falling it broke the bedroom window next to Mom's bed." Myrtle and two brothers went outside, where they found several tracks, "really huge, but narrow, with big toes. We knew that nobody around there had big feet like that."

Later that night, the family's dogs began barking, "like they're really scared," Anelon says. "Mom tells the boys to take a bright flashlight, and shine it where the dogs are looking. When they did, they saw two real hairy things; they thought it was two bears standing on their hind legs. They come running in saying, 'Give me a gun, a knife, anything,' but my mom says, 'Don't kill anything. You don't know what they are. They might be human.'

"The boys go back out and don't shoot, but they start chasing those things all over the place. They said the things ran like humans, not bears, but were full of hair, and fast. They came around three nights in a row, even looked in our windows. Mom said they were probably wild people, and if we don't harm them, they won't harm us. So we never bothered them anymore, and they kind of quit coming around. I never saw them, but my brothers did."

Several theories have been proposed to explain Hairy Men. One is that they're simply humans who've gone wild. Out in the forests and mountains they become larger, faster, and more hairy, though no one knows how, or why.

"Through the years, we've had people just disappear, with absolutely to trace," says Shirley Nielsen, a lifelong resident of the Bristol Bay Iliamna region. "The thought is that these people have gone back to the wild, but who knows? In a village like this, there's lots of superstition. And we always used to say that one way parents can control their kids is by saying, 'You have to be in by dark, or the Hairy Man will get you.'"

Van Daele, the wildlife biologist, recounts a more supernatural explanation that bears a vague resemblance to the Dracula legend. "What I've heard is that some folks wander off, get lost and are caught by Hairy Man, who eats their livers while they're still alive. After their livers are eaten those people also become a Hairy Man, and have special powers."

Another, less common belief holds that Hairy Man, like Sasquatch, is some sort of primate-like creature that's neither human nor ape, but an entirely different species.

But to Ted Angasan, and many others, no explanations are necessary. "I have no ideas what stories are behind it," he says, "All I know is that Hairy Man exists."

A co-editor of this book, Bill Sherwonit has never seen a Hairy Man, but he believes in the possibility of their existence.

MIKE GRUDOWSKI

✦ ✦ ✦

Would You Be, Could You Be, Won't You Be (and Why in the Hell Does Anyone Want to Be) My Neighbor?

What's worse than cabin fever? Tenement fever.

THERE'S A PAINTING HANGING IN THE HALLWAY OF THE school in Whittier, Alaska—a framed, folk-art, children's-book vision of the town as seen in winter from Passage Canal, the finger of Prince William Sound on which Whittier sits, fifty-seven miles southeast of Anchorage. The picture gets it right, give or take. White mountains loom over town, adorned with curlicued waterfalls (accurate, though not in winter). Wet-suited divers clutch red king crabs. Apple-cheeked children ride sleds or beam out the windows of a chugging train. Snowflakes hover among the evergreens (dead-on accurate: there's as much as twenty feet of snow each winter). And right at the center, something leaps out garishly from the storybook tableau: a huge, somber, jaundiced-beige high-rise, with row after row of square brown windows. A mistake, you might think; somehow the sketches for *Wow! It's Winter!* got shuffled in with *My Book of Housing Projects.*

But that towering hulk actually does exist in the town. In a sense, it is the town. Almost every one of Whittier's year-round residents—about 300 officially, though skeptics say that's inflating it—calls one of its fourteen floors home. Main Street? That would be the elevator. Town square? Try the lobby.

There's a virtual city ensconced among the polished tiles, institutional-yellow concrete walls, and uniform brown doors. The 13th and 14th floors house (in part) June's Vacation Condo Suites, a bed-and-breakfast. The Whittier Baptist Church parsonage is on 7, the medical clinic on 3. The 2nd floor features the garbage room and the public library, the latter padlocked until further notice for lack of volunteers. A basement tunnel leads to the school, which has a basketball court with green-painted lanes—home of the Whittier Eagles—and a high-ceilinged, concrete-walled playground, where the younger of the thirty-eight students play on the slide and swing set year-round without fear of getting swallowed by a snowdrift. The 1st floor includes the Country Store (a miniature grocery), city offices, a U.S. Post Office, and Cabin Fever Cures, a small enterprise run by a woman named Esperanza. From six to nine there most evenings, townsfolk—Whittiots, some call themselves—can browse the shelves of rental videos or simmer in a tanning booth in the closet-size room adjoining. Also on the first floor is a tiny laundromat, where cabin fever finds a less congenial outlet. A stenciled sign outlines the laundry rules, including this one, hinting that in such close quarters even Our Town neighborliness has its bounds: Clothes that are left in machines after the cycle has been completed by thirty minutes may be dumped on the floor by the person waiting.

Why, someone might reasonably ask, does almost all of Whittier live under the same roof? They have little choice. When the U.S. Army bulldozed Whittier into existence during

World War II, spacious housing didn't top its wish list. It chose this one-square-mile delta of glacial silt because of its advantageous quirks. Passage Canal never freezes, making it the closest fail-safe port to Anchorage. The junction of the Chugach and Kenai ranges traps clouds, making perpetually overcast Whittier a tricky target for bombers. Soon troops and supplies were shuttling through town en route to the Aleutian Islands, host to the war's only combat on U.S. soil. The Army also blasted out two train tunnels—the longer almost three miles—until recently the only land route in and out of Whittier. And after the war, the military put up two hulking concrete monoliths that remain the signature of Whittier: the Buckner Building, a seven-story dormitory that broods, gray and ominous, at the edge of town, abandoned since the Army bailed out in the sixties; and the fourteen-story warren that most of Whittier calls home, Begich Towers Incorporated, better known as BTI.

BTI is a somewhat cozy place, but even if it weren't, people would think twice before venturing outdoors. The climate makes Whittier a forbidding place to winter, even by Alaskan standards. Anchorage boat owners who dock in Whittier's harbor usually hire locals to shovel off their craft after blizzards. One owner's boat was neglected this winter. It sank.

Weather isn't the only plague. Most residents make their living off tourists—sea kayakers, fishers, glacier gawkers—who scatter, along with their money, after summer. Construction crews working on tunnel improvements sometimes make it impossible to leave town. And Whittier's southern flank of mountains makes it impossible from late November on to see the sun from town; not until February 4 (or the next clear day) does it reappear. Together, these combine into a powerful recipe for funk, or worse. "If you're not stable to begin with," says Jan Latta, the school's office manager, "things here might push you over the edge."

If you watch daylight slowly fade into Whittier from the 14th floor of BTI, the place looks like a toy-train village might if they made toy-train sets to resemble Soviet fishing towns circa 1950. On the sound side of the tracks, a few blocks away, boats sit silently in their slips. On the near side, ten-foot snow piles divide a dozen or so bland, low-slung buildings. "In some ways the winters are more beautiful than the summers," someone remarked to me. "The snow covers a lot of ugliness—rusted hulks and things."

Sometime between nine and ten o'clock, though, the dark surface of the sound and the all-encircling peaks come into focus, and then you better grasp what draws people here. Bald eagles slice through town like sparrows. Otters and sea lions bob around the harbor. Last summer a black bear infiltrated the school. A few years ago, a family of moose migrated in through the tunnel. And Prince William Sound and its 2,000 miles of coastline—endless bays and bights and spectacular beaches—all of that is Whittier's front yard.

"You go out on these coves—maybe three miles out there," says Kirk Loeffler, a thirty-five-year-old former software analyst who moved to Whittier four years ago with his wife, "and you'd swear no one had ever been there before. This place in the summer is the most beautiful place you can imagine." Loeffler told me of a time shortly after he moved to Whittier when a storm churned up six-foot seas. "Maureen and I are staring out at this chaos, and all of a sudden a killer whale came in. He was so close you could've thrown a stone and hit him."

For some, alas, such beauty is scant compensation for the hardships of the town or the oddities of its housing situation. A few winters ago, Whittier had no local police, so state troopers rotated in. One day when the skies cleared, Babs Reynolds, a longtime Whittiot who owns a dockside hamburger stand, spotted a trooper brushing snow off his car outside BTI during the brief sunny interlude.

"Boy," she shouted to him, "it doesn't get any better than this, huh?"

"Lady, you been here too frickin' long," came the reply. "It gets a lot better than this."

Each day of my week-long reconnaissance visit to Whittier, I awoke to the piercing beep of heavy snow-moving machinery backing up in the dark down below. From my 14th-floor bed-and-breakfast aerie, I took a gander at the town through the binoculars thoughtfully included in the living room. Occasionally I'd greet the

> From my campsite I watch boats heading into and out of Whittier—the State Ferry *M.V. Bartlett*, the *Klondike Express* and other tour boats, pleasure craft and fishing boats. Climbing the hill above the beach, I'm embraced by temperate rainforest. Sitka spruce and hemlock shade saturated ground from which the improbably huge leaves of skunk cabbage emerge. Rain is the lifeblood of this northernmost temperate rainforest. Whittier receives 160 inches more precipitation per year than Anchorage, which is only fifty miles away as the raven flies.
>
> —Jon R. Nickles, "Paddling Solo in the Fiords of the Far West Shore"

day by playing one of the eight-track tapes also provided: Bobby Goldsboro, Donny Osmond, Helen Reddy's "Ain't No Way to Treat a Lady." I'd venture into the bathroom, startled awake by the military-issue pink tiles. ("I've talked to a few guys who tried to rip 'em out," a BTI resident later told me, "and they said, 'Wow. The Army did a hell of a job puttin' 'em in.'") My daily shower commenced only after the bathtub faucet first spat out a few ounces of Coke-colored liquid, which I assumed—hoped—was some residual Cold War rust in the pipes.

The hallways of BTI can resemble someone's parody of a suburban subdivision. BTI rules state that you can't paint your door, so individuality arrives in more subtle form: a lingering wreath, an anchor door-knocker, a Scotch-taped notice of an exterminator's upcoming rounds. Neighbors gossip on the elevator while taking their dogs down for a stroll. Here in this town there are no lawns, of course, unless you count the artificial turf in the sixty-yard tunnel to the school. Here keeping up with the Joneses means acquiring the latest coveralls from Carhartt, or some really nice calf-length rubber boots. And here, winter's eventual demise is joyously heralded by the arrival of seasonal Mexican and Filipino fish-processors to their rental rooms in BTI: Whittier's answer to the swallows of San Juan Capistrano. "Everybody's happy to see them," says Dodi Protzman, who with her husband has lived in Whittier off and on since 1947. "It's like you know spring is finally here."…

"There's a lot of people that lose it," Jerry Noran announces to me one evening across a table at the Anchor Inn, Whittier's sole restaurant/bar open all winter. "I lost it."

Jerry, a slightly pudgy thirty-six-year-old harbor technician with mousy brown hair, once made Whittier history by barreling through the Whittier tunnel in his '99 Chevy Tahoe before there was a road. Even the Anchorage paper picked up the story. "I made front-page Metro," Jerry says with a hint of pride.

The episode began when the erratic train schedule didn't mesh with the office hours of Jerry's doctor, causing him to run out of antidepressants for several days. "A lot of people here are on 'em," Jerry says. Desperate, he resorted to a few cocktails, thereby unleashing the proverbial hounds.

"It was 2:30 in the morning," he says matter-of-factly, between spoonfuls of glutinous vegetable-beef soup. "I figured the tunnel crews would be done working." It's dinnertime, and the Anchor's regulars line the bar. Arcade-size video games take up one wall, a few of them functioning. Neon signs glow in the windows: "Anchor Inn," "Budweiser," "Food," the last perhaps meant ironically.

"I started out at about twenty, but that was too rough," Jerry continued. "So I got her going about sixty-five, seventy. I high-centered when I was trying to go around the gondola car they backed in to block me. I whitewalled the tires, but that's the only damage I did."

Even before this incident, Jerry played a key role in Whittier's rich heritage of spontaneous buffoonery. "My second or third winter here, I drove a truck off the train," he says. "Then on a Super Bowl Sunday I got hit by the train driving a bus. I was sober then." He pauses to reflect. "Me and that train don't get along very good."

Others have chipped in to this legacy. The volunteer fire chief accidentally set the firehouse aflame. A railroad engineer backing up onto the barge dock dumped some train cars into the drink. The self-proclaimed former "town drunk" told me he would habitually stay at the Anchor until closing time, then not feel up to walking the two blocks home to BTI. So he'd sneak into the police station across the street, find the key to the jail, curl up for the night there, and quietly let himself out in the morning.

For better or worse, the isolation that has made Whittier what it is today will soon vanish forever. In May 2000, the revamped tunnel will open to automobile traffic. A thousand people have joined a waiting list for harbor slips, anticipating expansion. An Anchorage speculator bought the decrepit old Buckner Building, despite rumors of bears in the basement, and vowed to raise $25 million to resurrect it (he's said to be having difficulty).

"People buying BTI apartments now, they're investors," says Ken Miller, who runs fishing charters in town. "They're not buying one; they're buying five or six. Four years ago you could've gotten one for $8,000, $10,000, $12,000. Now they're going for $45,000 to $60,000."

One person's renaissance is another's hostile invasion, however. "There seems to be so much suspicion and animosity," says Carrie Williams, the city manager. "More than anywhere else I've ever seen."

The road's most rabid opponent is Jerry Protzman, Dodi's husband, who for decades has served as Whittier's crustier version of George Bailey. His shipping and snow-clearing firm, Dojer Ltd., is the largest employer in town, and he's known for putting borderline drunks and welfare cases (among others) to work. He's also known for shouting down adversaries at

---

L ife in Whittier has changed little, if at all, since the much-anticipated (and in some quarters, dreaded) road into town was completed in May 2000. Yes, visitors and residents now have three ways of getting in and out of Whittier (by road, rail, and boat). But the expected flood of tourists has remained a trickle. And residents remain isolated—psychologically, if not physically—while continuing to deal with "tenement fever" during the long winter months. Still, many locals are optimistic that the tunnel road will eventually bring big changes.

—Ellen Bielawski

council meetings and writing frothing letters to state officials. ("The DOT is saying SCREW THE PEOPLE OF WHIT-TIER!!!" one of them noted recently.) "Everybody in Anchorage is gonna drive in here one time—been there, done that," he told me in his office. "The only people I could see coming down more than that is somebody shacking up with somebody else's wife, hiding out for the weekend."

He shakes his head. "You got half the people here that are on drugs and welfare, and drunk; and then you got the people who work for a living. About half the town can think, and about half the town can't."

He shakes his head again. "Funny place."

There were dozens of other stories I heard during my stay—the man who fired his rifle at the barge because it was making too much noise at night; the time the wind spun a Labrador retriever down an icy street like a curling stone—and the days passed quickly. Finally, on a Friday morning in a blinding blizzard, I boarded the eight o'clock train out. At first the only sounds on board were the thrum of the locomotive, someone's cat mewling, and some muttered comment about "the damn public defender." But once the train lurched into motion, a woman with her two grandchildren in tow struck up a conversation with another passenger. A year had passed, she said, since she'd last tasted alcohol. She began to reminisce at high volume about her drinking days: about how she'd once found herself on a barstool at the Anchor Inn talking to a woman, with no idea how she'd gotten there; about the time she lit out for the tunnel on foot with a pint of brandy in hand. I don't know how that story turned out, because right then my mind drifted off to an amazing sight I'd seen out by the harbor a day or two before. It was an otter, a land otter. He had bounded over a snowdrift and scampered west on the slushy road, agile as a greyhound. I can only guess, but he seemed to have had his fill of Whittier: He was headed for the tunnel.

Mike Grudowski is a freelance writer living with his wife Kelly in San Luis Obispo, California. A former senior editor at Outside, *his work has also appeared in* Men's Journal, Smithsonian, The New York Times Magazine, Fortune, Sports Illustrated Women, *and* Rocky Mountain.

TOBY SULLIVAN

✦ ✦ ✦

Leaving Land Behind

*Dark water, darker thoughts haunt
a Bering Sea fisherman.*

I COULD TELL YOU WHAT BEING AT SEA LOOKED LIKE, the view across the water on a sunny day, of an empty world beyond the sight of land, or a distant horizontal white line of frozen coastline, when land was close enough to see. The skidding clouds, the waves echoing each other, the mast ticking back and forth as the boat rolled, like a metronome clocked down to some kind of essential proto-rhythm, all of that was part of what we saw and understood. When we were beating it out in a storm a hundred miles from the lee of any kind of shelter in the middle of the Bering Sea, the motion became amplified and distorted, a massive download of experience that was so overwhelming it drove everything else from our minds. The horizon then became an abstract idea hidden by heaving mountains of water for all but the few moments when you crested a wave and could see across the backs of thousands of its brothers, and it read like the jagged line of a seismograph, or the teeth of a saw. But even when it was calm, when we were sliding across the Gulf of Alaska on the flat calm ocean of a long and brilliant summer day, there was always that ceaseless motion, that underlying rhythmic core of the experience. And even on utterly windless days, when the surface of the ocean was like a polished table top, with the volcanoes of the Aleutians reflected on it like some frozen, spiky version of the grassy bank of a millpond, nothing was for certain. Even when it seemed the boat was perfectly stable and your life on it was a sure thing, you knew in the back of your mind that there was a softness to the edges of that stability, that what you were seeing was a temporary illusion, and that if the boat turned, or someone swung the crane across the deck, the boat would drop a shoulder and heel over a few degrees, and remind you that the world was liquid, that everything could change in a moment.

We were always taking pictures of each other holding up king crabs and wolf eels, or pink mountains far away on some painfully beautiful morning. But the prints always came back with something essential missing, as if the thing we had meant to catch had ducked away just before the shutter snapped. We took videos too, and they at least showed the waves rising, the water surging across the deck, demonstrated that the world we lived in was moving, that it was always moving, a dimension the photographs could never show. But even video couldn't quite fit it all in. "If I just had the right lens," a friend of mine once said, but we both knew no lens would ever be quite wide enough to show the thing we knew but could not explain.

A series of pictures ran in a magazine once, shots of some crab boat in the middle of the Bering Sea in February, with the rails and the rigging sheathed with six inches of ice. The men on deck were dwarfed by black waves looming just off the bow, their orange rain gear in high contrast against the water, and all of it was achingly familiar, and true as far as it went. But the part that was missing, the thing the camera couldn't catch, was how our fingers got so cold from being on deck all day in 10-degree weather that they burned for hours while we lay in our bunks trying to sleep afterwards. Or the burned-out adrenalized feeling we got from standing in the wheelhouse all night in a storm, the back of our eyes reverberating from hours of staring at thirty-foot waves coming up out of the darkness, the curling lips shimmering white in the irradiated purple light of the sodium vapor deck lights.

I have a picture of us hanging onto the chart table with both hands to keep from being thrown across the wheelhouse on some wild night trying to get into the shelter behind the north side of Unimak Island. We are grinning madly at the camera, our eyes red in the flash, the green glow of the radar screen and the orange dial lights from the radios and Lorans behind us. It looks exactly right as far as it goes, but just looking at the picture you cannot hear the wind screaming through the rigging above us so loud we had to shout

About one-half of the entire U.S. seafood catch is taken in the Bering Sea, with pollock—a mild whitefish used in fish sticks and surimi—topping the list. Crabbing, the most dangerous occupation in America, rivaled pollock fishing before it hit a recent slump. Crab fishermen work the Bering Sea in winter months, braving high waves, ninety-mile-per-hour winds, and freezing spray that can make a boat heavy enough to roll. Why risk such conditions? Fast profits. At the industry's peak in the 1980s, a crewmember onboard an elite crab-fishing highliner might have taken home "a $100,000 paycheck in a single two-month season," according to Spike Walker in *Working on the Edge*.

—Andromeda Romano-Lax

to hear each other above it. You cannot feel the shudder of the hull slamming into the waves, or smell the stench of diesel smoke back-drafting up out of the engine room as the wind jams it back down into the stack. And definitely the picture does not show the scratching thought that really, this might not be very cool at all, that right now the last wave of our lives was forming up out there in the wind—the seventh son of the seventh son. Our own personal last wave, the wave that would come through the windows and sweep us all away in a million tons of water as black and hard as basalt, leave us smashed, bleeding, and sinking in a swirling white trail of foam.

And missing, too, is the other end of the experience spectrum, the basic animal joy at simply being alive and present in the world as the sun came up out of the sea after a long night. The smell and heat of cups of the first fresh coffee since midnight in our hands, a full load under the hatches, a good forecast for traveling, all of that was part of our lives, too. So little of any of that came across in any of the pictures we took, the emptiness and exhaustion of countless freezing hours on deck before dawn, or the redemptive scent of bacon and eggs and coffee at sunrise. The good, the bad, the horrific, and the sublime, none of that ever got recorded in a way we could bring home and show to people on a screen after dinner. And even the stories we told, that other, older way to explain our lives at sea to people on land, to our girlfriends on the phone from the dock in Dutch Harbor, as wild and exaggerated and true as they were, were like trying to describe the taste of a lemon, or what sex felt like, to people from another planet.

Things happened that seemed too bizarre and too horrible to be true. People would just smile and nod their heads politely when I told them about the helicopter rescue where the pilot had to fly into the wind at eighty knots to keep station above the four men floating in the water below him, after their boat had sunk 150 miles off Yakutat. How he had to fly up and down in thirty-foot dips at the same time to get the basket down to them, because they were rising and falling on thirty-foot waves. All of this at three in the morning, in snow so heavy the crew chief could only see the floodlit deck below him intermittently through the snow squalls.

They got two guys up with the basket in two hoists, but when the third guy came up they couldn't get the basket to swing into the helicopter. It kept hanging up on something on the lip of the door, and the chief and the medic kept pulling hard, and then real hard, before it swung in. But as they did, they watched in horror as the last man dropped off the bottom of the basket and fell a hundred feet into the water. They lowered the basket to him but he was unconscious or too broken to climb in. They were redlining on fuel, and it was eighty miles to the beach and the pilot had to call it. They left with the waves breaking over the red hood of the survival suit down there in the water, the arms outstretched, the white face staring up. The air station in Sitka sent another helo out at daylight, but everyone knew what they'd find, which was nothing but wind and snow and water. They flew a grid pattern all morning and then headed back, light on fuel, nobody talking, as they stared out at the water below them.

Seven hundred miles west of Dutch Harbor, 1,400 miles from Anchorage, almost at the end of the long arc of the Aleutian chain which divides the Pacific Ocean from the Bering Sea, was the island of Kiska, and the harbor it enclosed. Kiska was closer to Asia than to the North American continent, but during the two winters I fished in the western Aleutians, we often anchored up there during storms. The Japanese had captured Kiska in June of 1942, in the northern prong of the same offensive that tried to take Midway, and they immediately began building a massive base around its deep natural harbor. A few weeks later they took Attu, the last island in the chain two hundred miles further west of Kiska, and they held both islands until the next summer. Kiska and Attu were as remote as the moon, but by forming an island chain linking Asia with America they were intensely strategic. They were also the only American soil occupied by foreign troops since the British captured Washington in the War of 1812, and during the fall and winter of 1942 and 1943, the Americans flew hundreds of B-24 bombing missions against them from bases near Dutch Harbor. Flying 1,500 miles round trip, through some of the worst weather in the world, the Americans lost far more planes and crews to storms and fog than to Japanese anti-aircraft fire, but they flew almost every day, and dropped 7 million tons of bombs. They sank dozens of Japanese troop ships in Kiska Harbor. In May 1943, the Americans and Canadians invaded Attu. The Japanese had been cut off from re-supply for months by a naval blockade, and in the end, hopelessly outnumbered and thousands of miles from home, they charged the Allied lines with banzai attacks and died for the Emperor. Of the nearly 2,400 Japanese troops defending the island, only 29 survived.

The Americans waited until August to invade Kiska, expecting a similar battle, but instead when they came ashore they found the island deserted. Five thousand Japanese troops had boarded transports and managed to disappear into a dense fog, a frequent occurrence in the Aleutian summer. It was one of the great withdrawals in military history. While the American destroyers chased phantom flocks of birds on their radar screens, the fleet of Japanese ships slipped through the blockade and sailed home to Japan.

✳

There was a video we used to watch, taken in the wheel-house of some boat out west during a storm, a tape that got passed around the crab fleet in the Bering Sea for a while. The first time I saw it I was sitting at the galley table while we waited out a blow, anchored up in Kiska Harbor. The masts of Japanese transport ships still stuck up out of the water along the west shore, where their wharves had been, sunk by the B-24s. Hundreds of Imperial troops were still down there, sur-prised in their sleep, or caught in daylight, all now drowned and forgotten, and we were always talking about going down to the wrecks, getting souvenirs, or just looking. But Kiska was a haunted place, awful and lonely even in daylight, and at night it was only worse, our twenty-watt mast light the only light in a bay full of dead soldiers, immense and treeless mountains rising up into the mist around the bay that made it an appro-priate place to watch a video like that, a video from the wheelhouse of a boat whose name we never knew. It was short, under five minutes, but on a certain level it described perfectly everything we knew about the Bering Sea but never found a good way to explain. It was a view of a wet nightmare through windows covered with wind-whipped spray, the an-odized gray steel of the anchor winch in front of the wheel-house, the black bow rails, the white-lipped edges of the waves, all blurred and indistinct, as streams of water across the windows smeared the view entirely for seconds at a time. The only sound was a high keening wail, the sound of the wind sucking at the corners of the wheelhouse, pulling on the an-tennas, with the odd comment from one of the men in the wheelhouse, or a squawk from the radios. Then there was one last shout from someone, and a quick visual snap as the bow

dipped and the last great wave came over the rail and through
the window. The tape ends there, with a screen full of silent
and patternless video noise, and the part that came after, a
wheelhouse full of water, electronics blown, steering and engine controls shorted out, none of any of that long list of bad
possibilities is recorded or revealed. And though the tape is
evidence that they made it, you can only guess at how far from
land they were, or what they had to do to get back from that,
bolting plywood over the windows, hand steering, relying
solely on a compass for navigation, dealing with injuries, who
knew. It was like a last dispatch from The Lost Patrol, out on
the far edge of the galaxy, and we used to love showing that
to the green guys. "Hey Jerry," we'd say, "How's your reflexes?
Think you could duck in time?" But when the green guys
asked, and they always asked, like we had wondered ourselves
at first, what happened to the boat, did everybody live, which
boat was it, what year did that happen? We'd laugh and tell
them to forget it, they were missing the point. Because they
were looking for hard details, the "facts," a way to understand
something that was essentially primal, beyond names, dates
and insurance reports. Maybe those existed somewhere, on
land, in a civilization we had left behind, but they were details
that had nothing to do with the true reality of the video for
us—just the wave itself, caught in the brief and ineffable moment of its power, the blank screen afterwards, and the fact, the
only fact that mattered, that there were no witnesses except
the men themselves, and that only by surviving was this video
even in existence as a record of the event. The men themselves
could have been any crew, on any boat, in any year since men
first sailed in ships. That they had lived to bring their cryptic
story back, that they had brushed up against the edge of the
thing we all knew surrounded us, and that it might just as easily have gone the other way, with just another missing vessel

alert from the Coast Guard, was what was true and significant to us.

In the early winter of 1998 a boat named the *Dominion* was fishing on the west side of Kodiak Island during the winter pollock season. They had just hauled a bag with 60,000 pounds of fish up onto the deck, and were pumping enough refrigerated sea water out of the tank to make room for the pollock. They started spilling the fish out of the bag into the tank, but they pumped too much water out too quickly and the water in the tank went slack, suddenly had what we called "free surface," and sloshed to one side of the tank, heeling the boat over. The bag of fish on deck spilled across the downhill side of the deck and the boat kept going, rolled completely over, and they were upside down in less than fifteen seconds. The deckhands walked up the deck, stepped over the rail onto the side of the boat and then up onto the keel like walking on a rolling barrel. They didn't even get wet.

A friend of mine was the hired skipper on there that winter, standing in the wheelhouse, looking out a window at the back deck when it happened. There was no outside door in the wheelhouse and when the boat rolled it went so quickly he didn't have time to climb down the ladder to the galley and run out on deck. He found himself paddling in 38-degree water in a corner behind his captain's chair with the boat upside down above him, the wheelhouse floor overhead, in an airspace just big enough to get his head out of the water. There was plenty of light coming in through the windows below him so he could see what he was doing, but when he tried to swim down and open them they were wedged shut. He came back to the corner, got some air and tried swimming up the stairs and into the galley but ran out of air again partway through and came back up into the wheelhouse. The air was going bad fast in the little pocket he was breathing from and he knew he had maybe one more try in him. He made it through the galley, pulled the floating refrigerator out of the way, and swam out the door and up to the surface. The other guys pulled him out and gave him some of their dry clothes to put on. It was January and cold, maybe twenty degrees, but it was flat calm, it was daytime, and there were two other boats fishing less than a mile away. They came over, and one of the boats came right up alongside the overturned hull, and they all just stepped across and were handed mugs of hot coffee.

My friend told me that story in his kitchen in Kodiak one afternoon about three months later. We sat on stools with our elbows on the tiled counter, drinking Coronas, looking out the window at the rain falling in the trees. From where we sat we could see out across Monashka Bay, see a squall moving into the bay from Marmot Island. His wife and kids sat out in the living room watching TV, the sounds of a game show coming in over the sound of the surf on the beach below the house. Though you'd never know it by the rain and by the ice still in the driveway, spring was coming, but they were moving back to New York; they'd be gone when summer came. "She freaked pretty bad over the whole deal," he said. "I'm not sure what I'm going to do in New York, but her mother's there, and her sisters. She wishes she never even knew about that part of it, about being trapped under the boat, and having to swim out like that." All I could do was take a hit on my beer and look out the window and nod my head. I could think of another way, the only other way it could have gone for her to never have had to listen to a story about her husband swimming out of a submerged wheelhouse with his last breath. But of course that possibility was the one she couldn't stop thinking about, the reason for the cardboard shipping boxes piled in the middle of the floor.

Somebody on one of the boats that came to the rescue of the *Dominion* had taken a picture of the crew just before they were taken off the overturned hull. They are standing on the keel like birds lined up on a floating log, and they ran it on the cover of *National Fisherman*. The picture has a very casual look to it, as if the men standing there are workers, painters maybe, taking a break. Inside there is a little blurb explaining it but from the picture alone there is very little to suggest what the odds might be of the weather being that nice, or of the other boats being that close by to take the picture in the first place, or indeed of what may have just happened at all.

One winter I was working on the *Irene H.*, fishing king crab. We had been fishing hard since the January start of tanner crab season, working in the shipyard all summer, and started king crab in September. We came into town only long enough to unload the crab and get food, fuel, and bait…. The unloading took all day. I finished my engine room chores, helped the other guys fix a burned out sodium bulb up on the mast and then in a small miracle found I had an hour to myself before the boat took off again. It had been weeks since I'd been ashore, three months since I'd had a day off.

I went across the street to the B&B Bar and sat on a barstool in the warm room, watching the girl moving behind the bar, listening to Willie Nelson on the jukebox, nursing a beer, feeling a hundred years old. In the mirror over the bar I suddenly caught a flash of a guy with his sweatshirt hood pulled up over his halibut cap walk past the street window and up to the door, as if he were coming in. There was a pause, but the door didn't open, and then the guy crossed in front of the window again, headed back down the street the way he'd come, and I saw a red beard peeping out around the side of the hood. For a second, still looking in the mirror, seeing a left

profile under the cap, I thought it was Jim Miller, the skipper
on the *George W.*, something about the red beard and the
white cap, but I knew that couldn't be right. The *George W.*,
a fifty-eight-foot trawler, had disappeared the winter before.
They were dragging for cod in the Shelikof and something
happened and the boat went down. A life raft with the two
deckhands was found drifting twenty miles off the south end
of Kodiak Island, many miles south of where they had been
working, but there was a hard northwest wind that week we
knew had blown the raft far from where it had been launched.
It was very cold and something had gone wrong with the
canopy and it had failed to inflate, and even with their survival
suits on the two crewmen had frozen to death lying on top of
it, exposed to the wind. The body of the skipper was never
found, nor was the boat, though if you follow the bottom
curve along that edge just right you can still see it down there,
an irregular red smudge on the orange bottom of the depth
sounder screen, a sudden hard spot on the soft sand of glacially
deposited moraine fifty fathoms down, where Uyak Bay opens
up into Shelikof Strait....

I sat there in the B&B, warm and drowsy with the beer I'd
drunk, wondering what I'd seen in the mirror, a stranger with
a red beard and a white hat who'd hesitated at the door of the
bar, and then decided to go back down the street to the boat
harbor, or something else.... I knew without being told that
one way or another the dead were as much a part of us now
as they had ever been when they were alive. And in a way I
knew, more deeply the older I got, that the glimpses of long-
dead men I saw turning corners around buildings in broad
daylight, or standing bright and forever young before me
when the room was dark or my eyes were shut, were really
them, not just my memory of them. And I knew too they
were with me for keeps, that they weren't going anywhere,

they were permanent visitors inside my head from all those last trips they'd never come back from....

I came out of the bar and stood in the parking lot in front of the cannery looking at the sky, trying to tell if it was going to blow hard enough to keep us in town, wishing hard that it would. All the accumulated debris of longing for warmth and the company of people other than the other guys on the boat came floating up out of the little box deep down inside where we all kept those pieces of emotion that had no place in the working environment at sea. My knees and wrists still hurt, I could have used a long nap up in my apartment in Aleutian Homes, and the thought of going out there again so soon was almost more than I was willing to take. For a minute I debated just walking away, telling the skipper he could fire me if he wanted, but I needed a trip off, I was

toast. Instead I just stood there breathing, knowing I was in it

---

The skipper was already in the wheelhouse, glowering at the fog that devoured his vessel's bow. The helmsman stared fixedly at the compass. His anxiety was palpable. I checked the radar screen for traffic, but we were alone. Boom. I stumbled slightly with the impact. The skipper muttered a gloomy "shit."

To starboard and to port, white zeppelins slipped past, grown large and menacing as our little ship penetrated the ice pack we blundered into at dawn. The fog bank began to thin. Within moments we could see the ship's bow, then glimpse the shattered ocean. It was littered with rubble-like shards of frozen milk below a hard blue sky. The skipper slowed to one quarter ahead and the helmsman did his best to avoid the larger ice rafts, steering a circuitous course around them.

—Dustin W. Leavitt, "Doublestar (Why I Write)"

till the season was over. I needed the money, and besides, anybody who might have wanted the job was either already on a
boat, injured, or not worth taking out....

For a long minute I stood there, looking back across the
boat harbor at the lights of town, thinking about the wind, the
ocean, the work, the hyper-reality of the lives we led beyond
the sight of land. I thought about how far all of that was from
the lives of the people on land I loved and who loved me
back, and then I turned and climbed up the stairs to the deck
of the processor and walked across to the ladder that led down
to the deck of the *Irene*. Twenty minutes later we were headed
down the channel past the canneries, tying up the lines behind
the house and securing the deck for the run to Chirikof.

Looking back at the houses of town as the evening
descended over them, I wondered if maybe someone was
watching us from up on the hill above the harbor, pausing
while they made dinner. Was someone looking down out their
kitchen window, watching our mast light disappear into the
gathering darkness of the open sea, wondering if we would be
all right? Would they remember that moment in a few weeks
as a last sighting before we disappeared with all hands, lost in
what the Coast Guard would call "Circumstances unknown"?

Years later I read a story by a reporter in Vietnam. A soldier
he met there told him about a squad of rangers that had
walked single file up a ridge one night and disappeared. The
reporter asked him what happened, were they killed, didn't
anyone go searching for them? But the soldier just looked at
him strangely and smiled and walked away, shaking his head.
It took the reporter years to realize he'd been told everything
he needed to know about the incident, that the soldier knew
if he didn't get it, well, he didn't really understand the war.

I read that story lying in my bunk one night in Kiska Harbor, with the rusted masts of the Emperor's ships rising from the dark water along the far shore, lost markers for those men who never returned to Japan to tell their wives and mothers and fathers and children what happened to them. I recognized it immediately in a spooky moment of clarity as the ultimate ghost story, for the truth it revealed about witnessing, and remembering, about bringing back, and giving, experience. And I thought about all the sea stories that never made it back from the places where they happened, to the places where people wait to hear them, thousands of stories for thousands of years. And I thought of all the ways those stories can be lost, the last frantic radio call ending in mid-sentence, the missed cannery schedule, the empty horizon where a boat should be. And I thought of all the stories that are just simply lost in the telling, survivors' stories forgotten as soon as they are told, or forgotten and lost before they are ever told at all. Unless we decide, deliberately, to remember our stories and to tell them, it will be as if they had never happened, or as if we had never returned to tell them.

I could tell you what the sea looked like on certain days, tell you about the things we did there, about the people we knew and carried with us and the ones we left behind when we had to leave. I could tell you all that and hope that some of it might become a part of you, a story that you might remember, a piece of my life now become a part of yours. Because it is all one story anyway, mine, yours, all of us connected by the stories we tell each other, and they are all true sea stories. The nightmare hundred-foot waves, the quiet moments in warm houses on the hill above the harbor, the last sight of the women who waited for us there—the universe breathes within all of us through all of them. And at some point, mariners all, we untie and slip out of the harbor one at a time, light falling at dusk, a single file of mast lights heading out into the oceanic darkness, looking back at the warm yellow lights of the houses along the receding shore, the first drops of cold sea spray beginning to rattle against the wheelhouse windows. Long before we get there we all know the salt blood water of the Gulf of Alaska, of the Bering Sea, of the Shelikof, even Kiska Harbor. We taste it on our lips, feel it seeping through the spaces in our hearts, like water filling the cracks of the bedrock beneath the sea, remembering it, carrying it with us, down, down, down, one last true story, into the center of the world.

Toby Sullivan is an author and a poet in addition to being an Alaskan fisherman. This story won the Grand Prize in the Anchorage Daily News *Annual Creative Writing Contest. He lives in Kodiak, Alaska.*

SHERRY SIMPSON

✦ ✦ ✦

I Want to Ride on the Bus Chris Died In

Was he a hero or a young fool?
Pilgrims seeking answers travel into the wild.

BEFORE WE STARTED OUR SMALL JOURNEY LAST YEAR to the place where Christopher McCandless died, I wondered whether we should be traveling on foot rather than by snowmachine. It was probably the last weekend before the sketchy snow would melt and the river ice would sag and crack. If we waited a few weeks, we could hike the Stampede Trail to the abandoned bus where his body was found in 1992. Wouldn't it seem more real, more authentic somehow, if we retraced his journey step by step?

No, I thought. This is not a spiritual trek. I refuse to make this a pilgrimage. I will not make his journey my own.

And so we set off on the tundra, snowmachines whining across a thin layer of hard snow. The five of us moved quickly, each following the other westward through the broad valley. To the south, clouds wisped across the white slopes that barricade Denali National Park and Preserve. I wore ear protectors to dull the noise of the grinding engines. When the sun burned through, we turned our faces toward it gratefully,

243

unzipped our parkas, peeled away fleece masks. It had been a long winter—warmer than most in Interior Alaska, but even so each day was filled more with darkness than light.

We kept on, the only motion against a landscape that seemed still and perfect in its beauty. It was the kind of day when you could think about Christopher McCandless and wonder about all the ways that death can find you in such a place, and you can find death. And then, a few minutes later, you'd look out across the valley, admiring the way the hills swell against the horizon, and think, "Damn, I'm glad to be alive in Alaska."

A few summers ago I rode in a shuttle van from Fairbanks to the park with a group of vacationers and backpackers. As we left town, the driver began an impromptu tour of McCandless's final days. In April 1992, he had hitchhiked to Alaska, looking for a place to enter the wilderness. The van driver pointed out a bluff near Gold Hill Road, the last place McCandless camped in Fairbanks. The driver talked about the purity of McCandless's desire to test himself against nature. He slowed as we passed the Stampede Road, the place where a Healy man had dropped off McCandless so the young man could begin his journey. He ignored all offers of help except for a pair of rubber boots. He did not take a map.

In the van, people whispered to each other and craned their necks to peer at the passing landmarks.

McCandless had hiked about twenty-five miles along the trail before stopping at a rusting Fairbanks city bus left there in the 1960s by a crew building a road from the highway to the Stampede Mine, near the park boundary. He had a .22 rifle and a ten-pound bag of rice. In the back of a Native plant lore book he scribbled brief, often cryptic entries.

In July he tried to leave but apparently was turned back by

the roiling Teklanika River. He did not know enough to search for a braided crossing.

By August, a note tacked to the bus pleaded for help from any passerby: "I am injured, near death, and too weak to hike out of here," it said in part. In early September, hunters found his body shrouded in a sleeping bag inside the bus. He had been dead for more than two weeks. Although he had tried to eat off the land, and had even succeeded in killing small animals and a moose, he had starved, an unpleasant and unusual way to die in America these days.

The strange manner of his death made the 24-year-old infamous in Alaska as authorities tried to puzzle out his story. A 1993 *Outside* magazine article by Jon Krakauer, followed by the 1996 best-selling book *Into the Wild*, made him famous everywhere else.

The van driver was maybe in his early thirties, mild and balding. As he drove and talked, he held up a copy of Krakauer's book, a sympathetic and compelling portrait of McCandless. The driver said he kept the book with him always because he felt close to the dead man.

"I understand his wanting to come here and go into the wild," he said. Like McCandless, he'd attended Emory University, and he and his wife had recently moved to Anchorage in search of whatever it is people want when they come to Alaska.

In a van full of out-of-state vacationers, the driver felt safe criticizing the response of Alaskans to the story of McCandless. "They called him a young fool who deserved what he got," he said. "There was not a positive letter to the editor written about Chris McCandless. It went on for days." He checked our reactions in the rearview mirror. "It was pretty chilling to read."

Through some strange transmogrification, Christopher McCandless has become a hero. Web sites preserve high school and college essays analyzing *Into the Wild*, which is popular on reading lists everywhere and frequently seen in the hands of people touring the state. A California composer has written a concert piece meant to convey the dying man's states of mind—fear, joy, and acceptance. A Cincinnati rock band has named itself "Fairbanks 142," after the bus where McCandless lived and died.

And then there are the pilgrims, the scores and scores of believers who, stooped beneath the weight of their packs and lives, walk that long Stampede Trail to see the place where Chris McCandless died—and never take a step beyond.

For two hours we rode along the rim of the shallow valley. Heat from the engines warmed our hands. We followed a trail used by dog mushers and snowmachiners; here and there other trails curved to the north or south. Russet

---

There's a thousand ways to die in Alaska, yet cheechako Michael Myers was unconcerned with them all. He seemed unusually at ease in this environment, this city kid from back East.... Turns out, he didn't know any better. And he had bigger concerns than the perils that confront adventurers in wild Alaska. His biggest fear was that one of us would go mad in camp and later dine upon his flesh. Once, as we hiked a well-trodden animal trail, he remarked on our good fortune in finding a man-made path. I replied it was Mr. Bear's trail, and punctuated my statement by stepping aside to reveal a fresh pile of scat. The scat, as scat will do, sunk in. Mike slowly realized that maybe, just maybe, his travel chums were less threatening than natural hazards. For at least the last evening of his trip, Mike knew he was on the right end of the serving spoon.

—John Woodbury,
"Reality Bites Back"

scraps of tundra patched the snow, and the packed trail wound across the ground like a boardwalk. We had barely beaten spring.

A Healy woman named Connie led most of the time because she knew the way. The others in the group were my friends Kris, Joe, and Charles. Kris and Joe live just outside the park; Kris, a freelance writer, covered the McCandless story when it first broke in Alaska, and she's the one who told me that people had been visiting the bus like it was Jim Morrison's grave in Paris. Joe had visited the site shortly after the body was discovered. Charles, a photographer, came along to document the bus and to make tasteless jokes. He wasn't alone. I suggested our journey should be titled "Into the Weird."

Now and then we rode by other trails looping across the snow, and an hour into our trip, two snowmachiners passed us before we reached the Teklanika River. They were friends of Joe's on their way northward to fix an off-road tracked vehicle that had broken a fuel line during a fall moose hunt. Their trail curved across a distant ridge, and I admired their ease and confidence roaming around out here, where machines can break down or dogs can run away and the walk home will be long and troublesome. You couldn't call it the middle of nowhere; the Stampede Trail has been mapped for decades. Still, you'd want to know what you're doing, so as not to make your next public appearance in a newspaper headline or as another statistic.

The Teklanika River ice had not yet softened, and we crossed its smooth expanse without trouble, just below where it emerges from a gulch. We cruised through Moose Alley, dipped into the forest, wound across the beaver ponds, and rose along an alder-thick ridgeline. Occasionally moose tracks postholed the snow. I tried to imagine hiking here in the summer, calling out to bears and waving away mosquitoes.

We rounded a bend and suddenly there was the bus, hollow-eyed and beat up, the most absurd thing you could imagine in this open, white space. Faded letters just below the side windows said "Fairbanks City Transit System." The derelict bus seemed so familiar because we had seen its picture many times in newspapers and on the jacket of Krakauer's book. For decades it had served as a hunting camp and backcountry shelter, a corroding green-and-white hull of civilization transplanted to a knoll above the Sushana River. Now it was haunted real estate.

We turned off the snowmachines and stood stretching in the sunshine and the kind of quiet that vibrates. A trash barrel, a fire grill, plenty of footprints, and frozen dog shit provided evidence of passing dogsleds and snowmachines. A wire chair leaned against the bus. I wondered how many people had posed there for photographs. The bus made me uneasy, and I was glad to be there with friends. It must have sheltered many people over the years who came to shoot and drink and close themselves up against the night.

Kris and I squeezed through a gap in the jammed door and climbed in. It was warm enough to remove our hats and gloves while we looked around, though an occasional draft swept through the broken windows. A bullet hole had pierced the windshield on the driver's side.

The bus was littered with messages scratched into the rusted ceilings and walls referring to McCandless's death, which seemed to bring out the earnestness of a Hallmark card in visitors: "Fulfill your Dreams, Nothing Feels Better," "Stop Trying to Fool Others as the Truth Lies Within," and "The Best Things in Life are Free." Also, "Keep This Place Clean You Human Pigs."

Scattered among the needles and twigs on the floor were bizarre artifacts: frayed hanks of rope, a mayonnaise jar lid, a camp shower bag, blue playing cards. The driver's seat was missing, but downy grouse feathers lined crannies in the dashboard. A few liquor bottles—big gulps remaining of the Jack Daniels and the Yukon Jack—crowded a small stand, which also held an electronic guitar tuner, a tin coffeepot, shotgun shells, a yellow container of Heet, and a can of Copenhagen Snuff.

Stowed beneath were worn Sorel boots and pairs of filthy jeans, one set patched crudely with scraps of a green wool Army blanket. Were these the jeans mentioned in the book? Hard to believe they were still here considering that locals joke about dismantling the bus and selling it on eBay. It was creepy.

A stovepipe lurched from a small barrel woodstove and poked through the roof. A green tent fly covered the rusted springs of a twin-size mattress. And here was the disturbing part: the bed lodged sideways against the bus's rear, mattress stained, straw-like stuffing exposed, the remnants of the cover torn and shredded. That's where his body was found.

On the wall beside the bed was a brass plaque left by his parents that read:

Christopher Johnson McCandless. "Alex." 2/68-8/92. Chris, our beloved son and brother, died here during his adventurous travels in search of how he could best realize God's great gift of life, with his final message, "I have had a happy life and thank the Lord. Goodbye and may God Bless All," we commend his soul to the world. The McCandless Family. 7/93

Three notebooks sat on the plywood table. They included a three-ring binder protecting a photocopy of Krakauer's original *Outside* article with its blaring headline "Lost In the Wild." It was a Monty Pythonesque moment when someone pointed out an unrelated title on the magazine cover: "Are you too thin? The case for fat." This kind of humor is one reason why Alaskans fear dying ridiculously: the living are so cruel to the foolish dead. It's a way of congratulating ourselves on remaining alive.

Kris and I began flipping through the steno notebooks, which had been filled with comments by visitors, the way people write in logbooks in public cabins or guestbooks at art galleries. The chronology began with the July 1993 visit by McCandless's parents. His mother wrote:

"Sonny boy, it's time to leave. The helicopter will soon arrive. I wondered briefly if it would be hard to enter your last home. The wonderful pictures you left in your final testament welcomed me in and I'm finding it difficult to leave, instead. I can appreciate joy in your eyes reported by your self-portraits. I too, will come back to this place. Mom."

These heartfelt words were followed by a single sentence from Krakauer himself: "Chris — Your memory will live on in your admirers."

"Oh, gag," Kris said.

Kris is not what you would call romantic about the wilderness. She and Joe are among the most competent Alaskans I know. They hunt, guide river trips, paddle whitewater all through Alaska and Canada, and travel frequently in the backcountry. In March, they had wanted to catch some of the Iditarod Trail Sled Dog Race, so they'd snowmachined from their house near McKinley Village through the uninhabited midsection of Alaska to Rainy Pass, winter camping along the 300-mile route. I was embarrassed about my modest survival gear when I saw how well-rigged their machines were with snowshoes, a come-along, and other useful equipment compactly stowed. To people like them, the adulation of Christopher McCandless is just one more reason to stay in sensible old Alaska.

✳

Beneath the bed was a small blue suitcase, a Starline, the kind your grandmother might have taken on weekend trips. The lid was busted off the hinges. Christopher McCandless's mother had filled it with survival gear and left it, and over the years other people had removed things or added to it. Joe dragged the suitcase out, plopped it on the bed and called out an inventory as he sorted through the jumble, beginning with a crumpled silver survival blanket: "The Jiffy Pop tinfoil thing. Look right here: saltwater taffy. Holy Bible. Cheesecloth. A map saying 'You are here. Walk this way out to get food.'"

He was joking, I think.

"Emergency first aid kit. The mittens. The headnet. Waterproof matches. The squirrels have gotten to the Ramen. Vaseline. Sewing kit. Jungle head net. Toothpaste. Cigarette papers. Princess Cruises Suntan Lotion SPF 30."

There was more: firestarter, tissue paper, soap, a can of tuna. Then Joe grew bored and went outside so Charles could take his picture posing by the famous bus with a can of Spam in his left hand.

"That's almost bad luck," Connie said quietly, and I had to agree.

Kris and I took turns reading aloud comments left by those who came after the visit by Krakauer and McCandless's parents. Some were epistles, others aphorisms. The earliest dated to January 1994 and was left by a pair of Alaskans who came by snowmachine: "Cloudy, & 42 degrees. Emergency supplies in good order."

In May, people started recording more intimate thoughts:

"Like Chris, I came to Alaska looking for some answers as I near my last year in college. A very emotional day and a highlight of my summer up here in the wild land of Alaska. Constant thoughts of my family and friends."

"I'll return next year and try to set myself free again."

"The vibes I felt from the bus made me sit and think for hours. I wasn't able to sleep until I felt every emotion possible: amazed, sadness, wonderment, happiness, and many more…"

Charles looked over my shoulder and read. "I wish I could come in here and have an inspirational moment," he said. "I wish my life was Zenned out."

"'Only time will tell how Chris McCandless's life has affected mine,'" Kris read. She snorted and looked up. "It's garbage! I mean, am I too cynical?"

We were. We were too cynical to read entry after entry from people looking for meaning in the life and death of a man who had rejected his family, mooched his way across the country and called himself "Alexander Supertramp" in the third person. I struggled to imagine the emotional currents that had carried people here to this bus, so far from their homes, to honor his memory. Later, a friend who had been born in Alaska and exiled to Maryland for five years tried to explain the overwhelming smallness and sameness of life on the suburban East Coast, where lawn care excites great interest; no wonder someone like Christopher McCandless seems adventurous and spiritual and inspiring, despite being dead.

Several visitors mentioned that *Into the Wild* had prompted their trips, but the book must have motivated nearly all of the pilgrimages, because why else would people attach any significance to the bus? They had come from Europe, California, Alabama, Michigan, Minnesota, Utah, Ontario, North Carolina.

One man made the journey after reading a book review while sitting in a doctor's office in Ithaca, N.Y. "It was then I knew the bus was a place I must visit," he wrote. "Christopher's story changed the way I look at a lot of things, moreover it changed my perception of 'need.' I will be forever in your debt Alex! May you wander your travels in peace."

A fellow from Belgium wrote: "I've come from Europe to follow the footsteps of a 'pilgrim,' as says Krakauer, and I'd almost say a prophet!" He then criticized the materialistic attitude of Alaskans and urged them to read Tolstoy "instead of prostituting their country to tourism."

I laughed at that. The Belgian and the others had themselves turned the bus into a perverse tourist destination now so well known that it's mentioned in *The Milepost*. They urged each other to protect the vehicle as a memorial, to leave things untouched. "His monument and tomb are a living truth whose flame will light the 'way of dreams' in other's lives," someone wrote. It was not hard to imagine that before long visitors would be able to buy t-shirts saying "I Visited The Bus" or "I Survived Going Into the Wild." So many people seemed to have found their way out here that an espresso stand didn't seem out of the question.

Astounded by page after page of such writings, we counted the number of people identified in the notebooks. More than 200 had trekked to the bus since McCandless's death, and that didn't account for those who passed by without comment. Think of that: More than 200 people, many as inexperienced as McCandless, had hiked or bicycled along the Stampede Trail to the bus—and every one of them had somehow managed to return safely.

Only one person even vaguely questioned this paradox: "Perhaps we shouldn't romanticize or cananize (sic) him.... After all, Crane and I walked here in no time at all, so Chris wasn't far from life...not really." But then, perhaps unwilling to seem harsh, the writer added, "These questions are in vain. We shouldn't try to climb into another's mind, attempting to know what he thought or felt."

Others criticized Alaskans for doing just that: "I am quite offended when I hear that people mock his story as one of stupidity and carelessness. Every man and woman has desires and hopes for happiness in life, but sadly, only few succeed."

A newcomer to Alaska wrote, "No wonder Alaskans did not understand the call to which most men feel at some point in their lives. No wonder they did not understand Chris McCandless. If you cannot fell it, mine it, or rape it, and in the very end profit from it, then it must be ludicrous and ill-conceived. Idealism, when harnessed for good unselfish acts, results in great men; the greatest and most influential of our times. Chris was on the verge of that path..."

Many people promised in their comments to call their families as soon as they could, so who's to say their journeys were wasted? Yet I felt exactly as a friend did as he read my notes later: repulsed and fascinated.

The practical entries, and there were just a few, were penned by Alaskans who noted the weather conditions, the river's depth, and so on—the sort of information useful to other backcountry travelers. Jon Nierenberg, a Stampede Trail resident, left a detailed description of how to cross the Teklanika River when it runs high—a problem that had defeated McCandless. Added in pencil was the advice, "Also, there's the park boundary cabin six miles away—upstream on the Sushana River. Food there. Don't trash the place."

A few people didn't feel obligated to join the soul-searching. "Too spooked to stay," one guy wrote. Another said, "This place is a mess." And another noted, "It sure is a long way out here. I'm glad I flew in."

But most comments were written by those experiencing some sort of emotional release:

"It's a good place to die."

"I cried so much I couldn't believe it."

"This bus has a sacred feeling to it and I feel grateful to be able to visit the place where Chris lived and died."

"I started my journey here hoping two things. 1) somewhere out there I would find myself 2) that I would find some hope for the future. Now I am here at the bus and I am happy because the future looks up. And I know who I am. Now it's time to go home to the ones I love and help bring truth to the light."

"The beginning of my journey is my departure from this abandoned bus. I feel alive and free—a freedom too beautiful to express in mere words."

"I didn't begin to understand Alex's quest until

An unwritten code of the North decrees that you don't steal, especially from a man's cabin. If an emergency forces you to hole up in a vacant cabin, you leave it as you found it—replenishing the firewood, replacing any food used, and somehow explaining your presence and expressing appreciation to the owner. Unless your life is in danger, you never take a rifle, axe, sleeping bag, or snowshoes from another's cabin... Now that the old-fashioned Code of the North is being discarded, a new man-made peril faces the wilderness traveler. The cabin into which a wayfarer stumbles at 40 degrees below zero may be without life-sustaining food, fuel, or sleeping bag.

And so a special quality of life in the Far North is being lost, and apparently our only recourse is to hire more policemen and use bigger locks just as every other state does.

—Edward J. Fortier,
Point McKenzie trapper
and Alaska journalist

today. Along the way I have discovered peace and tranquility and realized for the first time that the journey is the best part. Unexpectedly filled with emotion upon finding the bus, choking back tears, I can return to life and civilization with fresh eyes. Alex, you have inspired me and changed my life forever. If only there were more like you. Left bottle of Jack Daniels."

"Chris may have fucked up, but he fucked up brilliantly. Nonetheless, family *and* freedom would have been better."

And on and on.

Among my friends and acquaintances, the story of Christopher McCandless makes great after-dinner conversation. Much of the time I agree with the "he had a death wish" camp because I don't know how else to reconcile what we know of his ordeal. Now and then I venture into the "what a dumbshit" territory, tempered by brief alliances with the "he was just another romantic boy on an all-American quest" partisans. Mostly I'm puzzled by the way he's emerged as a hero, a kind of privileged-yet-strangely-dissatisfied-with-his-existence hero.

But it's more complicated than that. I can almost understand why he rejected maps, common sense, conventional wisdom, and local knowledge before embarking on his venture. Occasionally when I hear others make fun of Christopher McCandless, I fall quiet. My favorite book growing up was Scott O'Dell's *Island of the Blue Dolphins*, based on a true story about a nineteenth-century Chumash Indian girl who survived for years alone on an island off the California coast. How often had I imagined myself living in that hut of whale bones, catching fish by hand and taming wild dogs for companionship? It's common, this primal longing to connect with a natural world that provides and cradles, that toughens and inspires.

Yet this is the easiest thing to criticize—the notion that wilderness exists to dispense epiphanies and spiritual cures as part of the scenery. Live here long enough, and you'll learn that every moment spent admiring endless vistas or wandering the land is a privilege, accompanied by plenty of other moments evading mosquitoes by the millions, outlasting weather, avoiding giardia, negotiating unruly terrain, and thinking uneasily about the occasional predator. Walking cross-country through alder thickets or muskeg may be the hardest thing you do all year, as you fight against the earth's tendency to grab hold of you for itself.

And of course it's hard to eat out there. A friend who trapped in his youth likens the bush to a desert, nearly empty of wildlife. One winter he ate marten tendons for days because his food ran out. Read the journal of Fred Fickett, who accompanied Lt. Henry Allen on a 1,500-mile exploration of the Copper, Tanana, and Koyukuk river valleys; it is the story of hungry men.

May 20, 1885: "One of our dogs found a dead goose. We took it from him and ate it." May 22: "Had rotten salmon straight for breakfast. It was so bad that even the Indian dogs wouldn't eat it." May 28: "Had a little paste for breakfast, rotten and wormy meat for dinner, rotten goose eggs and a little rice for supper... about 1/4 what we needed." May 30: "Indian gave us a dinner of boiled meat from which he had scraped the maggots in handfuls before cutting it up. It tasted good, maggots and all."

There's a reason the Natives sometimes starved in the old days—and they knew what they were doing. There's a reason that many homesteaders and bush rats collect welfare to supplement hunting and fishing. There's a reason we gather in cities and villages. So many people want to believe that it's possible to live a noble life alone in the wilderness, living entirely off the land—and yet the indigenous peoples of Alaska know that only by depending upon each other, only by forming a community, does survival become possible.

People have been dying in the wilderness for as long as people have been going into it. There are always lessons to be learned from such sad stories, even lessons as simple as: Don't forget matches, don't sweat in the cold, don't run away from bears. But sometimes there are no learning moments, no explanations. From an account in the *Nome Nugget* of July 30, 1901:

"The death of George Dean by starvation at the mouth of the Agiapuk River and the narrow escape of his two companions, Thierry and Houston, from the same fate makes a strange story. Without wishing to criticize the survivors, it looks as if they did not make that hustle for life which men should. They were so near the course of navigation that they could hear the voices of men as they passed up and down the river."

Why didn't they…why couldn't they…why wouldn't they? And the wise *Nome Nugget* avoids this trap by shrugging away such unanswerables:

"But it's a strange country, and strange things happen in it."

In 1930, not far south from the Stampede Road, park rangers found the body of prospector Tom Kenney on a bar of the McKinley River. Kenney had disappeared July 19 after separating from his partner. On September 3, searchers discovered Kenney lying on his back with his arms at his side. One shoe was off, and searchers concluded he had been salving his foot — "which would indicate that he had been in his right mind up to the last," the newspaper reported.

Kenney had traveled about eight miles downriver, making several campfires. He and his partner had been searching for a lost gold placer mine, but toward the end, Tom Kenney surely would have traded all the gold he could carry for the sight of another person, for some clear notion of the way home. He must have eaten berries. He had killed and eaten several porcupines. At his final camp, rangers found a large pile of unburned dry wood. "It is known that Kenney always kept a diary, but as his pockets were not examined before burial it will never be known whether he set down an account of his wanderings or not," the *Alaska Weekly* reported.

You can hear the pain of letting go in the words of a prospector and trapper named Tom O'Brien, who died of scurvy in the summer of 1919 on the Whiting River near Juneau. In the book *The Dangerous North*, historian Ed Ferrell includes O'Brien's diary entries that describe teeth rattling in his sore gums, his fever and his aching joints, which conspired to keep him from collecting water, firewood, and food. Day by day he ate one meal of unheated rice or potato soup. He weakened and his mental faculties faded. Finally he realized he was suffering from scurvy, but his relief measures came too late. After two months of recording his trials, he left behind a final entry: "Life is dying hard. The heart is strong."

So many ways to die in the North, in manners grand and surprising and sad. A moment's inattention, the proverbial series of small miscalculations that add up to one giant screwup, delusion about one's abilities, hubris, mental imbalance, plain bad luck—that's all it takes.

For a few weeks last spring, I kept track of news articles reporting outdoor deaths. Over the winter, more than thirty Alaskans died in snowmachine accidents, a record. They had lost their way in blizzards, fallen through ice and drowned, been buried in avalanches, collided with each other. An intoxicated man perched on a boat's gunwales fell into the Chena River in downtown Fairbanks when waves rocked the vessel; his body did not emerge for days. Two men suffocated from carbon monoxide poisoning after they brought a charcoal grill into their tent near Chena Hot Springs. Two young kayakers were missing and presumed dead in the Gulf of Alaska. Campers found the bones of an eighteen-year-old soldier who disappeared while ice fishing near the Knik Arm fifteen years ago. And even as searchers looked for a man who had disappeared in the Chugach Mountains came the news that seventy-year-old Dick Cook, an extraordinary woodsman described by John McPhee as the "acknowledged high swami of the river people," had drowned in the Tatonduk, a river he knew intimately. Some days it seemed surprising that people survive the outdoors at all.

And yet there we were, we crude Alaskans, scoffing and making jokes in Fairbanks 142, shaking our heads and posing with cans of Spam. We want it both ways. We want to impress others and ourselves with scary tales of death defied at every turn, to point out that Alaska is so

---

A rmy Air Force co-pilot Leon Crane parachuted from a crashing B-24 bomber on the Yukon River drainage in December 1943. Thirty years later, Yukon River residents told writer John McPhee about a man who had walked out of the bush in winter: "Guy jumped out of an airplane, and he would have died but he found a cabin." McPhee tracked Crane down in Philadelphia through military records and told Crane's story in *Coming Into the Country*. Only Crane survived the crash. He waited eight days for rescue, with his parachute for shelter. When he realized no one knew where he was, he started walking. Crane happened on two cabins, one well-stocked with food and equipment, during the eighty deep winter days he spent surviving and making his way out of the wilderness.

—Ellen Bielawski

unforgiving that a person could die just a few miles from help, and still we scorn those drawn to that mystique, those poor, foolish slobs who manage to die out of ignorance or stupidity or even bad luck. Perhaps that's because we know that one day—just like that, really—we could so easily become one of those poor, foolish slobs ourselves.

Occasionally I paused while flipping through the note-books and looked out a busted window to watch how the mid-afternoon sun glazed the snow. We needed to return before dark, so I started skimming the entries, my eyes catching only certain words: Peace. Solitude. Meaning.

It was hard work, resisting the longing that rose from the scribbled words. I spent some moments puzzling over this comment written by a man from Ontario: "[Chris] gave his life in exchange for knowledge and his story is his contribution to the world. I feel complete now to put this story behind me as it was on my mind for quite some time."

This may be our oldest, truest survival skill: the ability to tell and to learn from each other's stories, whether from Aesop's fables, quest narratives, Greek mythology, the Book of Genesis, office gossip, the wisdom of elders, or made-for-TV movies. In some ways, Alaska is nothing but stories. We have constructed many of our ideas about this place, and about ourselves, from creation stories, gold rush stories, hunting and fishing stories, pioneer stories, family stories, clan stories. Even the animals told tales in the old Story Time, which is long behind us now.

Pay attention to what people say in bars and across dinner tables and around campfires, and often they are really telling survival stories of some sort or another: how I crossed the river, how I lost the trail, how I got my moose, how I fixed my boat, how I left home for the north, how I beat the storm, how I made it through another cold and lonely winter, how I became a true Alaskan. What all these stories mean, though—that's up to you, the listener.

We can't know exactly why Christopher McCandless died. What matters now is what people want to believe about his death. Krakauer hypothesized that toxic seeds of the wild potato plant weakened him, and early test results seemed to support that. But chemists at the University of Alaska Fairbanks further studied wild potato seeds, as well as seeds from the similar-looking wild sweetpea, and their work seemed to eliminate the poisoning theory.

"I would be willing to bet money that neither species had toxic metabolites that would account for the fate of McCandless," chemist Tom Clausen told me in an email. His conclusions appeared in the *Fairbanks Daily News-Miner* but never received wide coverage. Clausen added, "I believe McCandless died not from toxic foods but from foolishness. I hate to be so blunt about the dead but he clearly went 'into the wild' unprepared."

But the idea that McCandless was poisoned accidentally has become critical to his legend, because it means he wasn't stupid, wasn't seeking death. When I mentioned the research to the bus driver, he gave me an obstinate look and said, "The question is still open." He could not surrender the "right" story.

The one thing we can say about McCandless is that his biggest mistake may have been his failure to listen to the right stories. He ignored advice about the scarcity of game, the practicalities of bear protection, the importance of maps, the truths of the land. He was too intent on creating the story of himself.

And yet, that story has such power, such meaning for so many people, that they feel drawn—called personally—to travel across the globe and hike the trail all that way to the bus to look for Christopher McCandless or Alexander Supertramp or themselves. They endure mosquitoes and rain and tough walking and bad river crossings and the possibility of bears. The burden the pilgrims carry to the bus is so heavy, laden with their frailties and hopes and desires, with their lives that don't quite satisfy. And when they arrive, they sit in that cold bus and think, and sometimes they cry from loss and longing and relief.

Well, so many of them are young, and they're lost, somehow, just as he was.

As he was dying, Christopher McCandless took a picture of himself propped against the bus. He held up a good-bye note, a smile on his gaunt face, and from this photograph Krakauer concluded that "Chris McCandless was at peace, serene as a monk gone to God." But only Christopher McCandless could have known what truth was in his heart, there at the end. All we can say is that whoever he was, he's not that person anymore. Jon Krakauer made a story about him, by way of telling his own, and every pilgrim since his death has shaped him into something different as well. I'm doing it right now, too.

For many Alaskans, the problem is not necessarily that Christopher McCandless attempted what he did—most of us came here in search of something, didn't we? Haven't we made our own embarrassing mistakes? But we can't afford to take his story seriously because it doesn't say much a careful person doesn't already know about desire and survival. The lessons are so obvious as to be laughable: Look at a map. Take some food. Know where you are. Listen to people who are smarter than you. Be humble. Go on out there—but it won't mean much unless you come back.

This is what bothers me—that Christopher McCandless failed so badly, so harshly, and yet so *famously* that his death has

come to symbolize something admirable, that his unwilling-
ness to see Alaska for what it really is has somehow become
the story so many people associate with this place, a story so
hollow you can almost hear the wind blowing through it. His
death was not a brilliant fuck-up. It was not even a terribly
original fuck-up. It was just one of the more recent and point-
less fuck-ups.

At 3 P.M., after we'd read through the notebooks, taken our
silly and disrespectful photographs and eaten our lunches, we
climbed back on our snowmachines and left. We rode against
the wind as the light softened and dimmed all around. It grew
colder, but it was still a good day to be outside, with spring on
its way. I could feel fond about winter, now that it was dwin-
dling. What I really wanted was to keep going beyond the bus,
across the Sushana River and maybe down into the park.

As we followed our tracks home, I kept thinking about
poor Christopher McCandless, entombed by the tributes of
his pilgrims, forever wandering between the world he wanted
and the world that exists, still trapped by other people's desires
to make him something he is not—which is why he came out
here in the first place.

Too late he learned that the hard part isn't walking toward
the wilderness to discover the meaning of life. The hard part
is returning from the consolations of nature and finding
meaning anyway, a meaning lodged within the faithfulness of
our ordinary lives, in the plain and painful beauty of our ordinary days.

Some day, I told myself, I might return. I'd do what few
people do anymore, which is to pass by that junky old bus
with only a sidelong glance and see what else is out there.

When she was a girl growing up in Juneau, Sherry Simpson's secret ambition was to walk the entire rim of Alaska's coast. Later she thought she could settle for trekking the border between Canada and Alaska, from the southern end all the way to the tippy-top. As it turns out, the older she gets, the happier she is simply exploring the North one mile and one page at a time. She is the author of The Way Winter Comes: Alaska Stories, *and her essays and articles have appeared in numerous anthologies and publications, including* Sierra, Backpacker, Alaska, Creative Nonfiction, American Nature Writing 1995 *and* 1997, Under Northern Lights, *and* Another Wilderness: New Outdoor Writing by Women. *She currently teaches nonfiction writing at the University of Alaska Anchorage in the Department of Creative Writing and Literary Arts. This story was originally published in* The Anchorage Press.

PART FIVE

THE LAST WORD

NANCY LORD

* * *

In the Giant's Hand

A long-time resident recalls
a place of perfect paradise.

ARRIGETCH, WE KNEW BEFORE WE ARRIVED, MEANT "fingers of the hand extended" in the language of the Nunamiut Eskimos, the caribou hunters who once broadly inhabited the land. The Arrigetch peaks in Alaska's central Brooks Range were anomalous gray granite upthrusts, mountaineers' hard-rock dreams, as dramatic a landscape as can be found anywhere on earth.

Today, their photographs grace one nature calendar after another, and a national park—Gates of the Arctic—surrounds them, the sparkliest jewel cluster in a many-jeweled crown. But in 1971, the Arrigetch were still off the maps of most Americans, still part of that great wild North that, even on real, topographic maps, existed only at the 1:250,000 scale. An inch spanned four miles, and still there were broad blank spaces marked only with contour lines and the earth colors of vegetation and rock. The blue threads of unnamed creeks wound through unnamed valleys under unnamed mountains, and there was nothing like a road or airstrip or even a trail in

269

sight. The Brooks and the Arrigetch were epic countries then, places of outermost dream.

A June day, that ancient year. The sky is blue. The air is warm. For the moment, there's enough breeze to keep most of the mosquitoes grounded in the tightly woven tundra. Snow patches still fill hollows and streak the north-facing slopes, but they're melting as I watch, tinkling as their skeletal crystals collapse against rock. Green spears and tiny, pastel alpine flowers rush to fill in behind the retreating snow. It's all like some heavenly garden as I work my way along the pathways of licheny rock slabs and nappy ground, down from the benchland where our tents flutter their bright primary colors, to the valley floor and the creek that creases its bottom. Rivulets of water run everywhere, down the faces of rocks, into cascading waterfalls, spilling from one basin into the next. Small birds flit, and bees buzz. One solitary caribou lifts its alert head and springs away on clicking hooves. The air is so incredibly clear, like looking through ice water—almost a magnification. Those silvery granite peaks rise all around, as though just yesterday some god or giant pushed them through the crust. Rumblings of rockfall attest to the work-in-progress nature of this nature; freeze and thaw, freeze and thaw, and gravity exerting its pull. Talus stacks up deeply, precariously, at the mountains' feet.

I climb to the top of a boulder and spread myself over its sun-warmed surface. It pleases me to think that I may be the first person ever to climb up and sit on top of that particular rock. The Nunamiut who roamed these valleys probably didn't do a lot of frivolous rock-sitting, and few other people have entered here—to my knowledge only one previous group of recreationalists. Everything about the entire valley and surrounding peaks, sky, and last, lost, never-never land pleases me; if I had to construct an image of paradise, this would be it.

From the distance comes the clear, clean ringing sound of a piton being pounded into rock. Others of my party have availed themselves of the practice cliffs close to camp, to test the rock and their own climbing skills. We are here, after all, as climbers—ten of us from a new little college in Massachusetts: two who teach in the school's Outdoors Program, the wife of one, and seven students who have just completed their own and the college's first year. Our leader, David Roberts, a veteran of numerous Alaska climbing expeditions, had taught us, back in the smoothed-over Berkshires, the rudimentary arts of negotiating rock walls and had, now, brought us to a place of Olympian proportion. David was, at the time, only twenty-seven years old. When I think back from middle-age—an age when anyone *under* thirty seems suspect, at the least frighteningly short on maturity—I'm astonished. Who allowed us all to go off and do something so grand?

Lest you think some disaster befell us, let me assure you that it did not. For five weeks the ten of us climbed, hiked, camped among bears, and swirled downriver in plastic rafts, and we suffered nothing worse than blisters, mosquito bites, and the occasional storm of irritation with one another.

We were, still, in wilderness, in a time before global positioning systems and personal rescue beacons that reported via satellite. We carried a substantial rifle—a 30.06—for bear protection, but no radio. Had any of us fallen sick or been injured, the closest help lay two days distant. There was not, in those days, even much plane traffic; in our weeks in the Arrigetch, the only plane we saw was the one that made our airdrop onto a rock field, bursting our boxes and spraying our one bag of sugar into oblivion.

David, when I last saw him, reminded me that, of everyone on that trip, I was the only one who approached Alaska as something more than an attractive summer playground. He remembered me going on, like someone immodestly in love, about how fabulous the country was, how paradisiacal, how there could be no other place on earth so exactly what I considered ideal and idyllic. I reminded David that, when I packed up and moved to Alaska two years later, he warned me against doing so. What he'd said was, *living in Alaska will rot your brain.*

See me there, on top of that never-touched-by-human-hands boulder, filling my whole self with that pure Alaska spring air, my heart so big in my chest it might push right through my ribs. See me leap down and nearly weep at the flutter of bell-shaped flowers. I drink of the running water, gaze at the lofty peaks, dream of remaining forever in that perfect valley.

Am I over the top in my enthusiasms? Absolutely. Even as I fantasize staying in the Arrigetch for all time, I must know that the brief summer interlude is just that, and that arctic winters are interminably long, sunlessly dark, and spit-freezingly cold. Still, I hold an image of myself curled up in an earthen house under caribou blankets, savoring moonlight and sculpted snowdrifts.

I was not, really, a climber. I had learned to enjoy attacking rock like a puzzle, trusting my body to find handholds and fist-jamming cracks, to stand on my feet. I was reasonably fearless when belayed from above, willing to try any move, capable of finding my way up easy routes. I liked the teamwork, the coaching and coaxing, the feel of rope at my waist and, while belaying another, feeding assuredly through my hands. I liked simply being on rock, pressing palm and fingertips to the grainy surface, admiring the way plants worked tenacious roots into the smallest cracks on the tiniest ledges; I loved, in the Arrigetch, being surprised by an exquisitely white snow bunting that shot out of its nest near the top of a cliff. But I was not ambitious when it came to climbing, and not particularly competitive. I had no great desires to reach the tops of those granite fingers—except, perhaps, to see over the other side, to gaze upon more of my beloved land.

I did climb some, there in the Arrigetch. I practiced on the cliffs and on boulders, and I partook of the one climb we all did together—up to the col between two peaks named the East and West Maidens, where we split into four groups, two for each peak. I summited the East Maiden, not much of a technical feat. We might have simply walked the ridge, but we were cautious; we roped up and protected the route. At the top we found the cairn and bottled note of the only previous ascenders, from 1964. The view of the vertical back side made me hold my breath—that deep dive to another green and river-braided valley and, beyond, more rows of blue mountains fading gradually to pale and paler, turning under with the earth's very curve. We ate our candy bars and retreated. Clouds moved in, and snow flurried down on us. We retraced our chopped steps down a long snow couloir and picked our way back over a longer and shifty boulderfield.

Other days, with various combinations of companions, I explored our valley, hiked to another col between two peaks, hiked to the pass at the head of the valley. The day that David and Ed Ward, our other climbing instructor, made a first ascent of a monolith called Shot Tower, I hiked to its base to watch them negotiate its difficult midsection. Back at camp, near midnight, I watched with binoculars as they, tiny as flies in the dome of a cathedral, finally stood on top and waved. In my innocence, I had never doubted that they would.

Four of us organized a five-day trek, from our valley over the pass, through the next valley and back to camp, about a twenty-five-mile circuit. We saw small numbers of caribou and traveled, at times, on their grooved trails lined with discarded antlers and dry bones, bits of caribou hair blowing in the breeze. Aside from another cairn and note at the top of the pass, left by the same party that had climbed The Maidens in '64, we saw no other sign of humans, not so much as a jet's contrail overhead. Laboring under my pack through heat, thunderstorm, and mosquitoes, I lost myself in the idea of valley after splendorous valley. We forded creeks and bathed in pools, studied our map and located the right pass to complete our circle. The last day we found ourselves deep in bushwhacking country, with no animal trails through the tangles and mosquitoes so thick we could kill forty with a swat. I thought I might die. But then we climbed out of the brush and the bugs, back to base camp, that place that still looked a lot like heaven.

I kept a journal that summer, a journal I didn't look at again until I decided to try this essay—only to discover that the pages were filled with overwrought teenage emotion rather than useful detail. I did not record the name of a single plant (except the fabulous fireweed) or bird (not even the snow bunting) or any other bit of natural history smaller than caribou. I also did not take any photos that summer— or even own a camera. The life of the moment was all I wanted, and I was sure that such moments would be mine forever—because I would never forget, and because I would return to the Arrigetch many more times. I would become, I wrote in my journal, a park ranger or an archaeologist or a camp cook.

My one concession to naming things lies at the heart of my journal—a map I drew of our valley, showing the circling of peaks, each with the name bestowed by climbers before us and known to David—Citadel, the Camel, Disneyland, Badile, Battleship, Pyramid, the Prong, sixteen altogether on my map. I show the creek running down the center of the valley, the pass at the head, and our four tents pitched on the bench below the Maidens. It's a fair representation, I think, and in my head today stands for the place itself, which otherwise would be far vaguer, shrouded in forgetful mist.

After three weeks in the mountains, we packed up our tents, sleeping bags, and climbing equipment, hoisted our loads, and hiked out, three days to a lake where we traded our climbing gear for plastic rafts with wimpy toy paddles. For ten days a slow current carried us down 180 miles of winding river. Fireweed blazed along the banks, we napped, we swam, we watched two young wolves playing. It rained, and we gathered around a driftwood fire and got smoke in our eyes while we ate more noodles with tuna and described for one another the tastes of fresh apples, peaches, asparagus. We reached an Athabascan village with a volleyball court and an airstrip, and we got on a scheduled plane and flew to Fairbanks and drove back to Massachusetts.

Two years later, with my fisherman-wannabe sweetie, I moved to Alaska. We chose a home nowhere near my perfect and implausible Arrigetch, but a town on the south coast; its dot on a map, at the end of a road, looked of a size that seemed "right" if you expected to find some kind of existing shelter, someone to pay you for doing something, and a post office where you might have an address. We've lived there ever after, and I've never returned to the Arrigetch or anywhere at all in the Brooks Range.

If you'd told me, in 1971, that I wouldn't see the Arrigetch again, I would not have believed you. What, short of death, would keep me away?

Well, the reality of living in Alaska impressed itself upon me rather quickly. In our seasonal economy, summer is the frantic period in which to work and earn money; one doesn't go off and scamper in the mountains. I also learned something about the rest of the year. Winter has its pleasures, but huddling in the cold and dark are not among them. Somehow, I did not become a mountain-mama outdoorswoman, and I did not build my own little log cabin in the Arctic, or even in the sub-Arctic. I did, for a summer, become a camp cook at a remote salmon hatchery, where I filled my spare time fishing for Dolly Varden and picking blueberries by the bucket. I *did* take up commercial salmon fishing, and I *have* seen some of Alaska's magnificent coastline and I *have* fallen in love with landscapes all over the state, from southeast forests to Alaska Peninsula volcanoes to barrier islands along the Arctic coast. Everyday, when I look out my Homer window at ocean, mountains, and sky, I marvel at the beauty I live within.

These days, my knees are rickety, and I doubt I'll punish them with any more voluntary backpacking, never mind technical climbing. I know that, although I could, I probably never will see the Arrigetch again. But I'm all right with that. I know something that I didn't know when I was nineteen, and it has to do with the limits of one life. I also know better some things I may have known even at nineteen, having to do with seizing opportunities and letting ourselves dream. The power of the Arrigetch, for me, lay not only in its splendor, its scale, and the possibilities it suggested. The Arrigetch taught me about the potency of place and why we need large landscapes that will forever be *more* than what we humans want to make of them.

I'm an Alaskan now, without delusion or much sentiment. Each new summer I meet young people backpacking through town, turning their ruddy faces to the hills. I overhear their plans for scaling this or running that and how, later, they'll find some old cabin to make-over for winter. They talk about Lake Clark and Katmai, about Denali, the Wrangells, and Kenai Fjords. They get out their maps and find the big spaces that still exist. At the end of the road and beyond, far off in the roomy reaches of our public lands, the newly arrived lie down in fields of fireweed or walk barefoot on smooth sand beaches, and they think they've found the places that will forever set the standards for what's loveliest and most necessary in the world. Each new summer I shake my smarter, graying head, but I can't keep back the smile that admits memory *and* moment, now joyfully joined.

Nancy Lord settled in Homer, Alaska thirty years ago and has only recently begun to explore Alaska again as she once thought she routinely would. Recent stops have included the Alaska Peninsula and Aleutians, Bering Sea islands including Pribilofs, and the Arctic Coast. She is the author of three short story collections and three non-fiction books, including Green Alaska: Dreams from the Far Coast, *which retraces and reimagines the Harriman Alaska Expedition of 1899.*

Index

Index of Contributors

Recommended Reading

Berger, Thomas R. *Village Journey.* New York: Hill and Wang, 1985.

Cahill, Tim. *Road Fever: A High Speed Travelogue.* New York: Vintage Departures, 1994.

Davidson, Art. *Minus 148°: First Winter Ascent of Mt. McKinley.* Seattle: Cloudcap Press, 1986.

Ford, Corey. *Where the Sea Breaks Its Back: The Epic Story of Early Naturalist Georg Steller and the Russian Exploration of Alaska.* Anchorage: Alaska Northwest Books, 1992.

Freedman, Lew. *Iditarod Classics: Tales of the Trail from Men and Women Who Race Across Alaska.* Kenmore, Wash.: Epicenter Press, 1992.

Gabriel, Moses P. *Gwich'in History.* Fairbanks: Yukon/Alaska Publishing Company, 1993.

Garfield, Brian. *The Thousand-Mile War.* New York: Doubleday, 1969.

Goldstein, Niles Elliot. *God at the Edge: Searching for the Divine in Uncomfortable and Unexpected Places.* New York: Bell Tower, 2000.

Halliday, Jan. *Native Peoples of Alaska: A Traveler's Guide to Land, Art and Culture.* Seattle: Sasquatch Books, 1998.

Hedlin, Robert and Gary Holthouse (eds.). *Alaska: Reflections on Land and Spirit.* Tucson: University of Arizona Press, 1989.

Houston, Pam. *A Little More About Me.* New York: W.W. Norton, 1999.

Huntington, Sidney. *Shadows on the Koyukuk: An Alaskan Native's Life Along the River.* Portland: Alaska Northwest Books, 1993.

Jans, Nick. *A Place Beyond: Finding Home in Arctic Alaska.* Portland: Alaska Northwest Books, 1996.

Kizzia, Tom. *The Wake of the Unseen Object: Among the Native Cultures of Bush Alaska.* New York: Henry Holt and Company, 1992.

Krakauer, Jon. *Eiger Dreams: Ventures Among Men and Mountains.* Guilford, Conn.: Lyons & Burford, 1990.

Krakauer, Jon. *Into the Wild.* New York: Villard Books, 1996.

Kremers, Carolyn. *Place of the Pretend People: Gifts from a Yup'ik Eskimo Village.* Portland: Alaska Northwest Books, 1996.

Kusz, Natalie. *Road Song: A Memoir.* New York: Harper-Perennial, 1991.

Langdon, Steve J. *The Native People of Alaska.* Anchorage: Greatland Graphics, 1993.

Lentfer, Hank and Carolyn Servid (eds.). *Arctic Refuge: A Circle of Testimony.* Minneapolis: Milkweed Editions, 2001.

Leo, Richard. *Way Out Here: Modern Life in Ice-Age Alaska.* Seattle: Sasquatch Books, 1996.

Lopez, Barry. *Arctic Dreams: Imagination and Desire in a Northern Landscape.* New York: Charles Scribner's Sons, 1986.

Lord, Nancy. *Fish Camp: Life on an Alaskan Shore.* Washington, D.C.: Shearwater Books, 1997.

Lord, Nancy. *Green Alaska: Dreams from the Far Coast.* Washington, D.C.: Counterpoint Press, 2000.

Marshall, Robert. *Alaska Wilderness: Exploring the Central Brooks Range.* Berkeley: University of California Press, 1970.

McGinnis, Joe. *Going to Extremes*. New York: Alfred A. Knopf, 1980.

McPhee, John. *Coming into the Country*. New York: Farrar, Straus and Giroux, 1976.

Mergler, Wayne (ed.). *The Last New Land: Stories of Alaska Past and Present*. Portland: Alaska Northwest Books, 1996.

Miller, Debbie. *Midnight Wilderness: Journeys in Alaska's Arctic National Wildlife Refuge*. San Francisco: Sierra Club Books, 1990.

Moore, Kathleen Dean. *Holdfast: At Home in the Natural World*. Guilford, Conn.: Lyons Press, 1999.

Morgan, Lael (ed.). *Alaska's Native People*. Anchorage: Alaska Geographic Quarterly 6(3), 1979.

Nelson, Richard. *The Island Within*. New York: Vintage Books, 1991.

Paulsen, Gary. *Winterdance: The Fine Madness of Running the Iditarod*. New York: Harvest Books, 1995.

Rich, Kim. *Johnny's Girl: A Daughter's Memoir of Growing Up in Alaska's Underworld*. Portland: Alaska Northwest Books, 1999.

Roberts, David. *The Early Climbs: Deborah and the Mountain of My Fear*. Seattle: The Mountaineers Books, 1991.

Roberts, David. *Moments of Doubt and Other Mountaineering Writings*. Cambridge, Mass.: The Mountaineers, 1986.

Romano-Lax, Andromeda. *Alaska's Kenai Peninsula: A Traveler's Guide*. Portland: Alaska Northwest Books, 2001.

Romano-Lax, Andromeda. *How to Rent a Public Cabin in Southcentral Alaska*. Berkeley: Wilderness Press, 1999.

Schooler, Lynn. *The Blue Bear*. Toronto: HarperCollins Publishers, 2002.

Servid, Carolyn. *Of Landscape and Longing: Finding a Home at the Water's Edge*. Minneapolis: Milkweed Editions, 2000.

Servid, Carolyn (ed.). *From the Island's Edge: A Sitka Reader.* St. Paul: Graywolf Press, 1995.

Sherwonit, Bill. *To the Top of Denali: Climbing Adventures on North America's Highest Peak.* Portland: Alaska Northwest Books, 2000.

Sherwonit, Bill. *Alaska's Accessible Wilderness: A Traveler's Guide to Alaska's State Parks.* Portland: Alaska Northwest Books, 1996.

Sherwonit, Bill (ed.). *Denali: A Literary Anthology.* Seattle: The Mountaineers, 2000.

Sherwonit, Bill and Jeff Schultz. *Iditarod: The Great Race to Nome.* Seattle: Sasquatch Books, 2002.

Simpson, Sherry. *The Way Winter Comes.* Seattle: Sasquatch Books, 1998.

Spencer, Page. *White Silk and Black Tar.* Minneapolis, Bergamot Books, 1990.

Walker, Tom and Larry Aumiller. *River of Bears.* Stillwater, Minn.: Voyageur Press, 1993.

Waterman, Jon. *In the Shadow of Denali.* New York: Dell, 1994.

Zwinger, Susan. *Stalking the Ice Dragon: An Alaskan Journey.* Tucson: University of Arizona Press, 1991.

Acknowledgments

Special thanks to all of the writers, who submitted so many remarkable stories, including ones that did not make it into this anthology. Thank you to David Roberts for his delightful and perceptive introduction, and to the editors and publishers at Travelers' Tales for their fine work and dedication to this book.

Additionally, the Alaska editors express appreciation to their families for ongoing support of their writing lives. Bill Sherwonit especially thanks his wife, Dulcy Boehle, and, mom, Torie Sherwonit; Ellen Bielawski thanks Kay Bielawski; and Andromeda Romano-Lax thanks Brian Lax.

"Sixty-Five" by Jeff Fair reprinted from the December 2000 issue of *Appalachia*. Copyright © 2000 by Jeff Fair. Reprinted by permission of the author.

"Surrounded by Bears" by Ed Readicker-Henderson published with permission from the author. Copyright © 2003 by Ed Readicker-Henderson.

"The Flyboys of Talkeetna" by Jon Krakauer excerpted from *Eiger Dreams: Ventures Among Men and Mountains* by Jon Krakauer. Copyright © 1990 by Jon Krakauer. Reprinted by permission of The Lyons Press, an imprint of Globe Pequot.

"Kayaking Through a Timeless Realm of Rain, Bugs, and B.O." by Barbara Brown published with permission from the author. Copyright © 2003 by Barbara Brown.

"Eating Edward Curtis at the Ugruk Café" by Daniel Henry published with permission from the author. Copyright © 2003 by Daniel Henry.

"The Only Place Like This" by Kathleen Dean Moore excerpted from *Holdfast: At Home in the Natural World* by Kathleen Dean Moore.

Selection from Rex Allen Rock, Sr. excerpted from *Growing Up Native in Alaska* by Alexandra J. McClanahan. Copyright © 2000 by The CIRI Foundation. Reprinted by permission of the CIRI Foundation.

Selection from "The Hard Way Home" by Steve Kahn published with permission from the author. Copyright © 2003 by Steve Kahn.

Selection from *Iditarod Classics: Tales of the Trail Told by the Men & Women Who Race Across Alaska* by Lew Freedman reprinted by permission of Epicenter Press. Copyright © 1992 by Lew Freedman.

Selection from "Paddling Solo in the Fjords of the Far West Shore" by Jon Nickles published with permission from the author. Copyright © 2003 by Jon Nickles.

Selection from "Paris! Rome! Deadhorse!" by Robin Cerwonka published with permission from the author. Copyright © 2003 by Robin Cerwonka.

Selection from "Plowing the Driveway" by Dana Greci published with permission from the author. Copyright © 2003 by Dana Greci.

Selection from "Reality Bites Back" by John Woodbury published with permission from the author. Copyright © 2003 by John Woodbury.

Selection from "Steambath" by Tim Troll published with permission from the author. Copyright © 2003 by Tim. Troll.

Selection from "A Time Machine Called the Chilkoot Trail" by Dana Stabenow published with permission from the author. Copyright © 2003 by Dana Stabenow.

Selection from "The Whale's Gift" by James Dorsey published with permission from the author. Copyright © 2003 by James Dorsey.

About the Editors

Born in Bridgeport, Connecticut, Anchorage nature and travel writer Bill Sherwonit first visited Alaska in 1974 while employed as a geologist. After switching from geology to journalism during the late 1970s, he returned to Alaska in 1982 as a sports writer for *The Anchorage Times*. Sherwonit worked at the newspaper ten years, the last seven as its outdoors writer/editor.

Now a full-time freelancer, he's contributed stories and photos to a wide variety of newspapers, magazines, journals, anthologies, and guidebooks. He's the author of several books on Alaska: *To the Top of Denali: Climbing Adventures on North America's Highest Peak, Iditarod: The Great Race to Nome, Alaska's Accessible Wilderness: A Traveler's Guide to Alaska's State Parks, Alaska Ascents, Alaska's Bears, Denali: A Literary Anthology, Denali: The Complete Guide*, and most recently, *Wood-Tikchik: Alaska's Largest State Park*. Bill also teaches classes in wilderness writing and travel/adventure writing at the University of Alaska Anchorage.

Sherwonit lives in the foothills of the Chugach Mountains with wife Dulcy Boehle and eighty-one year old mom, Torie Sherwonit, a recent transplant from Virginia. There he writes about the wildness to be found in Alaska's urban center, as well as in the state's backcountry wilderness.

Andromeda Romano-Lax drove to Alaska from her native Chicagoland in December 1994 with her husband Brian, baby son Aryeh, and dog. During the month-long trip, their car broke down seven times, they maxed out every credit card they owned, and they spent Christmas Eve with nothing to eat but frozen jalapeño peppers. They've been too afraid and too broke to risk driving the Alcan Highway again, and so Anchorage has remained their home. By air, they also travel to Mexico, where Romano-Lax and family (including a second child, daughter Tziporah) have paddled and sailed the Sea of Cortez, and Puerto Rico, where she studied the cello as research for a forthcoming novel. Romano-Lax is the author of five books, including four guidebooks to Alaska and Mexico, and a travel narrative, *Searching for Steinbeck's Sea of Cortez: A Makeshift Expedition Along Baja's Desert Coast*. She teaches creative writing at the University of Alaska Anchorage and in children's workshop settings.

Ellen Bielawski was born in Alaska and still prefers northern life to any other, although she has worked as an archaeologist in West Africa and trekked in Tibet. Her two sons have accompanied her from Ghana to Grise Fiord. They refuse to drive the Alaska Highway with her one more time. Her editing credits include scientific papers as well as essays. She is the author of *Rogue Diamonds*, an account of diamond miners and aboriginal people on Canada's Barren Lands, and *Life in Ancient Alaska*, as well as numerous magazine articles.

TRAVELERS' TALES

THE SOUL OF TRAVEL

Footsteps Series

THE FIRE NEVER DIES
One Man's Raucous Romp
Down the Road of Food,
Passion, and Adventure
By Richard Sterling
ISBN 1-885-211-70-8
$14.95

"Sterling's writing is like spit-
fire, foursquare and jazzy with crackle...."
—*Kirkus Reviews*

LAST TROUT
IN VENICE
The Far-Flung Escapades
of an Accidental
Adventurer
By Doug Lansky
ISBN 1-885-211-63-5
$14.95

"Traveling with Doug Lansky might result in
a considerably shortened life expectancy...but
what a way to go." —Tony Wheeler,
Lonely Planet Publications

ONE YEAR OFF
Leaving It All Behind for a
Round-the-World Journey
with Our Children
By David Elliot Cohen
ISBN 1-885-211-65-1
$14.95

A once-in-a-lifetime
adventure generously shared.

THE WAY OF
THE WANDERER
Discover Your True Self
Through Travel
By David Yeadon
ISBN 1-885-211-60-0
$14.95

Experience transformation through travel
with this delightful, illustrated collection by
award-winning author David Yeadon.

TAKE ME
WITH YOU
A Round-the-World
Journey to Invite a
Stranger Home
By Brad Newsham
ISBN 1-885-211-51-1
$24.00 (cloth)

"Newsham is an ideal guide. His journey, at
heart, is into humanity." —Pico Iyer, author
of *Video Night in Kathmandu*

KITE STRINGS OF
THE SOUTHERN
CROSS
A Woman's
Travel Odyssey
By Laurie Gough
ISBN 1-885-211-54-6
$14.95 ─ ★ ★ ─

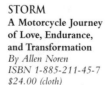

ForeWord Silver Medal Winner
—*Travel Book of the Year*

THE SWORD
OF HEAVEN
A Five Continent Odyssey
to Save the World
By Mikkel Aaland
ISBN 1-885-211-44-9
$24.00 (cloth)

"Few books capture the soul
of the road like *The Sword of Heaven*,
a sharp-edged, beautifully rendered memoir
that will inspire anyone." —Phil Cousineau,
author of *The Art of Pilgrimage*

STORM
A Motorcycle Journey
of Love, Endurance,
and Transformation
By Allen Noren
ISBN 1-885-211-45-7
$24.00 (cloth) ─ ★ ★ ─

ForeWord Gold Medal Winner
—*Travel Book of the Year*

Travelers' Tales Classics

COAST TO COAST
A Journey Across 1950s America
By Jan Morris
ISBN 1-885-211-79-1
$16.95

After reporting on the first Everest ascent in 1953, Morris spent a year journeying by car, train, ship, and aircraft across the United States. In her brilliant prose, Morris records with exuberance and curiosity a time of innocence in the U.S.

TRADER HORN
A Young Man's Astounding Adventures in 19th Century Equatorial Africa
By Alfred Aloysius Horn
ISBN 1-885-211-81-3
$16.95

Here is the stuff of legends —tale of thrills and danger, wild beasts, serpents, and savages. An unforgettable and vivid portrait of a vanished late-19th century Africa.

THE ROYAL ROAD TO ROMANCE
By Richard Halliburton
ISBN 1-885-211-53-8
$14.95

"Laughing at hardships, dreaming of beauty, ardent for adventure, Halliburton has managed to sing into the pages of this glorious book his own exultant spirit of youth and freedom."
— *Chicago Post*

UNBEATEN TRACKS IN JAPAN
By Isabella L. Bird
ISBN 1-885-211-57-0
$14.95

Isabella Bird was one of the most adventurous women travelers of the 19th century with journeys to Tibet, Canada, Korea, Turkey, Hawaii, and Japan. A fascinating read for anyone interested in women's travel, spirituality, and Asian culture.

THE RIVERS RAN EAST
By Leonard Clark
ISBN 1-885-211-66-X
$16.95

Clark is the original Indiana Jones, relaying a breathtaking account of his search for the legendary El Dorado gold in the Amazon.

Travel Humor

NOT SO FUNNY WHEN IT HAPPENED
The Best of Travel Humor and Misadventure
Edited by Tim Cahill
ISBN 1-885-211-55-4
$12.95

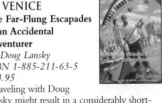

Laugh with Bill Bryson, Dave Barry, Anne Lamott, Adair Lara, and many more.

THERE'S NO TOILET PAPER...ON THE ROAD LESS TRAVELED
The Best of Travel Humor and Misadventure
Edited by Doug Lansky
ISBN 1-885-211-27-9
$12.95

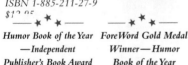

Humor Book of the Year
—*Independent*
Publisher's Book Award

ForeWord Gold Medal
Winner— *Humor*
Book of the Year

LAST TROUT IN VENICE
The Far-Flung Escapades of an Accidental Adventurer
By Doug Lansky
ISBN 1-885-211-63-5
$14.95

"Traveling with Doug Lansky might result in a considerably shortened life expectancy...but what a way to go."
—Tony Wheeler, Lonely Planet Publications

Women's Travel

A WOMAN'S PASSION FOR TRAVEL
More True Stories from A Woman's World
Edited by Marybeth Bond & Pamela Michael
ISBN 1-885-211-36-8
$17.95

"A diverse and gripping series of stories!" —Arlene Blum, author of *Annapurna: A Woman's Place*

A WOMAN'S WORLD
True Stories of Life on the Road
Edited by Marybeth Bond
Introduction by Dervla Murphy
ISBN 1-885-211-06-6
$17.95

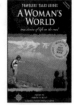

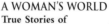

Winner of the Lowell Thomas Award for Best Travel Book— Society of American Travel Writers

WOMEN IN THE WILD
True Stories of Adventure and Connection
Edited by Lucy McCauley
ISBN 1-885-211-21-X
$17.95

"A spiritual, moving, and totally female book to take you around the world and back." —*Mademoiselle*

A MOTHER'S WORLD
Journeys of the Heart
Edited by Marybeth Bond & Pamela Michael
ISBN 1-885-211-26-0
$14.95

"These stories remind us that motherhood is one of the great unifying forces in the world" —*San Francisco Examiner*

Food

ADVENTURES IN WINE
True Stories of Vineyards and Vintages around the World
Edited by Thom Elkjer
ISBN 1-885-211-80-5
$17.95

Humanity, community, and brotherhood comprise the marvelous virtues of the wine world. This collection toasts the warmth and wonders of this large, extended family in stories by travelers who are wine novices and experts alike.

FOOD (Updated)
A Taste of the Road
Edited by Richard Sterling
Introduction by Margo True
ISBN 1-885-211-77-5
$18.95

Silver Medal Winner of the Lowell Thomas Award for Best Travel Book—Society of American Travel Writers

HER FORK IN THE ROAD
Women Celebrate Food and Travel
Edited by Lisa Bach
ISBN 1-885-211-71-6
$16.95

A savory sampling of stories by some of the best writers in and out of the food and travel fields.

THE ADVENTURE OF FOOD
True Stories of Eating Everything
Edited by Richard Sterling
ISBN 1-885-211-37-6
$17.95

"These stories are bound to whet appetites for more than food." —*Publishers Weekly*

Spiritual Travel

THE SPIRITUAL GIFTS OF TRAVEL
The Best of Travelers' Tales
Edited by James O'Reilly and Sean O'Reilly
ISBN 1-885-211-69-4
$16.95

A collection of favorite stories of transformation on the road from our award-winning Travelers' Tales series that shows the myriad ways travel indelibly alters our inner landscapes.

THE WAY OF THE WANDERER
Discover Your True Self Through Travel
By David Yeadon
ISBN 1-885-211-60-0
$14.95

Experience transformation through travel with this delightful, illustrated collection by award-winning author David Yeadon.

PILGRIMAGE
Adventures of the Spirit
Edited by Sean O'Reilly & James O'Reilly
Introduction by Phil Cousineau
ISBN 1-885-211-56-2
$16.95

—— ★*★ ——

ForeWord Silver Medal Winner
— Travel Book of the Year

A WOMAN'S PATH
Women's Best Spiritual Travel Writing
Edited by Lucy McCauley, Amy G. Carlson & Jennifer Leo
ISBN 1-885-211-48-1
$16.95

"A sensitive exploration of women's lives that have been unexpectedly and spiritually touched by travel experiences.... Highly recommended."
—Library Journal

THE ROAD WITHIN
True Stories of Transformation and the Soul
Edited by Sean O'Reilly, James O'Reilly & Tim O'Reilly
ISBN 1-885-211-19-8
$17.95

—— ★*★ ——

Best Spiritual Book — Independent Publisher's Book Award

THE ULTIMATE JOURNEY
Inspiring Stories of Living and Dying
James O'Reilly, Sean O'Reilly & Richard Sterling
ISBN 1-885-211-38-4
$17.95

"A glorious collection of writings about the ultimate adventure. A book to keep by one's bedside—and close to one's heart."   —Philip Zaleski, editor,
The Best Spiritual Writing series

Adventure

TESTOSTERONE PLANET
True Stories from a Man's World
Edited by Sean O'Reilly, Larry Habegger & James O'Reilly
ISBN 1-885-211-43-0
$17.95

Thrills and laughter with some of today's best writers: Sebastian Junger, Tim Cahill, Bill Bryson, and Jon Krakauer.

DANGER!
True Stories of Trouble and Survival
Edited by James O'Reilly, Larry Habegger & Sean O'Reilly
ISBN 1-885-211-32-5
$17.95

"Exciting...for those who enjoy living on the edge or prefer to read the survival stories of others, this is a good pick."
—Library Journal

Special Interest

365 TRAVEL
**A Daily Book of
Journeys, Meditations,
and Adventures**
Edited by Lisa Bach
ISBN 1-885-211-67-8
$14.95
An illuminating collection
of travel wisdom and
adventures that reminds us
all of the lessons we learn while on the road.

THE GIFT
OF RIVERS
**True Stories of
Life on the Water**
*Edited by Pamela Michael
Introduction by Robert Hass*
ISBN 1-885-211-42-2
$14.95
"*The Gift of Rivers* is a
soulful compendium of wonderful stories that
illuminate, educate, inspire, and delight."
—David Brower, Chairman of
Earth Island Institute

FAMILY TRAVEL
**The Farther You Go,
the Closer You Get**
Edited by Laura Manske
ISBN 1-885-211-33-3
$17.95
"This is family travel at its
finest." —*Working Mother*

LOVE & ROMANCE
**True Stories of
Passion on the Road**
*Edited by Judith Babcock
Wylie*
ISBN 1-885-211-18-X
$17.95
"A wonderful book to
read by a crackling fire."
—*Romantic Traveling*

THE GIFT
OF BIRDS
**True Encounters
with Avian Spirits**
*Edited by Larry Habegger
& Amy G. Carlson*
ISBN 1-885-211-41-4
$17.95
"These are all wonderful,
entertaining stories offering
a *bird's-eye view!* of our avian friends."
—*Booklist*

A DOG'S WORLD
**True Stories of
Man's Best Friend
on the Road**
*Edited by Christine
Hunsicker*
ISBN 1-885-211-23-6
$12.95
This extraordinary
collection includes stories
by John Steinbeck, Helen Thayer, James
Herriot, Pico Iyer, and many others.

THE GIFT OF TRAVEL
The Best of Travelers' Tales
*Edited by Larry Habegger, James O'Reilly
& Sean O'Reilly*
ISBN 1-885-211-25-2
$14.95
"Like gourmet chefs in a French market, the
editors of Travelers' Tales pick, sift, and prod
their way through the weighty shelves of con-
temporary travel writing, creaming off the
very best."
—William Dalrymple, author of *City of Djinns*

Travel Advice

SHITTING PRETTY
**How to Stay Clean and
Healthy While Traveling**
*By Dr. Jane Wilson-
Howarth*
ISBN 1-885-211-47-3
$12.95

A light-hearted book about
a serious subject for millions of travelers—staying
healthy on the road—written by international
health expert, Dr. Jane Wilson-Howarth.

THE FEARLESS SHOPPER
**How to Get the Best
Deals on the Planet**
By Kathy Borrus
ISBN 1-885-211-39-2
$14.95

"Anyone who reads
The Fearless Shopper will
come away a smarter, more
responsible shopper and a more curious,
culturally attuned traveler."
—Jo Mancuso, *The Shopologist*

GUTSY WOMEN
**More Travel Tips and
Wisdom for the Road**
By Marybeth Bond
ISBN 1-885-211-61-9
$12.95

Second Edition—Packed
with funny, instructive,
and inspiring advice for
women heading out to
see the world.

SAFETY AND SECURITY FOR WOMEN WHO TRAVEL
*By Sheila Swan
& Peter Laufer*
ISBN 1-885-211-29-5
$12.95

A must for every
woman traveler!

THE FEARLESS DINER
**Travel Tips and Wisdom
for Eating around
the World**
By Richard Sterling
ISBN 1-885-211-22-8
$7.95

Combines practical advice
on foodstuffs, habits, and
etiquette, with hilarious accounts
of others' eating adventures.

THE PENNY PINCHER'S PASSPORT TO LUXURY TRAVEL
**The Art of
Cultivating Preferred
Customer Status**
By Joel L. Widzer
ISBN 1-885-211-31-7
$12.95

Proven techniques on how to travel first
class at discount prices, even if you're not
a frequent flyer.

GUTSY MAMAS
**Travel Tips and Wisdom for
Mothers on the Road**
By Marybeth Bond
ISBN 1-885-211-20-1
$7.95

A delightful guide for mothers
traveling with their children—
or without them!

Destination Titles:
True Stories of Life on the Road

AMERICA
Edited by Fred Setterberg
ISBN 1-885-211-28-7
$19.95

FRANCE (Updated)
Edited by James O'Reilly,
Larry Habegger &
Sean O'Reilly
ISBN 1-885-211-73-2
$18.95

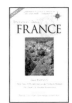

AMERICAN SOUTHWEST
Edited by Sean O'Reilly
& James O'Reilly
ISBN 1-885-211-58-9
$17.95

GRAND CANYON
Edited by Sean O'Reilly,
James O'Reilly &
Larry Habegger
ISBN 1-885-211-34-1
$17.95

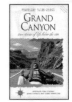

AUSTRALIA
Edited by Larry Habegger
ISBN 1-885-211-40-6
$17.95

GREECE
Edited by Larry Habegger,
Sean O'Reilly &
Brian Alexander
ISBN 1-885-211-52-X
$17.95

BRAZIL
Edited by Annette Haddad
& Scott Doggett
Introduction by Alex
Shoumatoff
ISBN 1-885-211-11-2
$17.95

HAWAI'I
Edited by Rick &
Marcie Carroll
ISBN 1-885-211-35-X
$17.95

CENTRAL AMERICA
Edited by Larry Habegger
& Natanya Pearlman
ISBN 1-885-211-74-0
$17.95

HONG KONG
Edited by James O'Reilly,
Larry Habegger &
Sean O'Reilly
ISBN 1-885-211-03-1
$17.95

CUBA
Edited by Tom Miller
ISBN 1-885-211-62-7
$17.95

INDIA
Edited by James O'Reilly
& Larry Habegger
ISBN 1-885-211-01-5
$17.95

IRELAND
Edited by James O'Reilly,
Larry Habegger &
Sean O'Reilly
ISBN 1-885-211-46-5
$17.95

SAN FRANCISCO
Edited by James O'Reilly,
Larry Habegger &
Sean O'Reilly
ISBN 1-885-211-08-2
$17.95

ITALY (Updated)
Edited by Anne Calcagno
Introduction by Jan Morris
ISBN 1-885-211-72-4
$18.95

SPAIN (Updated)
Edited by Lucy McCauley
ISBN 1-885-211-78-3
$19.95

JAPAN
Edited by Donald W. George
& Amy G. Carlson
ISBN 1-885-211-04-X
$17.95

THAILAND (Updated)
Edited by James O'Reilly
& Larry Habegger
ISBN 1-885-211-75-9
$18.95

MEXICO (Updated)
Edited by James O'Reilly
& Larry Habegger
ISBN 1-885-211-59-7
$17.95

TIBET
Edited by James O'Reilly,
Larry Habegger, & Kim
Morris
ISBN 1-885-211-76-7
$18.95

NEPAL
Edited by Rajendra
S. Khadka
ISBN 1-885-211-14-7
$17.95

TUSCANY
Edited by James O'Reilly, &
Tara Austen Weaver
ISBN 1-885-211-68-6
$16.95

PARIS
Edited by James O'Reilly,
Larry Habegger &
Sean O'Reilly
ISBN 1-885-211-10-4
$17.95